ATHENS

INSIGHT *City* GUIDES

Edited by Martha Ellen Zenfell
Editorial Director: Brian Bell

APA
PUBLICATIONS

ATHENS

First Edition (Reprint)
© 1991 APA PUBLICATIONS (HK) LTD
All Rights Reserved
Printed in Singapore by Höfer Press Pte. Ltd

ABOUT THIS BOOK

The challenge posed by *Cityguide: Athens* was clear: how do you write a useful travel book to a city which can be, in the words of one contributor, "impossible to love"? The writer continues in this same vein: "Athens is not a city that deliberately puts its best foot forward to greet visitors. Its overall architecture is undistinguished, its geography difficult to grasp, partly due to smog and partly to the local passion for putting up endless lines of billboards."

Once established, the solution to the problem became equally clear: not to pretend that Athens is a beautiful tourist centre like London, Paris or Manhattan, but to see it as a vibrant metropolis with headaches and attractions which remain primarily hidden.

Project editor **Martha Ellen Zenfell** was under no illusions about Athens. When approached in London by editorial director **Brian Bell** to edit a sequel to her *Insight Guide: Greek Islands*, her initial response was a mite less than enthusiastic. Countless trips to Athens an editor and writer had exposed her to the city's highs and lows, and it was only after an assurance that she could present a balanced picture that a contract was signed.

Frantic Efforts

The rest of her duties fell rapidly into place: to assemble a crack team of writers and photographers who could explain not only *why* Athens often seems so unlovable at first sight, but who could sort out the fascinating from the merely frantic to ensure a more satisfying visit.

Writing accurately about a city is easy. Writing about it well is quite a different matter. The description at the beginning of this piece is from **Sloane Elliott**'s introduction to the book, "An Athenian Outlook". Publisher of the English-language monthly *The Athenian* and an elegant essayist himself, Elliott manages to be frank about Athens' "initial disappointment" while in the next breath clarifying and redefining its attributes. In fact, his introduction achieves that difficult feat: to make readers like and appreciate the city more than they might have previously. See if you agree.

A city with a past spanning 5,000 years obviously places emphasis on history. This formidable task fell to **Rowlinson Carter**. Classical Greece provided the springboard for both channels of Carter's career: philosophy and history. His subsequent calling as a war correspondent took him to Indo-China, the Middle East and Africa, but his interest in Greece was revived by a one-year sabbatical in which he investigated clandestine operations and guerrilla warfare in the Balkans during World War II. "The closer one looks at history," he says, "the more surprises it throws up." Carter has steered the historical sections of this book towards the discoveries which he found most appealing. They are rarely the most obvious choices.

The history question posed to **John Carr** was an intriguing one: "Are there any similarities between the ancient Greeks and the modern Greeks?" His well-argued response can be found on page 79. History aside, Carr, with a Greek mother and a British father, is a profoundly contemporary man, combining music and journalism (*The Wall Street Journal, Billboard*), with presenting English-language news bulletins on Antenna 97.1 FM stereo radio. Carr also wrote the very modern

Zenfell   *Carter*   *Carr*

piece on Athens' first woman train driver called "Railway Woman".

For the record, just who are these modern Greeks? In one of her columns for *The Athenian*, **Elizabeth Boleman Herring** wrote: "We are vain and humble, sensual and distant, demanding and patient to a fault." As deputy editor of the same magazine and a South Carolinian by birth, Herring has first-hand experience of the contradictions which make up the volatile contemporary Athenian. She suggested for the essay on this subject the columnist **Alec Kitroeff**, an Alexandrian Greek whose activities have ranged from service in the navy and merchant marines to journalism, public relations and advertising. Herring herself tackled the weighty subject of Greek food and, together with J. A. Lawrence, took to the streets to document much of the "Places" section. Many thanks for her contributions at all levels.

J.A. Lawrence, a New Yorker by birth, lives with many cats in an old schoolhouse in an inner-city Athens village. A writer of guidebooks, science fiction, romances and historical novels, she tackled Syntagma Square alone and came up with this quote about the mini-skirted soldiers who guard Parliament: "These dedicated chaps should not be taken as merely decorative: they are in fact highly trained special troops, albeit with extra-fine legs."

To round out the "Places" section, two more people were recruited. California-born **Marc S. Dubin** graduated from Berkeley and promptly began travelling. Years spent transiting Athens en route to other places, including a spell as a tour guide, developed an inadvertent knowledge of, and grudging affection for, the city. He knows of no better place to have boots or camera fixed. Dubin wore out large numbers of both in the course of researching *Greece on Foot*, a walker's guide and taking photographs for a variety of books, including *Insight: Greek Islands*, and was the obvious person to research the piece on walking Mount Parnitha. Piraeus and the Athens Festival fell to **B. Samantha Stenzel**, a dedicated cinephile and the Greek correspondent for *Variety* and the *International Film Guide*. She likes to unwind after a day's work with a friend in one of the *rembetika* (Greek blues) clubs. Her articles on movies and music clubs reflect those twin passions.

Nigel Lowry has lived in London, Yorkshire, Australia and Athens. A journalist for many publications, he has recently specialised in shipping. Seaside offices in Piraeus made Lowry the logical choice to write about sailing and city beaches. **Carol Reed**, an erstwhile freelancer, tackled the hotly debated subject of tourism for *Insight: Greek Islands*. For this book she has contributed another hard news story, this time on pollution, demonstrating how Athens is coping with the dreaded *nefos*.

Put In The Picture

So many photographers contributed to *Cityguide: Athens* that they cannot all be singled out by name. Special thanks, however, to **János Stekovics** of Hungary and Munich, **Marcus Wilson-Smith** in London, and **Pierre Couteau**, **Markos G. Hionos** and **Michele Macrakis** for providing pictures from Greece.

Thanks, too, must be extended to **Olympic Airways** for providing flights to Athens, often at short notice, and to the **National Tourist Organisation of Greece.**

Herring *Kitroeff* *Stenzel* *Dublin*

CONTENTS

PLACES

TRAVEL TIPS

AN ATHENIAN OUTLOOK

It is probably impossible to love Athens at first sight. It is not a city that deliberately puts its best foot forward to greet visitors. Its unruly aggressiveness, noticeable at once, almost feels like a slap. It takes a little time and patience to feel its first caress.

That initial slap, however, is well-intentioned, the kind that tries to bring the befuddled to his senses. Almost rudely, Athens brushes aside preconceptions people have of it and roughly proclaims its very own reality.

Athens is more polluted than most European cities, more congested, noisier. Its parks are few. Avenues lined with trees are rare. Its overall architecture is undistinguished, its geography difficult to grasp, partly due to smog and partly to the passion for putting up endless lines of billboards.

Street wisdom: The city's disorganised sprawl is immediately apparent and so is its look of improvisation and incompleteness. This is typified by the forests of iron rods sticking up above slabs of concrete in anticipation of floors which may (or may not) be built. In Athens, nothing is certain except that the future promises to be as disorganised as the present. At the same time, Athenians are on record for being the most optimistic city-dwellers in Europe. This must be due to their looking at life in a fluid, take-it-as-it-comes sort of way. Four thousand years of continuous civilisation may be difficult to find in Athens, but the street wisdom it has produced is visible everywhere.

The great renown of Athens in history is yet a further reason for initial disappointment. If it were just another city like hundreds of others, there would be no cause for complaint. But where, in this particular jungle of concrete, is "the glory that was

Greece", "the cradle of democracy", the true measure of man"?

Modern Athenians are no help in answering these questions. They are too busy talking, running about and carrying things. One of the astonishing sights of Athens is what is being transported from here to there. In normal cities, most people carry handbags or briefcases. Not in Athens. On a single block pedestrians can be found carrying birdcages, standing lamps, a toilet seat, a stack of

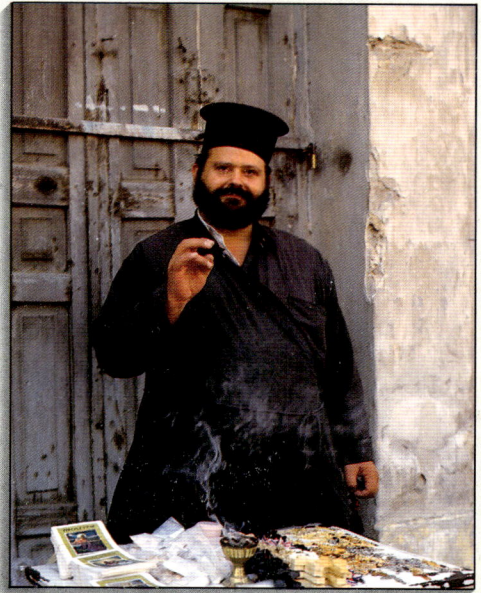

magazines, a large gilt frame without a picture in it and a bicycle tyre. Rich in detail, Athens is full of anomalies, and the day the visitor is amused rather than baffled by what he sees, then he has begun the adventure known as Getting to Know Athens.

This phenomenon is even more arresting in the street, where trucks and smaller three-wheeled vans carry whole households. There, in vehicles festooned with Christmas lights, encrusted with collections of seashells, armed with horns that play the theme song from *Never on Sunday* and plastered over with faded photos of John F.

Preceding pages: welcome aboard; back to the future; *Evzones* march past the flower market; Athens lies in a valley surrounded by mountains; 75 percent of all Greeks go to church; shedding new light on Plaka. <u>Left</u>, Athens has been on record as the noisiest city in Europe. <u>Right</u>, an orthodox fragrance.

Kennedy, Pope John XXII and Marilyn Monroe, sway, piled in the back of the truck, mirrored mahogany wardrobes, Louis "Kez" dining sets, chandeliers, bowls full of goldfish, and TV screens protected by Leonardo's *Last Supper* in tapestry on which teeter piles of 78 r.p.m. records and vintage sewing machines. In Athens, where history is so long, things are not valued just because they are old, but because they are loved. So, caught in one of its dreaded traffic jams, passengers can learn the history of the city just by looking at the contents of the truck in front of them.

Athens in general is full of unexpected ity. Monuments erected a thousand years apart stand cheek-by-jowl, and two built in the same era may be divided by housing thrown up two thousand years later.

At heart, Athens does not cater for tourists. It doesn't pretend to exist for anyone other than Athenians. That is why directional signs, written in a vague medium of communication locally thought of as English, can lead a tourist on a wild goose chase or sometimes just in circles. Inaugurating the Olympic Stadium many years ago, the authorities put up hundreds of signs to help foreigners find their way there. Most of these signs remain, but few point towards the antiqui-

sights. Characteristic is the first glimpse of the city. The sight of the overwhelmingly familiar Acropolis half-obscured by a jungle of television aerials might well be distracted by a much taller elevation that few visitors have ever heard of. Right away, one is confronted by a city whose antiquities are difficult to grasp with a fresh eye for being too well-known, and the rest of it impossible to judge because it isn't known at all.

Although it has, of course, spectacular sights for tourists, Athens makes few efforts to display them. The past is scattered here and there without much thought for continu- ties. The writing on many signs has been effaced by weather; others point straight up in the air. This is due to very strong winds that sometimes blow like cyclones through intersections.

Major attraction: Athens puts on no airs. It has a take-me-or-leave-me way about it that may disconcert at first but soon becomes one of its major attractions. The city does not have picture-postcard good looks, which is one of the reasons why there is so little variety in tourist views. The irony of this is that often the most appealing parts of the city are cropped by photographers who don't understand what foreigners like about the place. At least it allows them a chance to discover Athens for themselves. It takes time for its charms to work their way under the skin, plus another quality which its inhabitants totally lack: patience, and enough leisure to let experience sink in.

Athenians are so careless of the past in their manic absorption in the present, one might conclude that history did not leave a deep imprint here. This is far from the case, but in one respect it is a good thing. The past gives the impression of lying lightly on the present. There is little feeling of the weight of time. The great monuments are either set

hovering overhead. Athens lies in a valley surrounded by mountains on three sides and open only towards the sea to the south. The refreshing *meltemi* blowing from the north rarely reaches the city and the sultry *livas* from the south, sometimes heavy with sand swept up off the Sahara, rarely misses it. So even Athens' atmospheric inversion is primarily classical.

Although Athenians love to complain about their city, even they admit that the climate of Attica is superb. Luckily, too, there are many clear days, for one of the pleasantest surprises of Athens is the great beauty of its setting. The Acropolis, and the

apart, floating like the Acropolis serene over today's hubbub, or engulfed like the little Byzantine churches which lie scattered around, half-submerged on an earlier foundation of civilisation, overwhelmed by traffic and fumes but, being always in use, themselves exhaling puffs of incense.

If Athens tries to obscure its history while being determined by it, this is true of its geography, too. It is made painfully clear by the frequent presence of the pollution cloud

more naturally imposing crag of Likavitós just to the north, are only two of the many geological outcroppings on and around which the city has been built. It is full of little *acropolises*: low, sharply eroded limestone eruptions, supporting cactus, perhaps a few pines, and a great profusion of wild flowers for which Attica is famous.

Of the greater, encircling mountains the silhouette of Hymettus is most impressive. Traditionally, it has always been called Mad Mountain without anyone knowing quite why. It is said to be the city's weather gauge and when clouds collect over it, it always

Left, copper pots are good bargains. Right, Athens in general is full of unexpected sights.

means a downpour. These inundations are very dramatic in Athens, due to the sheerness of its little acropolises, the lack of vegetation to hold back water and the inadequate drainage. The floods can be quite biblical with massive street-light failures, stranded cars and no telephone service for hours.

More likely, Mad Mountain is so named for the dramatic change in colour and contour it goes through in a single day. Lying across the whole eastern side of the city, in the morning with the sun rising behind it, Hymettus looks as smooth and flat as a long strip of cardboard. Towards midday, its grey-blue tone turns rosy and then golden in

larly in winter, when the famous light of Attica can be enjoyed—though very few, as was common in years past, when the air is so clear that the flutings on the columns of the Parthenon might well be seen half-way across the valley.

If Athens' rather makeshift, sloppy, unfinished look seems disconcertingly haphazard at first, it is necessary to see this scattered metropolis as a whole to understand that it could not be other than it is. In the first place, more than most capitals or chief cities, Athens is the embodiment of its country in highly concentrated form. It exemplifies a way of life, which Athenians themselves,

the afternoon. At the same time the smooth surface begins to crumple and finally grows gutted and wrinkled towards evening as the last rays of the setting sun penetrate its deep ravines.

So Hymettus seems to progress from smooth-faced youth to ravaged old age in the course of a few hours. Yet it is most beautiful at twilight when the sunset coincides with the full moon rising over its flank, turning a surprising shade of purple, a phenomenon which earned from the poet Pindar the famous epithet, "Athens, violet-crowned". Luckily, there are still many days, particu-

rarely at a loss for words, can only call "Greek Reality". It is a complex, but definable, combination of attitudes which makes the country tick—and, often as not, not tick. Whatever private aesthetic opinion may be, Athens is what almost all Greeks want a city to look like, since there are so many smaller versions of it scattered around the country, and one suspects that every town would be the same if the tourism people allowed it.

The reason Athens looks improvised is that Greeks look at life as an improvisation, and one has only to take a cursory look at the Minoan palace at Knossos to understand that this has been mainstream popular Greek philosophy for the past 4,000 years. Since Greece, unique in the West, has survived all these millennia, this implies that its inhabitants have very good reason to live the way they do.

One of the delightful ironies of Athens physically is that the modern city was laid out by western (and, in particular, German) planners. In other words, the people who had survived thousands of years from asking the right questions were, by historical circumstance, made victims of people who had all the answers because they had no serious history at all. Although there are pretty

can attitude of an earlier period and the grab-as-grab-can of later urban developers is what define the rest of the city today. Throughout contemporary Athens the most appealing areas are those which nobody gave much thought to and which planners overlooked.

It's odd for a people who devote themselves to a lifetime of self-expression that the city looks so uniform. So much energy is spent on being what one is that no one seems to care about where one lives. Five or six similar architectural designs account for an overwhelming number of apartment blocks where individuality is expressed on what residents make of the balconies which hang

neo-classical buildings which have survived this period, it can only be admitted that the planned parts of Athens are its least congenial. The glory that was Washington D.C. and the grandeur that was Leningrad just didn't work in this unpretentious city that had thousands of years of wisdom behind it.

The central squares are uninspired spaces and the avenues that connect them are uniformly drab. The great charms of the old part of the city are left from the catch-as-catch-

off these concrete slabs like unclosed bureau drawers. They help give Athens its personal, rumpled look, like some enormous unmade bed still warm from body heat and the blankets thrown over the railings.

Life is far too serious and strenuous a matter for Athenians to give much time to making things look pretty. Life being something that you do, Athenians devote all their energies to doing it. Another reason for the uniform look of Athens is the absence of ghettos. There are few really run-down areas and the fashionable quarters are more distinguished by the expensive cars parked in the streets than by the buildings that line them.

Uniformity of look and singlemindedness about the present are the main reasons why it is difficult to find a sense of historical continuity. Centuries at a stretch have left little or no mark and the oldest part of this ancient city was not built until the second third of the last century. Even so, the expansion of Athens has been spasmodic and three distinct periods of sudden growth account for its appearance today.

The first period followed the War of Independence which had left Athens desolated with fewer than 1,000 inhabitable houses. It was proclaimed capital of Greece in 1832

solely on its great reputation in antiquity. Athens was then to be transformed into a stately capital, but in spite of the efforts of foreigners to do so, native Athenians whose survival had depended on tenacity and an unwillingness to change, were able to preserve the sprawl of a Levantine market town. Much of this atmosphere and the way of conducting business has been preserved today in the heart of Athens.

In the manner of a bazaar, merchandise of a similar kind is sold together in a single location. So, as the city grew, the number of similar shops simply increased. Today,

therefore, one will find dozens of florists selling the same varieties of flowers next door to each other, a long cul-de-sac offering nothing but plastic toys, a whole section of town devoted to retailing automobile spare-parts and a street from start to finish marketing nothing but buttons.

In one very large square block, the central meat market comprises more than 100 stalls offering no greater variety of cuts than can be found in a town one-hundredth the size of Athens. It is yet another reminder that Athens is not really a city, but a hundred towns, all similar.

The second great period of growth took place suddenly in 1922, following a war with Turkey disastrous for Greece, when there was a massive exchange of populations. As a result, Athens more than doubled in size in less than a year. Fortunately, these refugees from Asia Minor were industrious, cultured, skilled as artisans and merchants. Instead of creating a ring of shanty towns around the city, they built prosperous communities. As inner city municipalities today, they have set the style of the present city more than any other urban development before or since,

Pride of place: The similar appearance of New Smyrna, New Ionia, New Philadelphia and more than a dozen other "news", with their large, draughty dun-coloured neo-Byzantine parish churches, neat squares in front, parks behind and tree-lined streets radiating from them, is misleading, for the founders brought with them their own music, their particular social habits and their regional cuisine. So they stamped each suburb with its own personality which today in many places has been retained. With this distinction comes pride of place.

The neighbourliness of Athens is one of its most distinctive and agreeable aspects. As a result of it, in the midst of disorganised sprawl, there is local tidiness; within the anonymity of urban architecture, the human dimension is maintained; away from confusion and rudeness of the thoroughfares, courtesy and openness prevail in local areas where everyone knows nearly everyone else. More than any other social factor, this accounts for the lack of crime and the relatively high degree of safety for which Athens is rightly admired. It must be one of the few cities left where a purse-snatching incident is thought newsworthy enough to be recorded in the papers.

This sense of village, this loyalty to locality, has created problems for the city as a whole. Strong community ties do not lend themselves to metropolitan awareness, and the Athenian, polite and attentive in his neighbourhood, may be transformed into an aggressive, booring, noisy lout when he sets foot on the anonymous avenue. When eye-to-eye, heart-to-heart contact is lost, the Athenian becomes as dehumanised as his surroundings. As a result, parts of Athens get

ment and, for another it stops vehicle traffic entirely. If blocked in an endless jam, it is wiser to join the demonstrators than curse them. They usually have a just cause.

Every association and labour union, every profession which complex modern civilisation calls for, demonstrates at some time or another in central Athens. From grammar school students to old age pensioners, from medical professors to street-cleaners, everyone is out there demanding something—from nuclear test bans to higher pay. Why argue around a bargaining table when one can be protesting and promenading and chatting at the same time? These affairs are

a terrible battering from its own inhabitants. People abuse much of the city's centre or they avoid it. Parking rules are ignored, manners become abrupt, pedestrians crossing avenues are terrorised and the law of the jungle prevails.

One thing, however, that all Athenians enjoy doing in the centre of their city is demonstrating. For one thing, it forces a human presence on this impersonal environ-

Left and right: political rallies, which may draw more than a million people, combine a regard for the outdoors with a profound love of noise.

enlivened by the chanting of slogans and martial music. They rarely get out of hand and may be the only well-organised things in the city.

Profound love of noise: Political rallies, which may draw more than a million people in and around Syntagma Square, are just a massive example of the same phenomenon. They combine a love of the out-of-doors with a strong sense of gregariousness and a profound love of noise.

Ancient Athens was know for its high decibel count, and noise was even associated with democracy. It suggests that without effusive public spiritedness, democracy cannot flourish. For years now, Athens has been on record as the noisiest city in Europe, but at the same time it is the only city that has creatively transformed it, like music, into an art form.

The third great expansion of Athens took place mainly in the 1960s and 1970s. Whole rural regions emptied out with people seeking a better life in Athens. Most have found it. If poorer neighbourhoods were created at first, these have been upgraded. Others have moved on to greater prosperity. Within the city today there are still large shifts of population. The chaotic, arbitrary spread of Athens is unfortunate, but the dismal regimentation of government housing, such an eyesore in many cities, is rarely found in Athens. It is a city that may annoy, but it never depresses.

Growth problem: This later population explosion created a whole new series of neighbourhoods still further from the centre. While the empty areas among these suburbs are filling in, the process will take years to complete, if it ever does. With nearly 40 percent of the country's population now, and an equal level of prosperity elsewhere, Athens cannot grow much larger.

Even so, there are prosperous small farms within the city limits, and flocks of sheep, with 30 or 40 animals, which can occasionally be seen grazing under the shadows of high-rises. Today's shepherd is not a refugee; he is native-born and fitted out in a designer sweatsuit and jogging shoes. Like all Athenians, he reads the newspaper and waits impatiently for the nine o'clock TV news so that he can stay in touch with international affairs.

Athens is not an art city preserved in amber for the fastidious connoisseur. No Disneyland anywhere in the world would want to have anything to do with it. With its incomparable past bodylocked into an unquaint but vital present, Athens is the real thing—a great human hodgepodge dedicated, as it has been continually for the past 4,000 years, to the business of living as fully as possible.

Right, Athens at night seen from Likavitós hill.

DALMATIÆ PARS

ALBANIA PARS ILLYRIDIS

Sintica

Orboli

MACEDONIA

Iori

Almopi

Pelagonia

Migdonia

Lamboli

Amphaxitis

Albani

Astræi

Linchest

Ematia

Paraxia

Tamoriza

Eordei

Comenolitari

Dassaretii

Douriopes

Pieria

Elymiotæ

Parthini

Macedonia

Candauii Montes

Orestæ

Stymphalis

Pelagonia Tripolitis

Pelasgiotis

Penestæ

Canina Elyma

Chimera

Atintani

Tymphæi

TESSALIA

Estiæotis

Iannala

Phtiotis

EPIRO

Parorei

Pindus M.

Thessaliotis

Pindus M.

Hellopes

Larta

Dolopes

Dryopes

Molossi

Athamanes

Doris

Phocis

Beotia nunc

Amphilochi

Agræi

Perrhe

Locri Ozolæ

ACHAIA

Despotato

Acarnania

Etolia et

Stramulpa

Ducato di At

Corfu I. et Corcyra

Cefalonia I. et Cephalenia

Val di

Golfo di Lepanto et Corynthiacus sinus

Euxia I. et Ægina

Golfo di Parrasso

Achaia Clarenza

Argolis

Saccania

Ietoia I.

Zante I. et Zacynthus

PELOPONNESVS MOREA

Arcadia

Belvedere

Messenia

Tzacconia

Braccio di Mainas

Laconia

Strivali I. Strophades Insulæ

MARE IONIO O DI GRECIA

MARE DI SAPIENZA

Sapienza I. et Sphagia

LA GRECIA
VNIVERSALE ANTICA
Paragonata con la Moderna da
Giacomo Cantelli da Vignola
Con le direttioni delle Carte Migliori e de piu accre-
ditati Scrittori di Geografia. data in luce da Gio.
Giacomo Rossi in Roma alla Pace l'anno 1689.
con Priu. del S. Pont.

Giorgio Widman Sculp.

THRACIÆ PARS oggi ROMANIA

CONSTANTINOPOLI Bizantium olim Stambul

Bistones
Braca
Nicopoli
Nestoria

Traianopoli et Zernis et Zirnes
Cicones
Maximianopoli
Beyla Asperos et Abdera

Doriscus campus
Eno et Enge

Lauro Odrisio
Bebryce

MARE DI MARMARA olim PROPONTIS

Scutari
Calcedona
Nicomedia Comidia et Nicor, et Unigimid et Ischmt

Tasso I. et Thassus et Aria

Samandrachi et Iamus et Samothrace
Lembro I. et Imbrus

Stalimene I. et Lemnos

ARCIPELAGO

oggi

MAR BIANCO

anticamente

ÆGÆVM MARE

Metelino I. olim Lesbus

ANATOLIA PROPRIA

Mysia Minor

Mysia Maior

Scio I. et Chius et Chios

ICARIOM MARE

Sciro I. et Syrus

Andro I. et Andros
Tino I. et Tonos

Nicaria I. et Scaria

Samo I. et Samos

Delos grande et Rhenea
Micolo I. et Miconus

Insulæ Cyclades

Thermia I. et Cythnus

Nicsia I. et Naxus

Paru I. et Paros

Spora des Insulæ

MARE MIRTOVM

Mare di Candia ol. CRETICVM Mare

Santorini S. Erini et Thera Insula

Scarpanto I. et Carpathus

MARE DI SCARPANTO olim Carpathium Mare

Isola di Rodi et Rhodus

CANDIA olim CRETA

Candia

Scala
Miglia d'Italia
Leghe comuni di Francia
Leghe comuni di Germania
Leghe d'un hora di camino

When the Acropolis was pristinely in the form to which it has been partially restored today, a foreign king on a visit to Athens decided it was time for a shave and haircut. Clean-shaven faces were then coming into vogue, a practice copied from Macedonia, which happened to be the king's domain. The choice was between a full beard or none at all. Only the wretched Gauls and other low barbarians went in for moustaches.

The way a man wore his hair said a lot about him. If closely cropped, it was the mark of a slave or a professional athlete. Too long was foppish, the sort of ostentation people generally deplored. The cavalry let it dangle in short ringlets, a mark of distinction between them and the infantry and navy, the latter being in a clear majority once the powerful families who dominated political life were persuaded that the city-state's security depended ultimately on naval power. The decision to invest heavily in *triremes*—war galleys rowed by three layers of oarsmen on either side (no guns, of course; instead, they rammed the opposition)—had been vindicated at the battle at Salamis in 480 BC when, against all odds, a second Persian invasion was repelled.

This famous naval victory, however, came too late to prevent the Persian land forces from laying waste to Athens, the inhabitants having decamped for safety to one of the islands. The completion of the Parthenon was the triumphant climax of a 40-year reconstruction programme which included the Agora, the commercial centre below the Acropolis where, among the wine sellers and other shops, the barbers stood at their chairs.

"How would you like your hair done?" the barber enquired solicitously. "In silence!" the king snarled. If a contemporary comedy by Aristophanes is to be believed, barbers were even then garrulous pests. King Arch-

elaus was recognisably a Macedonian, and patriotic clairvoyance might have persuaded the barber to let the razor slice into his customer's throat. One of the king's successors was Alexander the Great, whose Macedonian troops would not long afterwards terminate Athenian supremacy in the Greek-speaking world, a position it did not regain until Greek independence more than two millennia later.

Athens between the Persian and

Macedonian invasions, a period of some 150 years, tends to steal the limelight from 5,000 years of Greek history. Looking back over that history from the present time, the acrimonious haircut falls almost at the halfway mark with about 2,500 years either way. In other words, what modern visitors see on the Acropolis is not the precocious beginning of Greek history but the end-product of a process which had been going on for as long as the time that has passed since. The earlier history of Greece swirled around Athens but only occasionally touched it.

The origins of Greek civilisation can be

Preceding pages: a 17th-century Italian map of ancient Greece. **Left**, the way a man wore his hair said a great deal about him. **Right**, the past is scattered throughout Athens.

traced to Crete. When it gained a foothold on the mainland, Athens was a part of it (as can be seen from the traces of a Mycenaean palace on the Acropolis) but not an important part. The Parthenon, symbol of the Age of Pericles, lay hundreds of years in the future. It would have been a remarkable architectural achievement by any standards at any time. How it came to be built in a city-state whose natural resources at the time of the Macedonian king's visit stretched to a silver mine, olive trees and not much else, is all the more extraordinary for that.

Attica, the state of which Athens was capital, was tiny: a fit man could cross it on

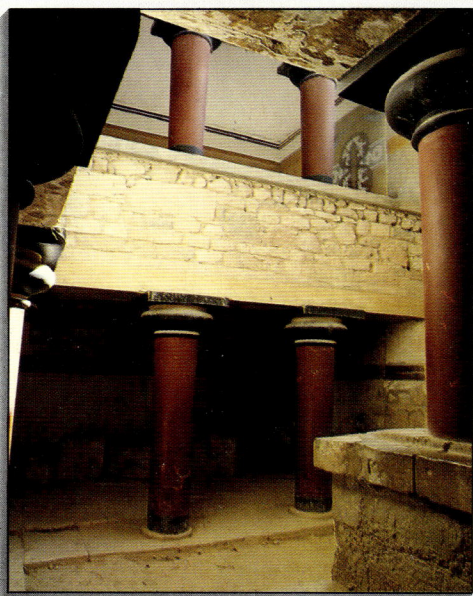

foot in any direction in a day or two. Moreover, it was only one of hundreds of independent Greek city-states scattered about on the mainland and islands, along the coasts of Asia Minor and as far afield as North Africa. In an ever-shifting pattern of tactical alliances, every one of them was equally friend or potential enemy. They shared a language and certain religious beliefs but were otherwise as remote as France is from Germany.

On the mainland, Corinth, Sparta and Thebes were at one time or another more powerful than Athens, but it was Athens which prodigiously mustered the intellec-

tual and artistic skills to set the course for Western civilisation thereafter, including democracy. In no small measure, the catalyst was an early example of creative accountancy—or daylight robbery, as far as many of the victims were concerned. This is a brief history of Athens rather than Greece as a whole, but to put this curious matter into a meaningful context it is necessary to turn the clock back, taking the story beyond the boundaries of what is now Greece, to Asia Minor and Egypt.

The Greek mainland faces east. The west coast, opposite Italy, is comparatively harbourless, the sea beyond a featureless horizon. The distance a ship could travel at a stretch depended on the stamina of the crewmen pulling at the oars. Storms could blow up without warning, and sailors were not happy to lose sight of land. As islands provided a reassuring chain of stepping stones across the Aegean, the earliest lines of communication naturally ran in that easterly direction, establishing contact with Asia Minor and Egypt.

It was the ability to produce and work metal, a skill long familiar in the East, that filtered across to Crete in the third millennium BC, providing the vital factor for the development of Minoan civilisation. Agriculturalists who had drifted overland from Asia Minor to the Greek mainland were still stuck with inferior tools made of stone.

Excavations in Crete at the turn of this century by Sir Arthur Evans exposed the trappings of the fabulous court of King Minos near Knossos, the largest of several such palace cultures on the island. Nothing comparable appeared on the mainland until much later, but in retrospect the Athenians pretended, and probably believed, that it had.

The tale recounted more fully in the Acropolis section (*pages 127–136*) refers to a kingdom in Athens during the reign of King Minos and an Athenian prince, Theseus, who was able to intervene in the matter of an annual tribute which Athens was obliged to pay Minos. This is wishful thinking, anticipating by many hundreds of years the point at which the mainland, having at last picked up some of the techniques of Minoan civilisation, was able to challenge

Cretan supremacy in the Aegean, especially in the Cyclades and (a discovery made only in 1967) on the island of Santorini.

The accomplishments of Minoan civilisation included palaces and pottery of a quality unprecedented in Europe. The Cretans enjoyed a kind of bull-fighting which consisted of grabbing a charging beast by the horns and leaping over it. The Cretans also invented flushing lavatories, an innovation which caused considerable excitement among scholars when the evidence was unearthed. "No truer sign of civilisation and culture than good sanitation," one of them intoned. "It goes with refined senses and orderly habits.

The impossibility of a supposed Athenian like Theseus turning up in Crete at the peak of Minoan civilisation is indicative of both the difficulties experienced by ancient Greeks in keeping track of their own history as well as tremendous advances in archaeology which enable us now to know rather more about their past than they did. The Cretans introduced to the Greek world a form of Egyptian hieroglyphics, called Linear A, which was adequate for drawing up lists but could not express language.

In what must have been a tragedy at the time but has turned out, for us, to be a stroke of great fortune, the palace at Knossos was

A good drain implies as much as a beautiful statue. And let it be remembered that the world did not reach the Minoan standard of cleanliness again until the great English sanitary movement of the late nineteenth century." Another pondered on the fact, again made clear by vase painters, that the dress of a well turned-out Minoan woman was artfully topless.

Left, Knossos. Above left, fresco from around 1500 BC. Above right, a Minoan bath. "No truer sign of civilisation and culture than good sanitation."

destroyed by fire. The heat baked a hoard of clay tablets which, when unearthed by Evans, revealed two kinds of writing, the unwieldy Linear A and something new, which was referred to as Linear B. It was not yet a proper alphabet with consonants and vowels (the Greeks later borrowed that system from the Phoenicians in what is now Lebanon) but it heralded the arrival of a pre-Homeric form of the Greek language.

Michael Ventris, a British architect, was shown an example of Linear B as a schoolboy. No one had yet been able to decipher it, and the young Ventris was fascinated. As an adult—in fact, in 1952—he cracked it. Confirmation that Linear B was a form of Greek underlined the important historical point that Minoan civilisation, originally a non-Greek import, had put down local roots.

The Knossos fire which preserved the clay tablets was nothing compared with the catastrophe which—it was learned only in 1967—spelt the end of the other Minoan palaces in Crete. Professor Spyridon Marinatos discovered on Santorini a hitherto unsuspected Minoan city buried under a mountain of ash in places 100 ft (30 metres) deep. (The frescoes and other relics rescued from the ashes, now in the National Ar-

Cretan expertise into what became known as Mycenaean civilisation, had returned to swallow the hand which had once fed them. It is with the advent of the Mycenaean age that Athens steps on to the world stage. Apparently unconcerned about the danger of invasion, the Minoans did not bother to fortify their palaces. Raiding Mycenaean Greeks took advantage of this vulnerability and in due course, when they built their own palaces on the mainland, were careful not to make the same mistake. They looked for naturally defensible hills on which to build their walled cities. In the area around Athens, the choice of the *acropolis* was automatic.

chaeological Museum, should be seen before they return to Santorini.)

The colossal volcanic eruption re-sculptured the shape of the island; it also, it seems, unleashed a tidal wave which roared down the Aegean and flattened the sister cities in Crete. The palace at Knossos, which had been rebuilt after the fire escaped, but not for long. Its subsequent destruction appears to have been an act of war, coincidentally a vindication of the spirit if not the letter of the story about Theseus and his pursuit of the child-eating Minotaur in the labyrinth.

The mainland Greeks, having assimilated

Athens, though, was a relatively unimportant element in the Mycenaean world. The principal centre was Mycenae itself, the city of the legendary Agamemnon, but those at Thebes, Tiryns and Pylos were scarcely less important. The fortified citadel was reserved for the king and a limited number of trusted nobles; the workers lived in villages outside. From the abundance of gold, jewellery, and other valuable objects recovered from tombs, mostly by the German banker-turned-archaeologist Heinrich Schliemann in the latter half of the 19th century, the Greeks seem to have been enormously prosperous between the years 1400 and 1250 BC.

It was in this period that a palace was built on the north side of the Athenian *acropolis*, adjacent to the site of the later Erechtheum, the whole being enclosed by thick, polygonal walls. Rich tombs on the south side were found to contain valuable objects from Crete, Egypt and Asia Minor.

The most vivid source of knowledge about Mycenaean Greece is derived from Homer's *Iliad*. Homer was born about 400 years after the Trojan War which the *Iliad* describes. He worked only from oral tradition, so some of the historical detail is suspect. According to tradition, the war was over the abduction of

Helen, wife of King Menelaus of Sparta, by Paris of Troy. It was her beautiful face which is said to have inspired the Greeks to launch a thousand ships, their purpose being to get her back. It was also the war of the wooden horse, which taught the lesson about not trusting Greeks who bear gifts.

The truth about the Trojan War was rather more prosaic. The extravagant tastes developed by the Mycenaean Greeks could not be satisfied locally. There was hardly any copper in Greece, no tin and therefore no bronze

Left and right, frescoes from Santorini.

for their prized weapons, which included spears with heads two ft (60 cm) long. The country was barely self-sufficient in food. Troy stood at the entrance to the Dardanelles and therefore commanded the shortest crossing between Europe and Asia and all the trade that passed that way. It also blocked access to the Black Sea, which the Greeks decided was an ocean of unlimited potential. Troy stood in the way of Greek commercial expansion; the war was, after all, about the sort of thing which has caused countless wars throughout history.

The Greeks won, but their victory did not produce the anticipated return. On the contrary, it was one of those wars which ruined all the parties concerned. Mycenaean power never recovered from the effort invested in it. It was too weak to resist an invasion building up on the northern frontiers.

Athens seems to have played an insignificant part in the Trojan War and therefore suffered less than those who threw their resources into it. Homer makes only passing reference to it, although that could be explained by the fact Homer was born and lived in Asia Minor and may never have been to Athens. The Athenians in their walled Acropolis were aware of the danger of invasion, and a flight of stairs was hastily cut into the rock to reach the additional sources of water that would be needed in a long siege.

The villagers living outside the city recognised the danger too, and they negotiated the right to seek shelter inside the walls in an emergency. In so doing, they were unknowingly formulating the rights and obligations of citizenship, the essence of the Greek city-state which would later evolve in Athens into the principle of democracy.

In the event, Athens was neither attacked nor conquered by the invaders, but the other Mycenaean cities were. The administrative system which they had inherited from the Minoans and refined into what would now be recognised as a government and civil service, collapsed. Greece fell backwards into a "dark age" which was to last for nearly 500 years; until, in fact, the invaders were assimilated in order to produce a more robust, hybrid "Greek" identity. The invaders were the Dorians.

DEMOCRACY IN THE MAKING

One of the surest ways to annoy modern Greeks, as Turkish politicians are sometimes bent on doing, is to doubt the existence of any link between them and those whom they claim to be their illustrious ancestors. The mischievous implication is that the descendants of Plato and Aristotle were diluted to extinction by a combination of emigration and repeated infusions of the blood of foreign invaders. As we have seen, the Athenians escaped the first of these invasions, by the Dorians, and survived stoutly as unadulterated Ionians. They too, however, were hostage to the almost comical Greek paranoia about national origin.

The ancient Athenians liked to think they were autochthonous, which is to say the original inhabitants of the area they occupied. This was to some extent a snub aimed at their great rivals, the Spartans, who were definitely Dorians and therefore, in Athenian eyes, *parvenus*. As the original inhabitants who had fallen to the Spartans were relegated to ignominious serfdom (the helots), the Athenians were not slow to point out that they had never suffered the humiliation of conquest. The historian Thucydides, incidentally, unkindly suggested that Attica was overlooked because it contained nothing worth conquering.

Aggressive troops: The Ionians tended to be short, dark-haired seafarers with a reputation for quick wits, shrewd commerce and aestheticism. The Dorians were of central European origin, taller and fair. They were aggressive troops who enjoyed harp music but were otherwise indifferent to the arts. They went to war in horse-drawn chariots and wore a full panoply of bronze armour with plumed helmets and studded belts. They carried long swords, iron-tipped spears and round shields with a central boss.

The Ionian resistance they encountered wore loin cloths or short breeches and fought

Left, the Temple of Olympian Zeus. A prediction at Delphi involving this site brought about the downfall of a king.

mainly with slings and arrows from behind large wicker-and-leather shields. Most of the Ionians had probably never seen a horse before. In their social arrangements, Dorian society was strictly patriarchal, but women enjoyed a fair measure of independence and respect. Ionian women, on the other hand, fared less well, which may have rankled in view of the affection which their men lavished on the female deity. In time, assimilation drew Ionians and Dorians closer together, and the old divisions tended to crumble when they were faced by a common, non-Greek enemy like the Persians. These bonds were strengthened by a shared

language and similar religious beliefs.

Their sense of joint "Greekness" manifested itself, too, in attitudes towards slavery. The prospect of one Greek enslaving another was considered unthinkable. Although slavery later became a commercial operation run by Greek pirates who raided shipping and scoured the coastal regions of Asia Minor and the Black Sea for suitable victims, the first slaves were mostly prisoners of war. When Greek fought Greek (and somewhere or other they were doing it all the time) it was kinder and more dignified to kill male prisoners. The same consideration did

not apply to "barbarians", a definition which fitted any non-Greek—or, for that matter, Greek women and children.

One of the great difficulties in providing a satisfactory answer to Turkish doubts about the ancestry of modern Greeks is the absence of any definable country called Greece before the 19th century. "Greekness" was language, religion and a sense of belonging, and as such it could be transported on the backs of "Greeks" wherever they chose to roam. And roam they did, so much so that Athens was only for a short period the centre of the Greek world. It was as likely to be in Asia Minor, where a large number of Ionians fled to evade the Dorians, as it was much later to be in Constantinople.

There cannot be an Athenian alive with a direct line of local descent from classical times. Apart from numerous and protracted foreign occupations, true Athenians were a smallish minority even in the Age of Pericles. In a later period, the city was suffering from severe depopulation and re-stocked with Albanians! At the time of Greek independence in 1834, Athens was a miserable village with a population of 6,000.

In one sense, then, there cannot be any surviving strains, certainly not one that has been continuously resident in Athens since the beginning. The Greeks argue that they are tied to their past and to one another by language, religion (although it was pagan for very much longer than it has been Christian) and their sense of being Greek.

It took the re-constituted Greeks nearly half a millennium to regain the strength and drive which the Mycenaeans lost as a result of the Trojan War. Just as the war was not really over a pretty face but over territory and money, the legend of Jason and the Argonauts looking for the Golden Fleece was an allegorical reflection of reborn political and economic forces. The Dorian invasions had depopulated the mainland to an alarming degree, but in due course the pendulum swung the other way and the Greeks—they were all Greeks now—began to experience land hunger. Jason was a symbol of new interest in the outside world for the purposes of trade and, a new twist, starting colonies.

The growth of trade had a profound effect

on the economies of developing city-states like Athens. Wealth had traditionally been invested in land, and it was the land-owning aristocracy alone which had the capital to develop the industries which produced the trading goods and to build the ships which transported them. The trade made them richer still, stretching the gulf between them and the poor. The aristocracy ran the state, perhaps under a titular king, but it was a selfish system with scant regard for the welfare of lesser mortals. There were no laws and no means to enforce them. The aristocracy were at liberty to preserve the social order as they saw fit, and that usually meant sending gangs of hired thugs into the streets with clubs to knock sense into anyone who seemed to be in need of it.

The unfortunates at the receiving end of such perfunctory justice began to think of starting colonies, possibly with the intention of emulating, once they got there, the bullies from whom they first had to escape. The new colonies invariably retained links with their homes bases, and it was to preserve the relationship that city-states organised regular festivals of games to which colonists could return like nostalgic "old boys". Athens staged the Panathenaic games, but these were never in the same class as a festival held in a comparatively barren part of the land, Olympia. Improvements in seafaring had opened up routes to the west, and some of the most important of the new colonies were in Sicily. As Olympia was on the western shores of the Peloponnese, it was convenient for colonists from Sicily and accordingly a popular sports venue.

Discontented citizens who did not join the flight abroad agitated for radical changes. The trend became noticeable in the second half of the seventh century and led to demands for written laws. Until then, anyone with a grievance had to settle it personally with the culprit. The state, such as it was, was concerned only with crimes that might offend the gods, and they, it seems, were oblivious to robbery and murder.

The codification of laws did not mean the

state was yet ready to take on the responsibility of prosecuting law-breakers. It was still up to the injured party to file a complaint. The judge merely put a stamp of approval on the penalty the plaintiff had in mind.

The penalties were dictated by custom and could be severe: enslavement for debt, for example, and death for stealing a cabbage. Draco, who was given the job of tidying up the legal process, has rather unfairly been saddled with the reputation of setting these penalties (hence the word "draconian"). In fact he, too, thought that many of them were excessive, and he said so.

The circumstances in which Draco was

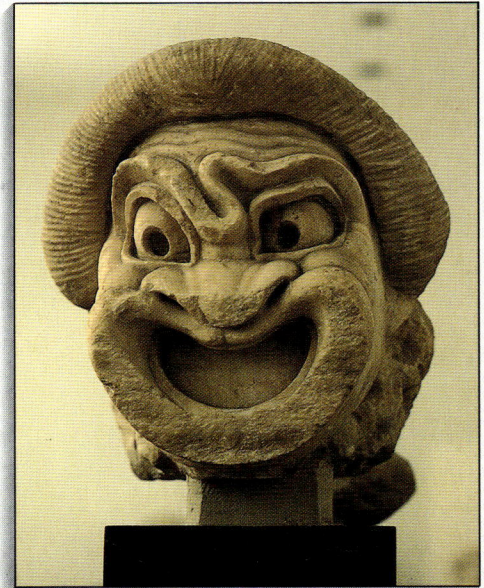

commissioned to sort out the law were indicative of the way things were developing on the political front. An Athenian noble, Cylon, had attempted in about 632 BC to seize power, which then lay in the hands of three officers elected annually from the great families. One of them was nominally a fixed-term king. His role, however, was limited to religious affairs and presiding over the Council of Elders, which was known as the Areopagus (after the hill, near the Acropolis, where the proceedings were held). The other officers were respectively chief justice and commander-in-chief of the armed forces.

Left, head of Asklepios. Right, an ancient gargoyle.

Cylon consulted the oracle at Delphi before making his bid and, not for the first or last time, the oracle responded with some thoroughly ambiguous advice. He was told to move during "the greatest festival of Zeus". A previous Olympic winner himself, Cylon assumed she meant the festival of Olympia. Wrong! The excuse, when the coup failed, was that she meant the festival of the Diasia, which was held where the Temple of Olympian Zeus now stands. As it happens, the festival of Diasia might have been a better bet. Most of the population turned out for an orgy of burnt offerings and drinking, and the venue would have left clear

the easiest line of attack on the Acropolis.

Cylon and his supporters managed to breach the Acropolis but were then trapped inside. He and his brother were able to escape; their supporters, however, were forced to surrender, which they did on the promise of safe conduct given by the Alcmaeonid family. As was to happen repeatedly to people who were forced to surrender when trapped in the Acropolis, the pledge was dishonoured and they were slaughtered on the way out. Cylon and his family were banished from Athens for attempting the coup but so, too, were the guilty Alcmae-

onids. It was a crime which appalled the gods to such an extent that it was thought certain to bring down a curse on the city.

The momentum towards democracy gained pace with the far-reaching reforms engineered by Solon. He seems to have understood that the old order was stirring such discontent that it was only a matter of time before another would-be tyrant like Cylon came along. "Tyrant" did not then carry all its later connotations; a tyrant was simply someone who grabbed power instead of inheriting it.

It was easily done. Cylon had shown what could be achieved with only a handful of supporters. What he had neglected to do was to secure more popular backing. Once in office, tyrants in other city-states were not necessarily worse than the kings or oligarchies they deposed, and in some cases were considerably better. Solon's reforms could not postpone indefinitely an Athenian tyrant, but compared with one of his contemporaries who was then roasting subjects alive in the belly of a large bronze ox, Athens was lucky in the one it got, Pisistratus.

Pisistratus was a great and popular champion of Athens. He promoted the Great Panathenaea, the festival which culminated in a procession up the Acropolis to present the goddess Athena with a new robe, which was to be the subject of Phidias's frieze on the Parthenon, as described in the section on the Acropolis. His architectural ambitions were so lofty that his greatest undertaking, a new temple of the Olympian Zeus near the Acropolis, was not completed for another 600 years, and only then by a philhellenic Roman emperor, Hadrian.

Pisistratus introduced a police force armed with bows and arrows and encouraged the worship of Dionysus. The main feature of the Dionysian feasts, among drinking and merry-making, was a musical contest between choirs behaving and dressed as goats. As the themes presented in song and dance became more wide-ranging, the goat-skins were replaced by the appropriate costumes. In a remarkably short space of time, the pagan goat ceremonies became tragedies presented by dramatists like Aeschylus—effectively the birth of theatre.

Pisistratus was succeeded by his son, Hippias. The Alcmaeonids, still languishing in exile after their heinous crime, were appalled at the prospect of a pre-emptive dynasty in the making and enlisted Sparta's help to get rid of him in favour of one of their own, Cleisthenes.

The plot worked but Cleisthenes, whose new position owed everything to well-lubricated nepotism, performed a notable *volte face* by declaring that there could never be any hope of political stability in Athens as long as tribally-based families were scheming to advance their own interests. His solution was to put responsibility for the affairs

The principles of fledgling democracy were protected by some curious safeguards. Once a year, for example, citizens were asked to place in an urn the name of the person they would most like to get rid of for 10 years. There were no formal political parties, and therefore no elections which would remove unpopular politicians from office. Ostracism, however, applied the same treatment to individuals, subject to a minimum of 6,000 disapproving votes. "Aristides the Just" was ostracised, for example, because people were bored with his sanctimonious posturing.

Marching orders were also given to Them-

of state and the re-organised army into the hands of a representative government elected on a regional basis which cut right across tribal lines.

Athens never achieved democracy in the modern sense. Every citizen had a vote, but the rules of citizenship were so tightly defined that power rested exclusively with a relatively small minority. Nevertheless, Cleisthenes had undoubtedly pushed Athens in a democratic direction.

Left, the youth of Antikythera. Right, pagan festivals lead to the birth of theatre.

istocles—a surprising choice because he could claim as much credit as anyone for elevating Athens to the top rank of Greek city-states. Persia had already encroached on the Greek colonies in Asia Minor and the appearance of Persian ships in the Aegean convinced Themistocles that Athens could be the next target. The vast Persian army would have been unstoppable on land, but Themistocles thought they would be vulnerable at sea. He therefore mounted a campaign to have all the state's resources put into building a navy.

Until then, the Athenians had not bothered

with a harbour as such; they had simply hauled their *triremes* on to the beach in Phaleron bay. Themistocles pressed for the fortification of the three natural harbours at Piraeus and the construction of a walled passage between them and the Acropolis. The walls were not yet ready when the Persians struck, and his fears for the safety of Athens were quickly confirmed.

Hopeless rebellion: As a token of Greek solidarity, Athens sent 20 ships across the Aegean in 498 BC to help the Ionians in their seemingly hopeless rebellion against the Persians, who were then intent on consolidating the Ionian settlements in Asia Minor into their burgeoning empire. The Athenian contribution was minimal. Its contingent of troops was retiring from an unsuccessful attack on a town when, by accident, a fire started and burned the town, Sardis, to the ground. The retiring Athenians were intercepted on their return to the ships, and scattered. They decided they had better go home.

That might have been the end of the story, but Darius, the mighty Persian commander, heard about the fire and asked who was responsible. One of his aides mentioned the Athenians. "The Athenians?" Darius was puzzled. "Who are they?" He asked a slave to make a note of the name for future reference. Even if the slave had forgotten to remind him, there was someone else present who would not. Hippias, deposed heir to the persistent Pisistratus, had devoted his exile to currying favour at the Persian court, and he could spot an opportunity to settle a score with the Alcmaeonid family. Cleisthenes, currently the liberal, reforming despot of Athens and also the direct cause of Hippias's misfortune, was one of them.

Hippias's scheming was a foretaste of the kind of Balkan intrigue which triggered World War I, and the consequences were no less convulsive. "Those ships," sighed the historian Herodotus, "were the beginning of the trouble between Greeks and barbarians."

Anyone with an interest in what happened next could do worse than read Herodotus, one of ancient Greece's finest products. It is said that Darius's slave made a practice of saying three times over every dinner: "Sire, remember the Athenians!" Darius was will-

ing to be reasonable with these obscure upstarts. He sent ambassadors to ask for an apology and a token of submission. The Athenians threw the visitors into a pit where they usually deposited the bodies of executed criminals. Darius replied with a punitive expedition. Hippias travelled with it, ready to reassume office.

To Darius's disbelief, the Athenians, whoever they were, saw it off. The battle of Marathon was immortalised, of course, by a runner, Philippedes, who was despatched to ask for Sparta's help against the Persians. The Spartans agreed, but religious convictions prevented them from moving until the full moon had passed. By then, the battle was over, and the victorious Athenians, while not as insignificant in their part of the world as they were in Darius's, earned a respect among the other city-states that they had never known before.

The Greeks glorified their heroes, as might be expected, but in Herodotus and some of the comic dramatists, like Aristophanes, they revealed a willingness to mock practically anything. Genuine heroes were not excluded. According to one story, Philippedes's best performance as a runner was not at Marathon but on another operation when the army unit to which he was serving was given general orders to retreat. Philippedes reputedly led the retreat at a pace which none of the others could keep up with.

Although Herodotus is full of wonderfully inaccurate gossip which tends to trivialise some of the issues he deals with, there were far-reaching global implications in what happened at Marathon. Strictly speaking, the Persians were Aryans and even spoke a language akin to Greek, but they were so under the influence of Semitic Babylonia and Assyria that the Greeks considered them wholly alien. Greek against Persian at Marathon set the precedent for the Aryan/non-Aryan, European/Asian and Eastern/Western confrontation which continued right through the Crusades into modern times.

When Xerxes succeeded Darius, the same slave, or conceivably his successor, was still mumbling over dinner, "Sire, remember the Athenians." Xerxes left no stone unturned in his preparations. Herodotus delights in listing the bizarre troops who assembled from every corner of the known world to form the biggest army ever, so big that when they stopped after a thirsty day's marching they were quite capable of drinking rivers dry. A bridge built across the Hellespont to carry them was broken in a storm; Xerxes ordered his men to pick up sticks and thrash the water for its impertinence.

Like almost every land invasion of the Greek mainland from the north the Persians had to funnel their way through the narrow pass at Thermopylae where formidable mountains reached to the sea. The pass between mountains and sea was in Xerxes'

avail. The Persian steamroller rumbled on and the civilian population of Athens was bundled off to the island of Salamis before the invaders entered the city.

Of all the buildings in Athens to which the Persians took their hammers, none would have given them more satisfaction than one in particular on the Acropolis. It was a temple, not yet finished, celebrating the Athenian victory over the Persians at Marathon 14 years before. But the last laugh rested with the Athenians, who later chose the very same spot to build the Parthenon as an enduring symbol of what lay in store for this new consignment of Persians.

Above, a *trireme*.

time barely wider than a chariot; by the 20th century, however, the sea had receded to widen the gap to more than a mile.

A mere 300 Spartans under Leonidas were deployed to defend the pass, and so confident were they about their chances against the Persians and their allies that they passed their time "bathing and combing their hair." The Persians discovered that a track through the mountains circumvented the bottleneck at Thermopylae, so the spirited defence put up by well-groomed Spartans was to no

The Persian navy, battered by storms on the voyage south, managed to reach the coast near Athens but was tricked into assembling in the narrow strait between Salamis and the mainland, where superiority in numbers was cancelled out, if not a liability. The citizens of Athens watched the battle from the island; Xerxes from a marble throne on a hill on the other side. Athens had provided at least half the ships for this momentous victory and took most of the credit, enough to crown the glory already earned at Marathon. Athenian supremacy among the Greek states was for the moment unassailable. But could it last?

Attica, as we have seen, was not rich. The naval construction programme which Themistocles had pushed through was paid for with revenue from the silver mine at Laurion, where the underground working conditions were so dreadful that they would, if better known, go a long way towards redressing the romantic view that the classical Athenians were in all respects saintly.

The measures taken to replenish and expand the state coffers after the victory were not beyond reproach either. The Delian League was established for the purposes of common defence against future foreign threats. Athens, exercising its prerogative as the hero of the moment, took charge of the money which members subscribed to the fund. The money was stored on the sacred island of Delos and was supposed to pay for the construction and maintenance of a fleet, but it was soon apparent that Athens was dipping into it for other reasons, like building the Parthenon.

Sharp practice: The contributors resented the sight of their money being squandered on the aggrandisement of a single member, particularly one who in the normal climate of Greek politics could not be trusted. The Athenian response to these complaints was to close down the treasury on Delos and transfer the money to the Parthenon "for safe-keeping". The way Athens handled the League's money was breath-takingly sharp practice, but 2,500 years later it is something for which visitors to Athens may wish to feel grateful. The Acropolis would have looked very different without it.

This period of great architecture and sculpture in Athens, the fifth and fourth centuries BC, was also a time of great literature and thought. Pindar's poems in praise of athletic victories may sound over-zealous to modern ears—the winner of a boys' wres-

tling match or some mule race was treated as if the victor had made an outstanding contribution to world history—but the poems were indicative of how the cult of the sportsman had taken root in a city where physical exercise was no longer associated merely with manual labour and whose citizens had the leisure time to indulge in it.

Euripedes, with Aeschylus and Sophocles one of the trilogy of great tragedians produced in this golden period, did not share

Pindar's enthusiasm for games. "It is folly," he wrote in *Autolycus*, "for the Greeks to make a great gathering to see useless creatures like these, whose god is in their belly. What good does a man do to his city by winning a prize for wrestling or speed or quoit-heaving or jaw-smiting? Will they fight the enemy with quoits? Will they drive the enemy out of their country without spears, by kicking? No one plays antics like these when he stands near the steel."

While Athenian intellectuals enjoyed a large measure of freedom to express their thoughts, there were limits. Socrates, forever

Left, boy with a goose. This statue is now in Athens' National Archaeological Museum. **Right**, a statue of Victory from the sacred island of Delos.

AN OLYMPIC TRADITION

The first indication of what was to become the Greek passion for athletic competition is contained in the Homeric legends, although at that time the contests were generally religious events connected with funerals and ancestor worship. The funeral of Patroclus, as described in the *Iliad*, included games staged at his tomb. The main events were a chariot race (first prize, "a blameless, accomplished woman"), shot put (first prize, a lump of iron) and wrestling (first prize, a tripod worth 12 oxen; second prize, "a clever woman").

Later on, the festivals assumed wider significance. They were, first of all, a logical development of the realisation that physical fitness was not merely the by-product of contemptible manual labour but also a respectable pastime for the leisured classes. There were running races over various distances, some for men wearing armour, and field events such as throwing the discus and the javelin.

The favourite among aristocrats was the pankration, a form of all-in wrestling between naked men with scarcely any rules apart from a ban on biting and gouging. It was not as dangerous as boxing, in which contestants wrapped their fists in leather thongs, although there were occasional casualties, such as the wrestler who won a bout with a hold that took so much out of him that he died just as he was being declared the winner. Kleomedes of Astypalaea, a boxer, killed an opponent with what was deemed to be a foul blow and was disqualified. The disgrace drove him mad, and on returning to his home town he wrenched the roof off a school, killing 60 pupils—the first recorded evidence, incidentally, of formal schooling.

Festivals of games were held in various parts of the country, the most famous being those at Olympia on the west coast of the mainland, a barren spot but a convenient venue for competitors and spectators who lived in Greek colonies in Sicily. They were held every four years, beginning in 776 BC, and nothing, not even wars, was allowed to interfere with them. By general agreement, states at war would allow participants to pass through unmolested.

The ancient stadium at Olympia, where games were held for more than 1,000 years, was not fully unearthed until 1961. The excavations revealed a running track but nothing of the awesome temples which had once stood near it. The games were abolished in AD 394 by the Byzantine emperor Theodosios I, partly because he objected to the nudity which had been a feature of the games ever since a sprinter, it seems, lost his shorts during the course of a race and presented a spectacle which delighted gods and mortals alike. Asian competitors were loath to remove all their clothing, an inhibition which Greeks took as a sure sign of barbarism. Theodosios II compounded the ban on the games by destroying the "idolatrous" temples.

The all-marble stadium in Athens, near the Zappeion, was built in its original form to provide for the contests of the Panathenaic festival. This festival, commemorated on the Parthenon frieze, had the usual track and field events but also incorporated an unusual kind of beauty contest. The city boroughs each paraded a team of 24 men who were judged according to "fine manhood". The climax was a procession up the Acropolis in which the entire population took part, the object being to present the goddess Athena with a new robe. After the presentation, the population trooped off to Piraeus for a regatta.

"Athlete" meant "prize-seeker" and, although the official prizes were of token value, winners were treated like fabulous heroes when they returned home, often being provided with free board and meals for the rest of their lives. When one of the despots won the chariot race, a highly dangerous event in which competitors considered themselves lucky to finish in one piece, the celebrations lasted a year.

It is a sad irony that modern Greeks do not win many prizes in modern, international Olympiads, but their competitive spirit lives on in an engagingly Greek way. The winner of the walking race in a recent festival of games restricted to Greek entrants was the man who crossed the line last. The judges decided that he was the only participant who didn't run!

challenging the ethical and political assumptions, discovered what they were. He was charged in 399 BC with corrupting the youth with atheistical doctrine and, declining to put up the defence of which he was more than capable, sentenced to death. In reality he was more likely the victim of political intrigue which was once again rampant in the city.

The historian Thucycides did not escape censure either. The subject which he tackled, the Peloponnesian War, cut short the peaceful and prosperous interlude after the defeat of the Persians. It was replaced by an internecine struggle which more or less divided the Greek world under the respective banners of Athens and Sparta and left the participants as weak as the Mycenaean Greeks had been after their prolonged campaign against Troy—with similar results.

The democratic institutions being fostered in Athens, first by Cleisthenes and then by Pericles, were viewed with great disfavour by the other city-states, whose kings (two at a time in the case of Sparta), despots and oligarchies saw no merit in sharing their powers. The transition in Athens had taken some revolutionary turns. Whereas members of government had previously been drawn by lot from a list of approved (but not representative) candidates, it was decreed that in future the names of all citizens would go into the hat as contenders for the so-called "Council of 500". As poor citizens who might be chosen by these means could not afford to give up their time to the state, state officials would receive salaries.

The concessions applied only to citizens, who were in a minority and, moreover, a shrinking minority. Coupled with a rise in the number of slaves and resident aliens, who were more heavily taxed than citizens, the qualifications for citizenship were tightened. No child was acceptable for future citizenship, for example, unless both mother and father were citizens and legally married. Under this rule, some of the city's most effective leaders in the recent past—Themistocles, Cimon and indeed Cleisthenes—would not have qualified because their mothers were foreigners.

Sparta, in particular, saw the rise of democratic notions as inimicable and actually anti-Spartan. The Peloponnesian War would probably have been remembered, or not remembered, as yet another of the interminal squabbles among notoriously quarrelsome Greeks had it not been the subject of Thucydides' detailed and absorbing history, the first of its kind. It dragged on from 431 to 404 BC largely because Athenian strength lay in the navy and Sparta's in the army, which made it practically impossible for the

two to get properly to grips with each other. It was brought to a conclusion by Athens committing its fleet to a madly pointless attack on Sicily and to Sparta going out and acquiring a navy of its own, from Persia.

Pericles died two years after the outbreak of the war, and the peace terms imposed on the defeated Athenians dismantled many of his achievements. Athens was effectively stripped of the empire he had built up, and the proto-democratic institutions were replaced by an oligarchical "Government of the 400". Assassination, surprisingly rare in what was generally a bloodthirsty climate, brought

Left, the Greek passion for athletic competition is highlighted in this statue of a discus thrower located near the Olympic stadium. **Right**, an "early owl" Attica drachma.

that government down after four months.

The Athenians ventured that they would like to revert to democracy, but Lysander, the Spartan victor, insisted they stick to old-fashioned, reliable oligarchy. Accordingly, the "Thirty Tyrants" came into being, but they also flopped. Lysander must have decided to let the Athenians pursue their democratic instincts, and Eucleides, the new archon, devised a socialistic scheme which put practically every person in the city on the state payroll.

The political debate had a hollow ring because of storm clouds gathering in the north. The Macedonians, who thought of

der, soon to become "the Great", took over. He had studied philosophy under Aristotle, but it was as a man of action that he was awesome. His all-conquering march to Egypt, across Persia, through Afghanistan and over the Khyber Pass into India has passed into legend. Even the southern Greek states were impressed. When Alexander asked their permission to call himself the son of a god, their response in as many words was that he could be the son of anyone he liked.

Alexander was probably mad in some ways, but he alone was capable of holding his prodigious empire together. When he died in Babylon in 323 BC, his generals

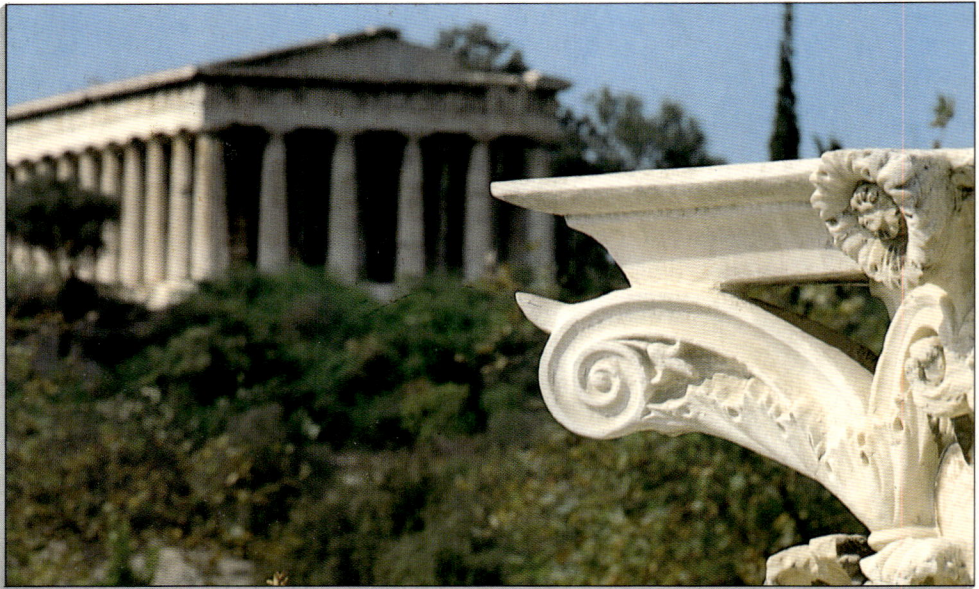

themselves as thoroughly Greek but were regarded by their southern brethren as somewhat uncouth barbarians, had preposterous imperial ambitions. Philip, successor to Archelaus who not so long ago had taken a seat in the Agora for a tight-lipped haircut, pounced on the northern areas and went on to defeat the south, bar Sparta, as well. Philip's presumption had Demosthenes in Athens spluttering, but Macedonia had rich resources in cereals, gold and timber, whereas the city states to the south had worn themselves out through warfare.

Following Philip's assassination, Alexan-

vainly tried for a generation to make it work. For a while, the whole of the world that mattered had been "Greek". Thereafter it was divided into three kingdoms, all of which remained nominally Greek: Macedonia, under various dynasties; Asia, under the Seleucids; and Egypt, under a long line of Ptolemies.

The rise of Alexandria in Egypt had the most direct bearing on Athens because it took away the latter's intellectual pre-eminence. The schools of philosophy in Athens continued, but scholars and scientists were attracted to the great library in Egypt which

Alexander had founded. Politically, Athens was allowed to pursue its idiosyncratic democratic inclinations, but the city had lost its place in the limelight.

Athens might have disappeared from the stage altogether but for one of those curious concatenations which history throws up. During the Second Punic War between Rome and Carthage (in what is now Tunisia), Philip V of Macedonia threw his lot in with the latter. The most familiar aspect of the Punic Wars is, of course, Hannibal's ascent of the Alps with his elephants, but far to the east the implications were that anyone who opposed Macedonia was therefore on

Athens enjoyed unprecedented peace and special privileges as part of the Roman state, but at times it seemed to labour under a death wish. Macedonia had been the author of its own misfortune by taking the wrong side in the Punic Wars; in 88 BC Athens emulated that folly by supporting Mithridates, king of Pontus in Asia Minor, in one of his military misadventures. Once again, the unequal adversary happened to be Rome, and the Roman general Sulla thereupon sacked Athens and levelled the walls of Piraeus.

Rome seems to have been remarkably tolerant of its troublesome charge. The Emperor Augustus was particularly sympa-

the side of Rome. Athens had never stopped sniping at Macedonia, so shortly after Rome's defeat of Philip in 197 BC, the Roman consul Flamininus turned up at the Isthmian Games to see how Rome's new-found Greek allies could be rewarded. For the moment, Athens was to be rescued from historical oblivion.

thetic, turning Greece into a province separate from Macedonia. The capital was not Athens, however, but Corinth, a sharp blow to Athenian pride because, while Corinth had once been an imposing rival, it too had been destroyed by the Romans for an unrelated misdemeanour and was still in the process of being put together again.

As if to compensate for the large number of Greeks who had decamped to Alexandria for their intellectual pursuits, Romans now flocked to Athens. Marcus Aurelius encouraged the trend by establishing a new university. The Emperor Hadrian (AD 117-38)

Left, the Theseion in the Agora. The Agora, full of stalls and shops, was once the site of a king's haircut. **Right**, two views of a statue of Emperor Hadrian (AD 117-38) located in the Roman Agora at the foot of the Acropolis.

looked at the plans for the temple of Zeus, a project which was over-ambitious at the time of its conception by Pisistratus and had proved too daunting to finish for a further 600 years, and made the necessary resources available. He also built the library and the arch which bears his name.

The extent to which Hadrian was consciously trying to put himself in the same league as the original creators of the city is revealed by his inscriptions on either side of the arch. One reads "This is Athens, city of Theseus"; the other, "This is the city of Hadrian and not of Theseus". The renewed fever of adornment affected some of the

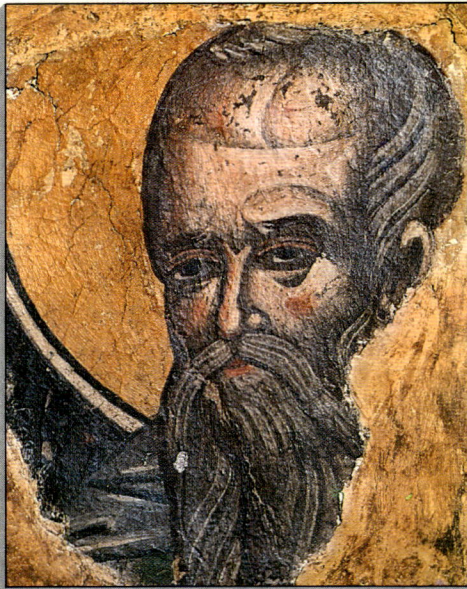

locals. Herodes Atticus, a rich citizen of Marathon, paid for the *Odeon* which is still named after him.

With hindsight, two unconnected events during the Greco-Roman era foretold the future of Athens. In AD 54, St Paul visited the city, although the time he spent in Corinth, which resulted in his two epistles to the Thessalonians, was to be more memorable. He won a few converts, but the full impact of Christianity was still some time in the future.

A similar time lag followed a raid into central Greece by a northern tribe called the Costoboci. The raid came to nothing, but 75 years later (around AD 250) saw the arrival of the Goths. Sensing the danger, the Emperor Valerian ordered the reconstruction of the walls around Athens, but they could not prevent the Goths from crashing through in AD 267 and pillaging the city. The Romans chased them out and for a hundred years or so all seemed well.

The Danube frontier, however, which had kept the aggressive northerners at bay, was beginning to show cracks. It broke down completely in the sixth century, and for more than 500 years thereafter the history of the Greek mainland is a chronicle of one invasion after another: Huns, Ostrogoths, Vlachs, Slavs of various stripe, Bulgars, Avars, Cumans, Patzinaks and one or two, like the "Getae", who popped up and then more or less vanished without trace.

A brief history of Athens cannot encompass the turbulent centuries of Slavic settlement in Greece. Isidore of Seville, writing in the seventh century, said "the Slavs took Greece from the Romans," and while that was probably true of much of the country, in Athens there seems to have been a repetition of the immunity which had enabled the city to sit relatively untouched through the Dorian invasions after the Trojan War nearly 2,000 years before.

Rather more pertinently, there was probably a repetition of the intellectual haemorrhage to Alexandria. The second time round it was to Constantinople which, originally the capital of just the eastern half of the Roman Empire, soon came to represent all that was left of it. The Byzantine empire centred on Constantinople was powerfully Greek in flavour. Just as the Ionians had once carried "Greece" in their luggage, as it were, to Asia Minor, the country now moved to Byzantium. Athens was an almost forgotten town in a provincial backwater, the more so after Justinian closed down its university, a stronghold of paganism, in AD 529.

The events in Athens between the departure of the Romans and the arrival of the Turks are likely to interest the modern visitor only insofar as they explain how and why the Acropolis was turned into a medieval fortress and became the home of a colourful collection of European dukes. The process began with the Fourth Crusade, which set out at the turn of the 13th century to liberate Jerusalem from the Moslem infidel but ended up attacking Christian Constantinople instead. The city fell in 1204, leaving the crusaders to share out the spoils of the Byzantine empire.

Athens, which most of the crusaders had never heard of, fell to a Burgundian noble named Othon de la Roche who passed it on after a few years to his nephew, Guy. For a while, Greece was a popular diversion for young French knights. "Some came to amuse themselves, others to pay their debts, others came because of crimes they had committed," according to the Venetian historian Marino Sanudo.

Banker takes all: Athens managed quite well under its young knight until he made the mistake of hiring some Catalan mercenaries to settle a local dispute. Later, there was a worse dispute about payment and the mercenaries found themselves owners of the city. They gave it to one of their previous employers, Frederick II of Sicily, but continued to live there. Their Athenian-born offspring did not inherit their fighting qualities, and in 1388 a Florentine banker named Acciajuoli took over the city. The Florentines were able to hang on for 50 years and demonstrated a certain flair for solving the labour shortage in a depopulated city by restocking it with imported Albanians.

In 1456, three years after Constantinople had fallen to the Turks, they were hammering at the gates of Athens and could not be denied. The Venetians twice occupied

Athens for short periods after that, which is how it came about, as described in the Acropolis section of this book, that a certain Schwarz of the Venetian artillery, under the direction of an officer with a more plausible Venetian name but no knowledge of artillery, contrived to blow a large part of the Parthenon sky high.

Lord Elgin, British ambassador to Constantinople, arranged to pick up many of the pieces still strewn on the ground like litter

150 years later. In so doing, he tidied up the Acropolis, but when the last Turkish garrison filed out during the Greek War of Independence—many to be butchered by the Athenian mob—they left behind what was little better than a slum.

The Duke of Wellington, a powerful voice at the European conferences which debated the shape of the future Greek nation-state, is said to have been not particularly concerned whether it included Athens, let alone that Athens should be the capital. The Romans, it may be recalled, preferred Corinth as the capital of their Greek province. To the vocif-

Left, *Greek Marriage* by Louis Dupré (*circa* 1820). **Right**, a naïve painting of leader Eleftherios Venizelos at the Balkan Wars.

erous Philhellenes who had been schooled in the Greek classics and had stronger romantic notions about the ancient Greeks than the Iron Duke or indeed the Greeks themselves, a Greece without Athens was inconceivable. Athens was duly incorporated in the new country and declared the capital while there was still a Turkish garrison in the Acropolis.

As the new capital of Greece (as opposed to Attica), the further history of Athens cannot realistically be separated from Greek history as a whole. A chronicle of events would generally reflect national issues, but there are some exceptions and it is on these that the story of Athens must concentrate.

The person who now filled the shoes of Cleisthenes, Pericles and Hadrian as the arbiter of what the city should look like was a 17-year-old Bavarian named Otho. When the Albanians later looked around for someone they could invite to become their king, their gaze lit upon the captain of the English cricket team. But he declined the job. The Greek throne was first offered to Prince Leopold of Saxe-Coburg, who accepted and then changed his mind. King Louis I of Bavaria did not want it either but thought it suitable for his son, the young Otho.

Athenians celebrated the king's arrival for days. A traveller complained in a letter: "The only thing wrong with these Greeks is their habit of rushing out into the street to sing and dance on any excuse!"

It has already been noted how Roman Emperor Hadrian observed a boundary between the Athens of Theseus and the new city he built. The young King Otho, or perhaps his regents, had the grace to turn down some enthusiastic architects who wanted to build him a palace on the Acropolis. Instead, the architects Cleanthes and Schaubert, commissioned to build a neo-classical city, were steered away from the historical sites.

Their proposals included an appraisal of the state of the king's capital: "The city of Athens numbers 6,000 inhabitants and is enclosed within a wretched wall which embraces 898 *stremmata*, of which barely two-thirds are inhabited…The greater number of houses are in ruins, and the rebuilt houses are mostly huts…There are 115 small churches, of which only 28 to 30 are in use, and four mosques, two in use, and two converted into baths."

The opportunities open to the architects were mostly insect-infected swamps, and it is said that the choice was narrowed down by hanging out pieces of meat and counting the maggots each accumulated. The yellow building along one side of Syntagma (Constitution) Square, the present Parliament building, was the original palace and denotes what was deemed to be the part of the city with the fewest pests. A second palace in Herod Atticus Street is occupied by king or president, as the case may be. Not without reason, the Greeks tend to view their monarchs as rather ordinary politicians whom they can take or leave as circumstances require. Greece is at present a republic.

Otho made the Greeks wonder about the institution of monarchy. His three regents were all Bavarians, and every department of administration and education was occupied by Germans. The Greeks thought that by then they ought to have some voice in government, but Otho refused to grant the constitution which would have given them that right. He was deposed bloodlessly in 1843 after a demonstration in Syntagma Square but was allowed back into office on the promise of adopting a more accommodating policy in future. In 1862 the Greeks decided he had not yet fulfilled that promise and he was forced to abdicate.

The country cast an eye over the underemployed royals on the European market for another palace tenant but decided that the choice would be made by plebiscite. An overwhelming 230,000 out of 240,000 votes cast were for someone who by international agreement was not eligible for the post, Prince Alfred of Great Britain, Duke of Edinburgh and second son of Queen Victoria. A Greek candidate, the only one, got six votes. The British government could not

egsakademie in Berlin and brother-in-law to the German Kaiser, supported Germany in World War I. Eleftherios Venizelos, the Greek Prime Minister, took the opposing view. Venizelos found himself running a pro-Allied breakaway government from Salonica while in Athens the king went his way. Both sides had armies and the Allies, who appreciated Venizelos's support but could not bring themselves to deal too sternly with Constantine, tried to keep the king and the prime minister apart.

When it appeared that Greece was threatened by a civil war, an Allied force of 2,000 French and British troops supported by ships

allow Alfred to accept, so it found an alternative in Prince William George of Denmark—like Otho, a teenager.

The arbitrary distribution of lesser European kingdoms around members of an extended family inevitably led to some testing divisions of loyalty. The problem manifested itself in Athens in the extraordinary events of 1 and 2 December 1916. Then King Constantine of Greece, educated at the Kri-

Left, the teen-aged King Otho, who left his mark on Syntagma Square. **Right**, a 19th-century water-colour of Athens.

was sent to Athens to act as a buffer. The king's forces took up positions just in front of the Acropolis in the knowledge that the Allied ships would hardly dare to bombard them at the risk of damaging it. Contact between the ground forces on 1 December led to a couple of hundred casualties on either side. The Allied troops withdrew the following day, but not before the French ships had bombarded the palace for three hours, sending Queen Sophia into the cellars. The royalist troops then began a systematic hunt for Venizelist sympathisers and killed them in cold blood.

The king's minister of war was more than satisfied with the outcome. "Our enemies," he told the troops, "must realise that such troops are invincible." The Allies promptly recognised the Venizelist government and, a few months later, sent word that they required the king's abdication. "Solicitous as ever of the interests of Greece," he went.

After the departure of King Constantine, who did not formally abdicate, Greece entered the war on the Allied side and therefore shared the spoils at the Peace Conference. Greece made substantial territorial gains, including eastern Macedonia, parts of the coast of Asia Minor and many of the Aegean

Byzantine empire could be re-established. Turkey might have appeared powerless when the Great Powers dismantled the vestiges of the Ottoman empire as war reparations, but it was not going to countenance Greeks helping themselves to whatever pieces of Turkey they felt they needed to realise their Great Idea, which presumed the seizure of Istanbul, *née* Constantinople.

In the event, the Greek army came within 60 miles (100 km) of Ankara, but thereafter the tables turned and the outcome, even Greeks have since acknowledged, was one of the worst military disasters in Greek history. In February 1922, the Turks took

islands. The population of a greatly expanded Greece exploded from fewer than three million to nearly seven.

The sense of a homeland recovered stirred foreign as well as Greek emotions, but the country had little chance of meeting the economic expectations of the population, many of whom were homeless. Conditions were especially dire in the countryside and villages, so all roads led to Athens, where they were hardly any better.

The wretched state of the country contributed to the "Great Idea", the extraordinary notion that all would be well if only the old

Smyrna, an area on the Turkish coast first settled by Ionians escaping the Dorian invasions and more or less given back to Greece at the post-war peace conference. They burnt it to the ground amid the ensuing chaos of escaping Greek soldiers and civilians.

A clause slipped into the peace treaty had provided for "the reciprocal and voluntary emigration of persons belonging to racial minorities"—in other words, the repatriation of ethnic Greeks stranded in Turkish territory after the re-drawing of the map and vice versa. The principle was brought into play to clear the human debris of the war of the Great Idea. In all, more than a million Greeks were repatriated, and again a large proportion found their way to Athens, a deluge which was to be repeated by refugees from the fighting in World War II and the civil war which followed it.

The façade of modern Athens would in any case have revealed the voids in its history when nothing happened. Once the Romans left and Greeks abandoned Athens in favour of Constantinople, the only building activity was on the Acropolis, and then little more than cosmetic. Pagan temples were converted first into churches and then into mosques. The Frankish and Florentine dukes

never had the luxury of such orderly growth. It had been a swamp when King Otho arrived and there was time to build only one commercial centre, the triangle formed by Syntagma, Omonia and Monastriki Squares, before the city was deluged by one influx after another.

The political repercussions of the disastrous Great Idea might have reminded Greeks that they had a tradition of despotism as well as democracy. A Colonel Plastiras— possibly the first but certainly not the last to be heard of 20th-century Greek colonels— led a coup which resulted in the prime minister, the commander-in-chief and other

senior members of government being tried by a court martial and shot. Political confusion split the country into republican and royalist factions.

Another soldier, a General Pangalos, took over with the intention of running the country personally. He postponed elections, suspended the constitution, imposed press censorship and threatened the civil service with the sack. He did not last long. Inviting comparison with the plotting that went on at the time of Hippias and Cleisthenes, he was replaced by a General Kondilis whom Pangolos had previously exiled.

added fortifications. But in terms of the Gothic and Renaissance, for example, which are a feature of other historic European cities, Athens has absolutely nothing.

Apart from the neo-classical architectural burst under King Otho, there is very little in the way of transition between ancient grandeur and modern scruffiness. Expanding cities usually fill in the gaps between outlying villages which lend their character to the part of the patchwork they occupy. Athens

Left, **Syntagma Square around 1865**. **Right**, **British troops liberate Athens in 1944.**

General Metaxas, next in the queue, could more flatteringly be compared with Cleisthenes. A dictator who had modelled himself on Mussolini, he turned against fascism and his mentor in particular with the most famous retort in Greek history. Mussolini, envious of German *blitzkrieg* successes, sought glory for himself by capturing Greece. The Italian forces began an advance from positions they had already occupied in Albania. Metaxas was given an ultimatum which, in effect, required him to give up Greece without a struggle. On paper, it was a grotesque mismatch, but Metaxas responded with one word: "No!" The anniver-

finally managed to achieve their objectives.

Herodotus sighted just 20 or so Athenian ships which were the start of the trouble between Greeks and barbarians. The small bands of Greek guerrillas who helped to delay the invasion of Russia may have put a mark on history as disproportionately large as those 20 ships.

Divisions between Greek guerrilla forces during the German occupation were the genesis of the civil war. The resistance, mainly in the form of hit-and-run attacks launched from the mountains, was as fragmentary as it had been against the Turks but eventually hardened into two bitterly hostile

sary of this famous rebuttal is celebrated each 28 October with a national holiday called "Okhi Day", *okhi* meaning "no".

Critical delay: The ferocity of the Greek defence drove the Italian army back into Albania where it had to be rescued by the intervention of Germany. The Germans occupied Greece but not as easily as might have been expected; in fact, the Greek resistance, led by crack British and Commonwealth troops, caused Hitler's invasion of Russia to be postponed for a critical six weeks which in turn caused the German troops to be trapped by the relentless Russian winter before they

groups, one Communist and the other loyal to the Greek government which, with the king, was in exile in England.

Sensing—wrongly, as it happened—that the fall of Italy and Allied landings in southern Europe would soon bring about the liberation of Greece, the Communists became less interested in the German occupation than in the swift elimination of potential rivals. Athens was liberated almost bloodlessly when the Germans withdrew northwards in October 1944, and the British commander ordered the dissolution of the guerrilla forces and the surrender of arms.

The Communists responded with a national uprising which at one point left the central district of Athens as one of the few parts of the country not under their control. The uprising was put down, not without difficulty, by British troops diverted from the fighting that was still going on in Italy. The Communists were split over what to try next. Some were inclined to accept their military defeat and to concentrate on infiltrating the political system; others took to the hills again, particularly in the north where they had the promise of cross-border support from the communists in Albania and, for a while, in Yugoslavia.

one day for the "fourth round". The Greeks never tire of denouncing the supposed barbarism of the Turks, but 40 years ago the Communists, at least, were emulating them in the matter of Janissaries, children removed from their families at an early age in order to be specially trained for military service.

This sorry chapter in Greek affairs was brought to an end largely by the split between Stalin and Tito of Yugoslavia. The latter closed the border to the Communist guerrillas, and without this vital route their revolution was doomed.

In spite of difficulties over Cyprus, Greece

The "third round" of the civil war was exclusively Greek against Greek and lasted three years. It was an atrocious business by any standards, and one which today the normally voluble Greeks are loath to discuss. When the Communists looked like losing, tens of thousands of children were taken from their homes and families and spirited to camps behind the Iron Curtain where it was intended that they would be imbued with the ideological purity which would equip them

Left and right, the Colonels seize power on 21 April, 1967.

made reasonable progress on many fronts after the civil war, and as early as 1951 the Communists were recognised as a parliamentary party. February 1964 was a subtle landmark: George Papandreou won with a clear majority of 53 percent of the votes cast, and it looked as if Greece might at last have torn itself away from the fragile coalitions on which previous governments had depended.

But Papandreaou's effort to advance the interests of his son, Andreas, especially after the latter had been identified with a group of allegedly revolutionary left-wing army officers in Cyprus, returned Greek politics to normal: "a cross between a coffee-shop and a whore-house," according to one of the cynical participants.

One crisis led to another until a group of unknown army officers took it upon themselves to rescue Greece from chaos and Communism. Their leader, Colonel George Papadopoulos, described Greece as "a patient strapped to the operating table" on whom he and his colleagues proposed to carry out some surgery. The treatment required the arrest of 7,000 political opponents almost immediately and included, for example, a ban on mini-skirts and an order to the civil service to answer all letters within three days. When the king tried to intervene with a feeble counter-coup, he was swiftly swept aside.

Public opinion abroad was outraged by the colonels, who were condemned as an affront to the birthplace of democracy. Ironically, it was in the birthplace of democracy that, once again, modern democracy was ailing.

The junta committed suicide in July 1974 by taking the country to the brink of war with Turkey. Other army officers, perhaps mindful of the Great Idea fiasco, forced them out and asked unconditionally for a civilian government. Constantine Karamanlis, who had run the country for eight years before the elder Papandreou, returned from exile in Paris for another six years in office. The Greeks were asked whether they wanted the king back; 70 percent said they did not. After negotiating Greece's admission to the European Common Market, Karamanlis was again voted out by a Papandreou, this time by the son, Andreas.

The colonels were still in prison in 1989 when Andreas Papandreou nearly died from a heart condition, made public his affair with a buxom air stewardess, fought and lost an election, married the air stewardess and was implicated in a financial scandal as big as any in Greek politics since Athens helped itself to the Delian League's money. The new government came into power on the promise that in future things would be different...

Greek officials promise that in the future politics will be different. Right, despite these claims, life in Athens continues much as usual.

64

A Day In The Life Of Ancient Athens

The Greeks who fought the Trojan War, according to Homer's description, were hearty meat-eaters and robustly heterosexual. By the fifth century BC, the Athenians were distinctly neither.

The switch in eating habits was forced on them. The domestic chicken had been introduced in some parts of the country, but meat was still hard to come by in Attica, which was agriculturally suited for little more than growing olive trees. After a breakfast of bread dipped in wine, the main meal was two courses: "a kind of porridge followed by a kind of porridge."

The more inspiring dishes served on special occasions were usually the work of cooks from one of the colonies where good food was the order of the day, notably Syracuse in Sicily. Wine was so cheap and plentiful that guests arriving for a meal might have their feet bathed in it, but it was never drunk with meals. Basic as the standard fare was, the epicurean Athenian must have been sorely tried by Pythagoras, the distinguished geometrician and religious reformer, who demanded total abstinence from beans, a popular source of protein.

Rituals of style: Almost all of these insipid meals were treated as a social occasion—although, unsurprisingly, the food counted for little. Plato and Xenaphon wrote about dinner parties without even mentioning what was served. Rather more importance was attached to the style with which men carried off the ritual of reclining on couches arranged around the table, their mantles off the shoulder down to their waists. Aristophanes had some advice for them: "Stretch out your knees and spread yourself in an easy and supple way among the cushions. Praise some article among the bronze-ware. Gaze at the patterns on the ceiling and admire the curtains of the courtyard."

They generally ate with their fingers and, instead of napkins, bread was specially prepared for the wiping of fingers. It was thrown afterwards, like everything else, on to the floor, either to be devoured by dogs or swept up at intervals.

The citizens of classical Athens, a minority among slaves and outlanders who paid an annual tax for the privilege of staying there, rose early and the men almost immediately prepared to go out. It was said that, to catch a man at home, it was as well to be waiting on his doorstep by dawn. Fixing a time thereafter meant referring to the length of the shadow thrown by a stick of standard length. "I'll meet you at six feet"—feet being the operative unit—obviously had to be qualified as either before or after noon, and confusion between the two was regular comic fare. Invited for a meal at a certain number of feet, hungry scroungers would always give themselves the benefit of the doubt and come before rather than after. One fellow arriving for a drink at an unholy hour claimed to have measured the shadow by moonlight.

Compared with the great public buildings on the Acropolis and in the Agora, private housing was drab, although some areas, such as a quarter known as Collytus, were more fashionable than others. No attempt was made to give houses an inviting façade. They turned their backs on the narrow, winding streets. The roofs sloped inwards, and the rooms looked on to a central courtyard.

By the fifth century, the reputation of women was at a low ebb. "A great pain for mortals," Hesiod called them. "In general, inferior beings," according to Aristotle, a fair-minded liberal. They were certainly not welcome to join male company at dinner unless, occasionally, as dancing girls. They were thought not to be up to the level of conversation. "If philosophic, it was above the women's comprehension; if not philosophic, it caused them no edification."

The odd theatrical jokes about women, however, imply a certain degree of affection. "Married!" a character splutters. "Did you say he was married? Incredible—only the other day I saw him alive and walking about." Theophrastus wrote about the Inopportune Man; in modern parlance, the type you can't take anywhere: "When he is a guest at a wedding he is the sort of man to run down the female sex."

Nevertheless, a man who was over-interested in women—sympathetically, libidinously or both—was definitely in a bad way; in fact, hopelessly "effeminate." The passive partner in male homosexual activity, incidentally, was not supposed to enjoy it. Although young girls took part in the sometimes naked pre-marital rites of the cult of Artemis Brauronia on the Acropolis, women generally spent their lives in the secluded

milk was from goats. Wine and water were always mixed, and getting the proportions exactly right was a serious matter. If too weak, it was dismissed as "a drink for frogs."

A book on symposium etiquette, *Professors at Dinner* by Athenaeus, analyses the problem of selecting the right kind of drinking cup for every occasion. The list of different cups runs for nearly 100 pages. A certain social cachet seems to have been attached to drinking deep without losing the ability to improvise a witty speech.

The Athenians clearly did drink a bit because their literature is full of sermonising about the virtues of not doing so. "This is the

world of the private courtyard. On waking up, their husbands could hardly wait to get out of it. They seem not to have been deterred by what must have been regular late nights at the symposia which followed dinner.

A symposium was not then the quasi-academic occasion now associated with the term; it was an after-dinner ritual of male conversation and entertainment. A formal invitation was not strictly necessary, the late-night company frequently being enlivened by gate-crashers. The choice of drink was between wine and water. There were no beverages such as tea or coffee, and the only

Greek way of drinking," according to one earnest authority, "to use moderate-sized cups, and chat, and talk pleasant nonsense to one another; the other course is swilling, not drinking, and it is deadly." Alternatively, and not nearly so earnest: "The first cup means health, the second pleasure, the third is for sleep, and then wise men go home. The fourth means rudeness, the fifth shouting, the sixth disorder in the streets, the seventh black eyes, and the eighth a summons."

The Athenians had their quota of euphemisms for being drunk, one of the more imaginative being "chest-protected." Citizens could afford to let their hair down because they were not inhibited by the prospect of having to turn up for work in the morning. A citizen could live adequately, which is not to say sumptuously, on handouts for performing state duties like jury service. The list of citizen-volunteers for jury service routinely stood at 6,000 and, as the legal system was always going at full tilt and each of the great juries required 500 members, they were kept busy. Citizens were obliged to attend the "democratic" assemblies which voted on government proposals and, rather like the present-day members of Britain's House of Lords, they were paid "expenses" for putting in appearances on a regular basis.

Cast out: Once a year, citizens were given the opportunity of nominating the person they would most like to see banished from Athens for 10 years.

There were no political parties in the usual sense, no conception of a loyal opposition, and no general elections for the constitutional hand-over of office. By putting unloved candidates out of the running for a decade, ostracism went some of the way to fulfilling the role of elections. It could also be wielded capriciously. Aristides was a Periclean example of the professional dogooder, and he was pleased to be called "Aristides the Just". In 482 BC the voters decided they had heard quite enough about this exemplary fellow and kicked him out to do good works elsewhere for 10 years.

The name of the unwanted person was inscribed on a piece of potsherd which was then placed in an urn. Many of these *ostraka* have been recovered, and identical handwriting demanding the banishment of a particular person is indicative of rigged ballots. Presumably, compliant citizens could earn extra money by helping one powerful family against another in their perennial plotting.

The growth of democracy and the re-distribution of wealth were inextricably linked, and between them they fashioned the style of life in Athens. Aristocracy by birth had

gradually been overtaken by an aristocracy of wealth, although the two were by no means mutually exclusive. Indeed, it was the landed aristocracy who were able to invest in the growth of foreign trade and therefore profit from it. They had the means to start the factories which produced the goods and to own the ships which carried them.

Citizens had deep-seated reservations about taking a job however much they could do with the money. Working regularly for someone else was tantamount to slavery. Slaves were exempt from the stigma of drudgery because, after all, they had no choice. A citizen did. "The type," said Theo-

phratus scornfully of a citizen who thought he might try working, "who would become an inn-keeper or a tax-collector; indeed, who would stop at nothing, not even taking a job as a public crier or cook." The objections were not the result of laziness, a later commentator observed, simply that "they detested that which made them acquire a stoop, or stunted the limbs, or misshaped the hands, or begrimed the person."

Apart from a few Ethiopians, slaves were white and preferably "barbarians", which is to say non-Greeks. Greeks were squeamish about enslaving fellow Greeks and, unless

Ancient Athenians clearly drank a great deal. Left, a gold cup from the temple at Vaphio. Right, an ancient and his friend.

they thought they could make some money out of ransom, were not inclined to take (male) prisoners in their internal wars. Women and children, of course, were a different matter.

Slaves were too valuable to be badly treated. They might take over the running of an aristocrat's estate or factory. Slaves who remained in domestic service—and there would seldom be more than a couple in a household—were expected to rise as early as their masters, because a citizen liked to have a slave handy at all times in case there was an errand to be run. Strolling down to the Agora with a slave in tow, the citizen attached considerable weight to appearances.

wear was the sandal—the favourite instrument of domestic corporal punishment, according to one English historian in an enthusiastic aside, "whether for children, slaves, or husbands." Shoes and boots could be white, bright red or black; if black, however, they should not be too highly polished. Slaves were notoriously slapdash about blacking a master's boots, so it was assumed that well-blacked boots were the work of the person wearing them, obviously someone who could not afford to keep a slave.

There were several such quirks about the figure an Athenian cut in public, not least the way he walked and talked. The great Aris-

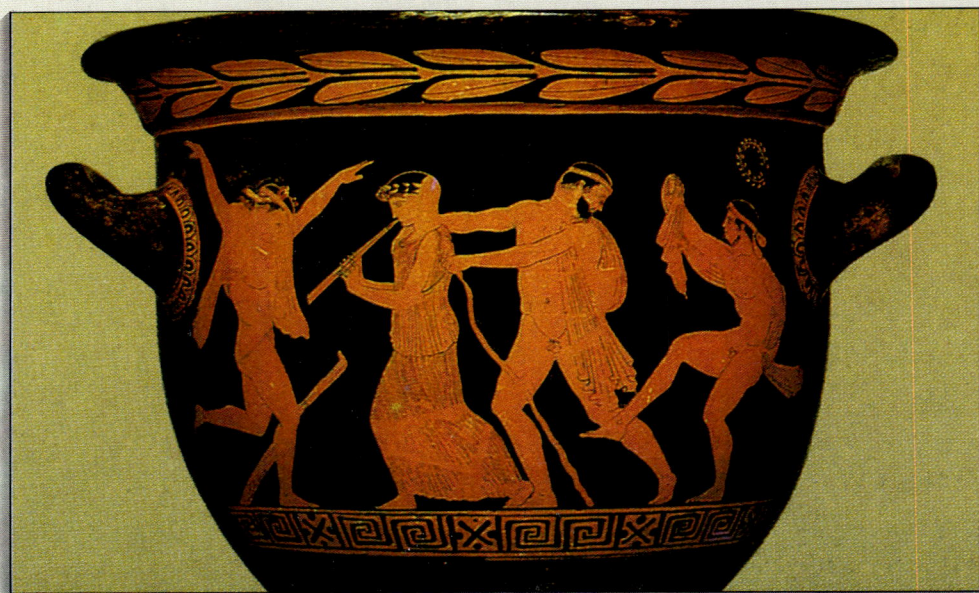

The tunic and mantle which men customarily wore were simply two oblongs of woollen cloth tied differently, but they had to hang properly and if necessary small weights were attached to the bottom to make sure they did. The length was important, too: about halfway down the shin. Clothing was generally white, although colours were not uncommon; only women, however, wore yellow. Men who wore lashings of jewellery were deservedly despised.

Some philosophers made a point of going about barefooted. The simplest form of foot-

totle pronounced on this matter, describing a respectable man as one with "slow movement, deep voice, and composed speech."

The business of the day was conducted in the Agora where, apart from market stalls and tradesmen, bankers sat at their tables. "Whose table do you use?" was the Athenian equivalent of asking after the name of someone's bank. Sparta, the great rival among city states, stubbornly retained iron bars as the only form of currency, whereas Athens, having borrowed ideas from the legendary Lydian billionaire, Croesus, offered a wide range of banking services, including exchange bureaux and letters of credit. The "tablemen" were invariably resident aliens but never the Jews who played a prominent role in banking elsewhere. Athens maintained a total ban on Jews.

The outlanders who were admitted filled the professional and commercial gaps left by the work-shy citizenry. Although many of them became immensely rich and influential, neither they nor even their children born in Athens could become citizens. The rights and perquisites of citizenship were jealously guarded by those who enjoyed them, and as time went by the qualifications—through marriage, for example—were progressively tightened rather than relaxed.

Afternoons were usually spent in one of the three gymnasia, early examples of the gentleman's club although with much greater emphasis on sporting facilities. Plato used the grounds of the Academy—"the groves of Academe"—to expound his views; Aristotle preferred the Lyceum. The Cynosarges was less exclusive and had the reputation of letting in persons of doubtful citizenship, although never slaves.

Various theories have been advanced for the Athenian's almost manic devotion to exercise, sport and the (male) Body Beautiful. One view attributes the cult to a change in military tactics. Under the old style of fighting, in which Ionian troops ran around in loin-clothes and fired off sling-shots, men had as much opportunity as they needed to show off individual prowess. The adoption of hoplite tactics, solid lines of infantry shoulder-to-shoulder behind a wall of massive shields, allowed none whatsoever, and the sports arena was a welcome antidote. A more prosaic thought is that the Athenians had merely shaken off the old idea that physical exertion was exclusively the concomitant of degrading manual labour and had decided it could be fun.

In any event, the store set by athletic feats gave rise to the professional sportsman, a hero of his times. The official prizes at the famous games were as symbolic as the present Olympic medals. The victors, however,

Left, pottery reproductions on sale in Plaka. **Right**, the genuine article.

could look forward to lucrative rewards from their sponsors, including free board and lodging for the rest of their lives.

The playing fields of the gymnasia, where younger members ran, wrestled, boxed and threw the discus and the spear, were surrounded by terraces and colonnades from which the older members looked on with, it may be assumed, close personal interest. The athletes were naked, as they were at the Olympic Games and similar festivals. The communal bathing after games was another demonstration of manliness in that Athenians thought the use of hot water effeminate.

There were no baths as such, rather a

stream of water gushing from a spout in a large urn or a dousing by an assistant with a bronze or earthenware vessel. Singing in the middle of all this was not effeminate, merely vulgar. After washing, members smeared themselves with scented olive oil which then had to be scraped off with a curved and hollowed instrument made out of bronze.

It seems to have been not a bad life—at least for the male citizen with a slave or two, an unprotesting wife, a passion for politics and exercise and, perhaps, a willingness to forgo the pleasure of beans. Anyone else might have expressed a few reservations.

LORD BYRON AND THE PHILHELLENES

On the morning of 5 January 1824, an exotic party disembarked from two ships at anchor off Missalonghi at the entrance to the Gulf of Corinth and were rowed ashore with an enormous amount of baggage which included five horses, a Newfoundland dog and a bulldog. They received a messianic welcome of artillery and musket fire from an assortment of Greek independence fighters, among them a very small, fat man dressed in tails and a flat cap.

Somewhat optimistically, because the rebellion against Turkey was not going at all well, he called himself the president of the Greek senate. A pair of extraordinary, pebbled glasses gave him the appearance of a myopic mouse. Prince Alexander Mavrocordato was not a real prince either, but he was a survivor and ended up, legitimately, as prime minister nearly a decade later.

Notorious libertine: The first of the visitors to step ashore, resplendent in a brand new scarlet uniform, was Lord Byron, famous poet and, as far as hordes of society women were concerned, even more notorious libertine. Such a reputation, however, meant less to the reception committee than the fact that he was both rich and committed to Greek independence. They had nothing. The entourage of their prospective benefactor included the brother of a recent mistress, his valet Fletcher who had been to Greece before and dreaded being back, a Venetian gondolier under the impression that his father had sold him to Byron, a pretty Greek boy dressed as a page, a physician and a black American groom who, in the records of this curious expedition, is never given a name.

To give him his due, Byron felt rather ridiculous. At 35 he was paying the price of converting the fame which had been showered on him as a prodigious poet into spectacular debauchery. The celebrated curly hair was thin and greying; his teeth were rattling in their gums. While Napoleon was on the rampage in Europe, Byron as an

Left, a young Lord Byron in Suliot dress.

Englishman (like citizens of other countries against Napoleon) had been denied the normal grand tour of Europe and had gone instead to a neglected and generally forgotten part of the world: Greece.

His poems, especially *Childe Harold*, about ancient Greek glory enslaved by Turkish barbarity, won enormous popular support (abroad, rather than among illiterate Greeks whose knowledge of history was shaky) and read like an incitement to revolution. When the Greeks indeed rose, Byron felt obliged to join them, even to die in battle for them. Byron arrived dressed for the part of a general, but militarily he was a total ignoramus.

His devotion to ancient Greece was undiminished, but he was appalled by what he saw as riff-raff who squabbled and if necessary murdered one another to get hold of the money he was doling out. Four months after his arrival, Byron was soaked by a downpour while riding, complained of pains in his back, and a few days later died a less than heroic death. Apart from the money and an intervention which saved some Moslem prisoners whom the Greeks would routinely have killed, he personally achieved nothing, and he knew it. "I do not lament," he said at the end, "for to terminate my wearisome existence I came to Greece. My wealth, my abilities, I devoted to her cause. Well, there is my life to her."

The extent to which Byron is venerated in Greece to this day clouds the more important, though often eccentric, contribution by foreigners on both sides. Byron's cry was taken up in fashionable circles in a manner which anticipated the crusading flavour of the International Brigade in the Spanish civil war a century later. Thousands of volunteers rallied to the cause, especially Danes, Germans, Swiss and British followers of the philosopher Jeremy Bentham (he, who on dying, was stuffed and mounted in the vestibule of his London college).

Most knew as little about soldiering as Byron, so luckily for them and perhaps for

Greece too, few of them actually arrived. Scattered among those who did, however, were volunteers and mercenaries whose participation has been as devalued in the war as Byron's has been exaggerated.

It was quite late in the war that Athens in general, and the Acropolis in particular, acquired symbolic status. Previously, according to a Greek account, "almost every [Greek] political or military chief was engaged in a plot to supplant or massacre some rival." A Turkish garrison sat out the turmoil in the Acropolis. They could not leave, but they were under no obvious threat until, in the unusually dry winter of 1821, their water

A brigand named Odysseus, whom Byron disconcertingly always called Ulysses, thereafter occupied the Acropolis, ironically offering his submission to the Turkish sultan in order to be allowed to keep it. The Turks were not yet spent, and in 1826, assisted by forces of the Egyptian ruler, Mehemet Ali, who was not an Egyptian at all but a former Albanian tobacconist, they regained control of almost the entire mainland. The Acropolis was under siege again, this time with Greeks holed up inside.

The Parthenon should not have survived the six months of besiegement. Despite an undertaking by the Sultan, the Turkish sol-

ran out. The terms of their capitulation were safe passage to foreign ships in Piraeus in exchange for their weapons and half the money they still possessed.

Of the 1,150 Turks who gave themselves up for herding to the Stoa of Hadrian where they were to wait, only 180 were fit men—the rest were refugees from the Acropolis village, elderly and maimed, women and children. The Athens mob chased them through the streets, and 400 were killed before finding sanctuary in foreign consulates. Atrocities by both sides were a common feature of this dirty war.

diers shelled it repeatedly. Unlike Schwarz, the Venetian gunner in 1687, they repeatedly missed. The lifting of the siege involved a full cast of eccentric Philhellenes. To begin with, inside the Acropolis was a furious French colonel, Charles Fabvier, who believed he had been the victim of a perfidious trick by his English arch-enemy, General Sir Richard Church, and the Greek government to get him out of the way. Carrying a sack of gunpowder, he had been persuaded to sneak through Turkish lines and enter the Acropolis with a private army he had diligently been training for special operations for years. He had expected to replenish the garrison's supplies and escape the following night, but the besieged Greeks took a different view. Thankful for reinforcements at last and deciding it was their turn to leave, they made a point of firing their guns to arouse the Turks whenever Fabvier tried to do so.

Although Church was English, he was a general only in the Neapolitan army and his knighthood was Hanoverian. Fabvier, a disciple of Napoleon who had never recovered from the shock of Waterloo, had travelled in disguise all over Europe hatching Bonapartist plots. He was a fierce republican and a principled, capable officer who gave his

Fleet, another Briton, Captain Lord Cochrane, heir of the Earl of Dundonald. Cochrane, like Church, had enhanced his rank in foreign service. A daring frigate captain in the Royal Navy at Trafalgar (what else to add to poor Fabvier's agony?), he was later imprisoned in Britain, and expelled from the House of Commons, for a hoax which enabled him to make a killing on the Stock Exchange by announcing, prematurely, that Fabvier's idol, Napoleon, was beaten.

He escaped, made his way to South America, and was successively commander-in-chief of the navies of Chile, Peru and Brazil. He was an unlikely looking South American

Bataille navale de Navarin, livrée le 20 Oct 1827

services to Greece free. He detested Church because he had fought not only for the despotic king of Naples but, moreover, against Napoleon. Trapped inside the Acropolis, Fabvier learned that over his head Church had been appointed Commander-in-Chief of the Army.

Fabvier's republican instincts did not allow him to form a significantly higher opinion of the newly appointed Admiral of the

Left, the sea-battle of Samos, a water-colour from 1824. **Right**, the Battle of Navarino was fought by countries not at war with each other.

admiral, a giant with a shock of red hair who was inclined to wield his telescope like a swagger stick and settled any sign of truculence below decks with a thumping fist.

Back home in Scotland and then in his fifties, Cochrane heard that the Greeks were looking for an admiral and, through stock market deals almost as dubious as his own, had money to pay for one. The fee he demanded—half in advance, the balance when independence was won—amounted to almost the entire national revenue of Greece for a year, but the Greeks went along with it. His agreed expenses, the even larger sum of

£97,000, would be supplemented by the right to all the prize money the navy won under his command, including the sale of captured ships. He said he would destroy the enemy navies and burn Constantinople given the fleet he specified, which included a yacht each for himself and his staff.

In their haste to be the first to dine in the Acropolis, Church and Cochrane, who supervised most of the action from their respective yachts, contrived to make what ought to have been a fairly simple advance from Pireaus to lift the siege into the worst single disaster the Greeks had experienced in battle. Against the local commanders' ad-

vice, they chose to make a new landing at the other end of Phaleron Bay. Instead of approaching under cover of olive groves, the men found themselves advancing totally exposed under a single Turkish howitzer.

Church and Cochrane, coming ashore from their yachts for what they imagined would be a victory celebration, found the remnants of their force tearing towards them with the Turkish cavalry in pursuit. The Neopolitan general and Brazilian admiral did an about-turn and waded into the sea up to their necks to reach their boats. The plan to relieve the siege was abandoned, and a few days later Fabvier, now black with rage, surrendered and led his men out.

Permanent possession of the Acropolis was decided, in the end, by the Anglo-Russo-French Treaty of London. The Greeks agreed to an armistice at once; the Turkish and Egyptian fleets only provisionally so. Cochrane was still on the loose, and they wanted an assurance that he would observe the armistice. Confusion reigned, and on 20 October the flagships at the head of the combined British, French and Russian fleet sailed into Navarino harbour and dropped anchor within a ship's length of the Turkish and Egyptian admirals and their fleet of 89 warships and about 50 transports. A British frigate sent a boat to ask a fireship to move. Someone let off a musket shot at the boat and hit an officer. An Egyptian ship fired a single cannon round at the French flagship; the Frenchman fired one back. That did it.

"Unabated fury for four hours," the British Admiral Sir Edward Codrington wrote in his dispatch, "and the scene of wreck and devastation which presented itself at its termination was such as has been seldom before witnessed." Codrington himself ended the day with two bullet holes in his coat and one in his hat. The British, French and Russian navies did not lose a ship, but most were damaged. At least 60 ships were written off.

The Battle of Navarino did not actually end the war. It dragged on for another five years while the Sultan bickered about the terms of the formal concession of Greek independence. Without a fleet to maintain his armies in Greece, however, all he could do was postpone the inevitable. In view of the impetus given to the rebellion in this first instance by the Philhellenes, it seems appropriate that foreigners should also be responsible for its practical conclusion.

In some respects, the Battle of Navarino was as singular an event as Byron's landing at Missalonghi. The entire battle was fought at point-blank range by ships at anchor, and none of the parties involved—Turkey, Egypt, Britain, France or Russia—happened to be at war with any other.

Left, the Lord and his dog Lion. Right, Byron was not the hero many historians claim.

Plato has preserved for us what must have been a touching little conversation that took place somewhere under the shadow of the Acropolis. Sophocles, a proud old man of 80, met a friend of about the same age who asked him—as twinkle-eyed old men are apt to do—whether he had any sexual desires left.

"Don't mention such things," the great tragic poet is reported to have replied. "I'm only too glad to be free from it all. It's like escaping from being tied to a raving madman." And he lived, thus liberated, for 10 more years, writing some of the world's greatest literature in the process.

Sophocles' words have a meaning deeper than what they seem on the surface. The ancient Greeks—condensed through the lenses of history into the few decades of the Golden Age of Athens in the middle of the fifth century BC—believed in the supreme good of wisdom in formulating the human being. Just as Sophocles freed himself (or rather, was freed by advancing years) from the "raving madman" of the flesh, lustrous contemporaries of his such as Pericles broke out of the temptations of partisan politics to the rarified air of shining statesmanship.

And in many ways, modern Greece—in its mere 170 years of existence—is trying to accomplish the same thing.

Overheated politics: Some parallels are striking. Domestic Greek politics are just as overheated as they were in ancient Athens: the right-wing oligarchs versus the left-wing democrats. And just as the Persians were the great foe, eternally threatening from across the Aegean when they weren't actually invading Greece, today the Turks are looked on with the same suspicion. In the past 15 years Greece and Turkey have come to the brink of war at least twice, and it could give the modern Greek some comfort to know that their forefathers finally disposed of the Persians through Alexander the Great.

It was three centuries after the Golden Age

that the Roman republic spread its legions over a Greece weakened by constant internal war. In the late 20th century AD, ironically, modern Greece is being similarly absorbed by what some thinkers consider to be a direct descendant of the Roman ideal of a unified Europe—the European Community. True, this time no hostilities are involved, and most Greeks believe the Community is beneficial to Greece (which joined as the 10th member in 1982). But will this land become Europe's bargain holiday beach, a nation of waiters and hotel keepers, overrun by hordes of tourists instead of Roman cohorts?

Meanwhile the Sophoclean madman is still very much in evidence as a kind of political sex drive that gives Greece more than its fair share of turmoil. Passions predominate in the neo-classical *Vouli* (Parliament), in party allegiances, in coffee-house talk, rising to regular vast orgasms every four years when election campaigns are on. Such wasting of energy has left the Greek people too tired to do any real work, as the telephone systems, public utilities and the general disorganisation woefully attest.

A cab driver who cannot be bothered to drive to a particular Athens suburb, a traffic policeman who runs for shelter in a few drops of rain, a bank manager who is grossly impolite to the old women asking for her pension, a cabinet minister who gives government jobs to his relatives, all are symptoms of a basic conflict in the Greek psyche: why must I work harder in a materialist world, when all my culture and outlook steer me towards a breezier way of life?

The ancient Greeks revered the life of the mind. The modern Greeks desire it as well, but are not given the chance. In the past 30 years Greece has been wrenched from an agriculture-based economy to the computer age, but the national mentality hasn't been given a chance to catch up. There is very little of the British-type politeness and efficiency, for example, simply because until the middle of this century it was never a social necessity.

Some might say that the modern Greek

mentality started to take shape while Pericles was on his deathbed and unstable, ambitious politicians angled for power. Pericles, in many ways the ablest statesman ancient Athens produced, has had his modern counterpart: Constantine Karamanlis, who gave modern Greece its periods of political stability in the late-1950s and late-1970s, who almost single-handedly restored democracy to Greece after seven years of military dictatorship (a miraculous, bloodless transfer of power), and who led the country into the European Community, preserving all the while an unswerving, dignified dedication to duty.

Pericles died of complications of plague; Karamanlis lives still, a Sophoclean figure, now in his eighties. Pericles did not live to see Athens' fortunes dragged in blood and dust in the 30-year Peloponnesian War by demagogues such as Cleon and Alcibiades. Today, to observe along with the rest of the world, scandal, intrigue and allegations of corruption during the recent administration of former Prime Minister Andreas Papandreou, who knows what other scenes Karamanlis will witness in the coming years?

After Rome rolled over the declining Greek states and annexed them to its empire, the advent of Christianity, through the efforts of St Paul, temporarily revived the Greek mind. We read of how Paul arrived in Athens and stood on the great rock a few hundred metres west of the looming Acropolis—a rock now polished shiny by tourists' sandals—while a few sophisticates snickered, calling him a "babbler". But they were a distinct minority; he was given a respectful hearing. Paul's astute mind had at once noticed that the ancient Greeks had lost none of their huge mental ability, for he saw an altar in the city dedicated to "The Unknown God". For a Greece yet dominated by the 12 Olympian gods, it was a revolutionary development, which Paul turned to his advantage.

After expounding the doctrine of Christ, Paul was given a polite brush-off. "We will hear thee again of this matter," the Greeks said, no doubt with a patronising pat on the back. After all, who was this Jew daring to challenge the Greeks on their own philosophical turf? But he had won. Walking away from that sermon were the first two Greeks who became Christians: Dionysios the Areopagite (the main road under the Acropolis is named after him) and a woman called Damaris (whose name now graces a long street in the district of Pangrati).

Nearly 2,000 years later, Greece is a devoutly Christian nation to a degree rare even in the Catholic countries. Ninety-seven percent of Greeks profess allegiance to the Greek Orthodox church, the oldest in Christendom. Despite the onslaught of Western ways and culture, the Orthodox spirit remains unchanged, and in fact, could be undergoing a revival as politics and social

concerns find no solution. Fashionably-dressed young people, of the sort who five years ago would have been more at home in a discotheque, are now seen standing reverently in the brilliantly-frescoed churches.

It was the Orthodox church that kept the idea of Greece, and the Greek language, alive during half a millennium of Ottoman Turkish occupation, from the 15th to the 19th centuries (some parts of Greece weren't freed until 1913) that is at the root of Greece's enmity towards Turkey. All Greeks today bewail the lethal influence of that alien rule as inculcating a social fatalism, a tendency to state corruption and graft, a temptation to bow the head, a fear of passionate crusading.

The Greeks are keenly aware of their psychological block and have given it a name: *ephthinophobia*, or fear of responsibility. A result of centuries of fickle rulers and uncertain times, it is what makes cabinet ministers and *Vouli* deputies appear to live in mortal terror of their party leader or prime minister. It is what makes a voter vote for his party even though his pockets are empty. It is what makes parliamentary rebellion in Greece a crime only one degree lower than high treason. The leader is king, as several

military dictators of this century have discovered to their satisfaction.

Greeks don't like independent politicians, and this is perhaps the most striking departure from the ancient Greek ideal. Social psychologists attribute the phenomenon to the great power of the in-group over Greek society. Social ostracism is seen as the ultimate evil, worse than death. That is why a Greek, ancient or modern, is rarely a traitor.

But when he is, he has to be spectacular

Classical symmetry: left, a Knossos fresco and **right**, a modern woman (*circa* **1930**).

about it, merely to find another in-group to give him vital social nourishment. Themistocles, after having saved Greek civilisation at the Battle of Salamis in 480 BC became so sickened at the treachery of postwar politics that he fled—right to his would-be enslaver, the Great King of Persia.

A generation later Alcibiades, in the midst of a disastrous war with Sparta, was stung unendurably by the political enmity of some of his fellow Athenians and walked right off to the enemy, even going so far as to bathe in the icy Eurotas River near Sparta—a far cry from his comfortable Athenian upbringing.

Fortunately, one today cannot imagine any Greek, however maligned he might be at home, going off to join the Turks. Modern Greek nationalism is here a definite improvement over ancient Greek fragmentation, when city-states could never manage to pull together in a common Greek cause.

But thousands of Greeks have gone—to form flourishing communities in North America, West Germany and Australia, to name the most congenial new homes. Like the colonists of ancient times who brought the blessings of civilisation to Spain and the Black Sea, like Alexander the Great whose troops rolled back the frontiers of the known world, modern Greek migrants might yet overcome the malaise of Themistocles and Alcibiades still lurking, one feels, in the shadow of the Acropolis.

A quiet life: True, Greece's constitution is undeniably democratic, and all the rights benefitting a free people are therein enacted. But the old tyranny of the psyche still drums its in-group message through the country's institutions. The Greek still isn't comfortable with a fast-paced way of life; he still longs for the siesta, the social gathering, a less structured existence.

When C.S. Lewis, the brilliant religious writer, visited Mycenae in 1960, the seat of the Greeks' most ancient civilisation, and gazed up at the 3,000-year-old Lion Gate of King Agamemnon, the old tales of the Greek tragedians surged back to him and he exclaimed: "My God! The curse is still here!"

But as Greece advances along with the rest of Europe, one feels, it won't be around for very much longer.

The most distinguishing thing about Greeks is their uniqueness. They don't belong to any of the more general groupings of Latins, Slavs, Anglo-Saxons, Scandinavians, Hispanics, Africans or Asiatics but stand entirely apart. Greeks are even listed as a separate race on immigration forms to enter the United States.

Their language is different from any other in the world and their religion is the *Greek* Orthodox faith. They have a history which contains the roots of western civilisation and a young king, Alexander the Great, who conquered the entire known world. This ancient history is a great source of pride to all Greeks and when they think about it (which they do quite often), it makes them feel a definite cut above their fellow-men.

Black Tuesday: On the other hand, four centuries of servitude under the Turks also left scars on the Greek character, most of which survive to this day. Just as an illustration of how deeply the collapse of Constantinople affected the Greeks, it is interesting to note that because the city fell on 29 May 1453, which was a Tuesday, Tuesday has remained as black a day for the Greeks as Friday the 13th is for the west.

No self-respecting Athenian will get married, start a new business, buy a new house or do anything important on a Tuesday because he is firmly convinced that the disaster that befell Constantine IX on that fateful day five centuries ago will be as sure to fall on him as it did on that unfortunate, last Byzantine emperor who was killed fighting on the walls of his capital.

During the 400 years of subjugating, and while those European neighbours who were not groaning under the Ottoman yoke were enjoying the Renaissance, the Age of Discovery, the Age of Enlightenment, the Spanish Inquisition, the French Revolution, the Industrial Revolution, and growing up to be-

come prosperous and sophisticated Europeans, it was all the Greeks could do to keep body and soul together. Those who did survive, and were able to pass their genes down to the Greeks of today, were those with the sharpest wits and easiest consciences; the most artful dodgers of the despotic laws of the oppressor.

One would have thought that after more than 150 years of independence, the "artful dodger" gene would have disappeared from

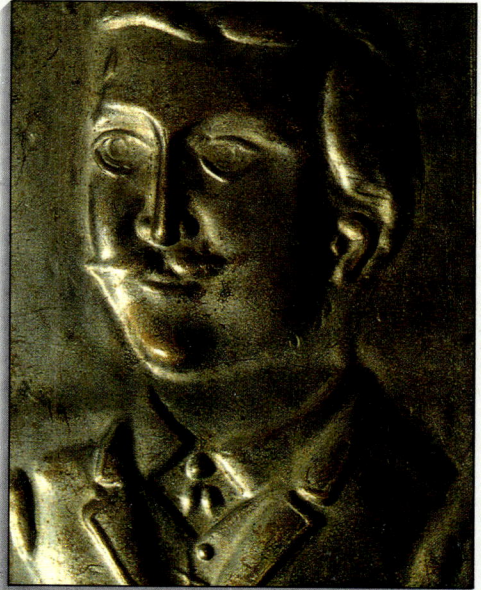

the DNA of the Greek male. But constant interference in Greek affairs by European powers, consistent misrule by imported royal families and misgovernment by the local political talent (sometimes elected and sometimes not), rather than blunting the sharpness of his wits and his disrespect for the law, have only served to make him more cunning and much more devious. Indeed, so acute is this in the modern Greek that a Jewish businessman is said to have ruefully remarked: "We may have the name but the Greeks have the talent!"

Unfortunately, this aspect of the Greek

character has made Athenians a very suspicious people. In most western European countries when someone meets a stranger, he automatically assumes the person is a moral and upright individual until proved to the contrary. When a Greek meets a stranger, perhaps he does not automatically assume that the man is a crook and a swindler, but he takes all precautions against that eventuality and lies warily in wait for the slightest sign that his suspicions are not unfounded. Observant westerners who meet a Greek for the first time can see this assumption in the way the Athenian narrows his eyes and looks at them speculatively as they shake hands.

in Greek affairs also nurtured another trait in the Greek character which still survives. The meddling often brought about disasters that were rightly blamed on the *xenos dactylos* (foreign finger). But when political, military and economic disasters were provoked by local talent—and there have been quite a few in the past 150 years—the "foreign finger" became a handy scapegoat for the guilty government. It has therefore become common practice for every Greek to refuse to accept any responsibility for his misdeeds or his failures and to blame them entirely on somebody else. His arguments in such cases are so ingenious that he ends up by believing

Most Greek girls and young women, too, will totally ignore a stranger who gives them a friendly smile, firmly convinced he is trying to pick them up. When a law was finally passed in 1952 giving women the right to vote in parliamentary elections for the first time, an enterprising American journalist went out in the streets of Athens, stopped the first woman he saw and asked what she thought of the new law. She glared at him indignantly, slammed her handbag in his face and shouted: "Get lost, you dirty scoundrel!"

The interference by foreign governments

many of them himself.

Yet another quality ingrained in the Greek character during the years of servitude to the Turks (admired when not carried to Mafia-like extremes), is the closeness of family ties and the loyalty that places the family above all other considerations, including law and the country.

Family unity was crucial in Ottoman times when even a friend or neighbour might betray confidences to the Turk if his own life depended on it, or, sometimes, if he merely bore a grudge. Members of the immediate family, therefore, were the only people in whom a Greek could have absolute trust. In return, they came first and foremost in his loyalties and his priorities. That feeling survives to this day and with very few exceptions, no Greek will ever break the code of family loyalty.

The Athenian Greek, in addition to all these characteristics, has those which he has acquired from a variety of backgrounds. Few of the local inhabitants over the age of 30 are born and bred Athenians, and those under the age of 30 have naturally been influenced by the exotic backgrounds of their parents. For, just as America was once the melting pot of Europe, Athens has become the melting pot

Even more Greek families poured into Athens from the countryside during the bitter civil war that ravaged the country in the years after World War II. The trend continued during the 1950s and 1960s when people left the neglected provinces and flocked to the capital to find jobs and a better future for their children.

Mass Exodus: More Greeks, members of the relatively small communities still living in Istanbul, were forced to leave from 1955 onwards to find refuge in Greece after life was made unbearable in Turkey following the onset of the struggle for union with Greece in Cyprus.

of the Greeks. In 50 years it has grown from a city of a few hundred thousand inhabitants into a sprawling metropolis of nearly four million, swallowing up the port of Piraeus and most of the surrounding suburbs.

The first to swell the ranks of the population of Athens were refugees from Turkey who came around 1922, following the defeat of the Greek army in Asia Minor by Kemal Ataturk, and the subsequent exchange of populations between Greece and Turkey.

Left and right, much Athenian life during the summer months is lived out of doors.

To them were added the Greeks from Egypt, members of a flourishing community several generations old, who had to leave when the Nasser revolution proclaimed Egypt for the Egyptians. Some were able to bring money out and start new businesses in Greece. Others found their smattering of languages, picked up among the polyglot foreign communities of Alexandria, Cairo, Port Said and Suez, made them invaluable to a burgeoning tourist industry in Greece which sorely needed foreign-language speakers to man hotel desks, airline offices, travel agencies and shipping companies.

The oil crises of the 1970s brought to Athens more waves of expatriates, this time workers and their families from Germany and from other west European countries who were no longer needed there. Other new arrivals were families who had emigrated to Australia, Canada and elsewhere and who had, for some reason or other, decided to return to the homeland.

These Greeks with foreign backgrounds are easy to recognise because they are generally more courteous and more obliging than the "Greekie-Greeks" (as foreigners living in Athens call the indigenous population). They also have better manners.

number of years for taxis with a fare to pick up more people along the way, who are going in the same direction. The cabbie collects the full fare from each independently "picked-up" passenger and so can make three or even four times the fare for the same distance at the same time. With a foreigner, he cannot do this because he cannot explain the practice to him or ask him to share the cab with somebody else.

To compensate, there are some Athenian cabbies—generous to a fault—who will go out of their way to take a foreigner to an obscure address and not charge for going round and round in circles searching for it.

For instance, Athenian cab drivers are generally surly, ill-tempered and rude. This is understandable for people who spend their working hours in a traffic-congested city and in a noxious smog that is largely of their own making. The airport taxis, like taxi-drivers everywhere in the world, are notorious for ripping off arriving air passengers, both Greek and foreign, sometimes charging as much as ten times the normal fare.

In town, however, they tend to avoid tourists for the simple reason that they make so much more out of their fellow-Greeks. This is because it has been common practice for a

Athenian cab drivers can be excused for not knowing the streets of the city primarily because they have come straight from the boondocks where they learnt to drive on a tractor and bought their cab and licence with money advanced to them by the Agricultural Bank to grow beetroots. Also, the names of the streets in Athens change regularly with every new regime that comes to power, as mayors fall over themselves trying to flatter the new bosses.

The staff in Athenian hotels is usually polyglot and efficient. Composed mostly of Greeks from Egypt or Turkey or repatriated emigrants from Canada or Australia, the staff members are polite and obliging, even more so if the hotel is a family enterprise and they are related to the owner. The same can be said for waiters in small restaurants who are unfailingly pleasant even if they do throw the cutlery for six in the middle of the table or plonk it down with the bread basket.

One of the things that perplexes many foreign visitors to Athens is the sight of grown men sitting in cafés during working hours. These people are not idling away their time. If the cafés are in the area of the law courts, they are the meeting places for lawyers with their clients and witnesses, on the

red-tape gagged Greek bureaucracy. The café is where they meet the middle-man or the lawyer before going into the government office together to smooth the path of the *hypothesis*.

The cafés in the Omonia area of downtown Athens are filled with ruddy-faced men, playing cards or backgammon, reading newspapers or chatting to each other. Again, these are no idlers. The cafés are the labour exchanges where building contractors hire building workers and skilled labour. There was a time, when the building boom in Athens was in full swing and skilled labour scarce, when such workers would pin a label

day their case is to be tried. There is no set time for a trial. Each case is assigned a number that is posted outside the courtroom in the morning, and a café is as good a place as any to sit until time draws near for the case to be heard.

If the cafés are in an area surrounded by ministries or government offices, then those who sit in them are likely to be people with business to conduct—a *hypothesis* as it is called in Greek—with the ponderous and

on the back of their coats, as they sat playing cards, with the wage they would accept written on it in large figures. This was to keep anyone offering less than the going rate from interrupting their game.

By far the most popular leisure-time occupation of the Greeks is eating out. This accounts for the huge number of restaurants and tavernas to be found throughout the greater Athens area. Also, working couples find it more convenient to eat out in the evening, and even take their children with them, rather than cook at home.

The second most popular form of enter-

Left, waiters can be unfailingly pleasant—or not. **Right**, cafés double as labour exchanges.

tainment used to be the cinema, until the advent of the video recorder and the proliferation of video clubs all over Athens. One thing the VCR hasn't been able to supplant, however, is the theatre. There are 54 theatres listed in the Yellow Pages of the Athens telephone directory and more than 40 functioning all the time. The fare is mainly French-type bedroom farces and satirical revues which lampoon the current political scene and the government. Serious plays are mainly translations of British, American or French hits and musicals like *Evita*, in Greek translation, have long runs.

There is a type of Athenian, also, who

by the management, and thus find release from all the frustrations of daily life.

In the summer, Athenians are lucky enough to be only a 45-minute drive away from a beach on the north or south coast of Attica and they can go swimming, windsurfing, water-skiing, motorboating and sailing on weekdays as well as on weekends. The other advantage of living in Athens is the proximity of the wooded mountains Parnes and Penteli, where Athenians can go hiking or picnicking for the day.

On Mount Parnes, too, there is a casino where millions of drachmas are gambled away every night. Many a home has been

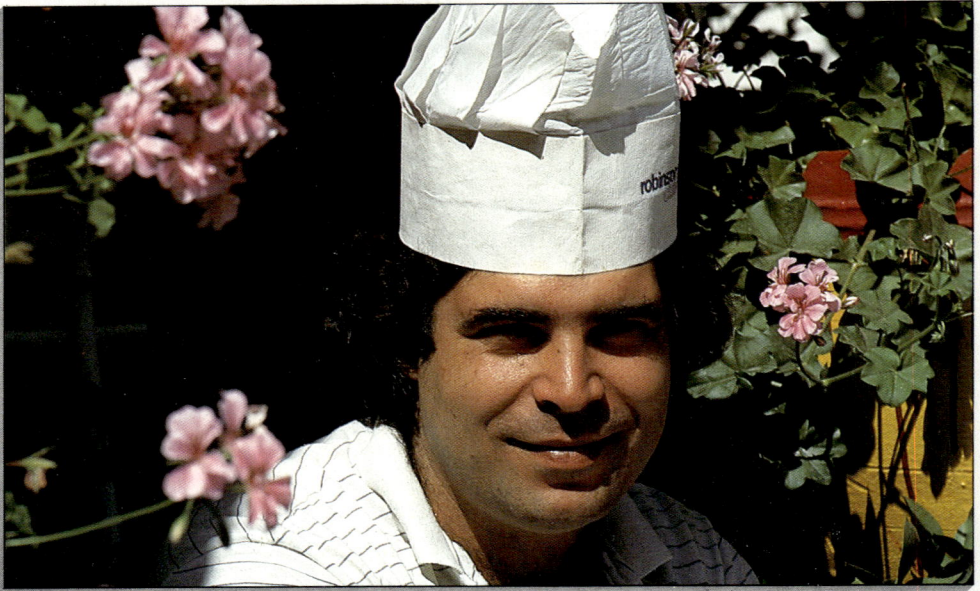

enjoys going to the *bouzoukia*. These clubs take their name from the *bouzouki*, (a stringed instrument that looks like a mandolin with a long handle) and are places where a six-piece orchestra sits in a single row with a singer in front who regales the audience with songs about sordid, low-life characters who come to sticky ends. Customers sit at tables and are served fruit and drinks at astronomical prices (good *bouzouki* singers are among the highest-paid entertainers in Greece), get high on the songs which are belted out at maximum volume, break unglazed plates that are thoughtfully supplied

wrecked and business ruined by the gambling streak that exists in every Greek to a larger or lesser extent. This gambling streak manifests itself in the love Athenians have for card parties in clubs, cafés or homes, where every imaginable card game, and every variation of each game is played, usually for high stakes, far into the early hours of the morning.

Another leisure occupation for Greeks of all classes is the mandatory call on a friend or relative on his or her nameday. This usually takes place at any time from 6 p.m. to 10 p.m., the caller dropping in unannounced (but very much expected) with a box of pastries or a bunch of flowers. He or she then sits in a circle in the living room of the nameday celebrant together with the other callers, chatting and gossiping for a couple of hours. At one point, the host or hostess produces a tray with sweets and serves a tangerine liqueur to all present. In more sophisticated households Scotch and soda or gin and tonic are substituted for the liqueur.

With a saint for every day of the Greek calendar, one would think this could be a full-time occupation. But people with ancient names like Achilles or Agamemnon, or a name like Byron (which is very popular), have no nameday and so it is mostly those fortunate enough to be named after St John, (the Yannises and Ioannas), the Virgin Mary (the Panayotises, Marios, Panayiotas, and Marias), the Annunciation (the Evangeloses, Angelos, Angelas and Angelikis), St Paul, St Peter, St Catherine and so on who are honoured with calls. Few Athenians know or can remember the namedays of the more obscure saints, after whom hardly anybody is named.

The Athenians—and all Greeks, for that matter—have great faith in their patron saint and usually have an icon of him or her in their homes to which they pray. More dangerously, Athenians will cross themselves piously every time they pass a church, whether on foot, in a bus or driving a car. The clergy has not budged an inch from the rites and forms of Greek Orthodoxy as laid down in Byzantine times and this traditional approach is reflected in the high attendance at christenings, weddings and funerals.

Another ceremony that is adhered to in most Athenian home is the cutting of the *vassilopitta*. This is a round, dry cake in which a coin has been hidden. On New Year's Day the *paterfamilias* gathers the family round him and cuts a slice of the cake for each member of the household, including one for Jesus Christ and one for the house. Whoever finds the coin in the cake is guaranteed a year of good luck. This custom has been extended to clubs, unions and associations and business firms (in lieu of the office party). As each Athenian belongs to more than one of these institutions, the pitta-cutting ceremonies go on well into late January and sometimes early February.

Finally, although most Athenians are hypochondriacs and take good care of their health (except for smoking, which they refuse to believe is harmful), they lose all sense of personal safety when behind the wheel of a car and generally drive like maniacs. Ninety percent of Athenian drivers are convinced that red lights are decorations left over from Christmas, and Greece has one of the highest accident rates in Europe.

Bashed and battered cars are a common

sight in Athens and the hospitals are full of bashed and battered people. The traffic police is mainly occupied in hurrying the traffic along by blowing constantly on shrill whistles, or unscrewing the number plates of cars illegally parked in the town centre. As these figure in the thousands every day, the police has its work cut out.

So why live here at all? When expatriates are asked why they have chosen to reside in Athens, among an irritable and irritating populace in a smog-bound disorganised city, they invariably give the same reply: "We live here because we are never bored."

Left, a chef outside his taverna. **Right**, despite domestic problems, the Greek flag waves on.

RAILWAY WOMAN

Train Number 19 is a five-carriage, red and silver job. At the controls is Evi Chroni, a short and chunky, but not unattractive, woman in her thirties. She's the only woman among the 190 commuter train drivers on the 16-mile (26-km) Piraeus–Kifissa line and, although the train number might change, Evi won't. The distinction of being the only woman among 190 males has proved to be a mixed blessing. It earns her publicity and renown, but also distrust from the older, male establishment in the rail company. Snappy in a yellow plastic raincoat, she nudges the control lever, and Train 19 moves forward.

Following the universal rule that anything in the vicinity of ports or railway lines must turn slightly seedy, inner Piraeus has few attractions. But a few minutes later the train emerges into an open space with the sea promenade on one side and the Karaiskaki football stadium on the other.

It was here in 1827 that General Karaiskakis, a Greek War of Independence hero, fell against a Turkish army in the closing years of the revolution. It was here also that, in 403 BC, an army of Athenian democrats under the command of Thrasyboulos charged down from Munychia Hill—yes, that's it just behind and to the right, with the small yellow houses of pre-war style—and defeated the Thirty Tyrants under Kritias at a place where the train approaches after leaving the Phaleron station.

Evi Chroni juggles the black control lever, reducing the train's speed to negotiate the curve that marks the end of Piraeus and the start of Athens. The actual frontier is what was long ago the Kephisos river, but is now an undisguised sewer. The bridge across it is not even that: a few planks and the rails. One wonders how the 37-ton train slips across it as lightly as it does. At 55 kilometres an hour Evi leaves the control and relaxes, for here the line runs dead straight for two stations, going due north. The Acropolis appears, small and white like an old, treasured trinket, straight ahead.

In the few dozen metres between the Thission and Monastiraki stations, Athens was born, lived, fought and died, to be resurrected in 1834 as Greece's capital. To the right stretches the ancient Agora, which needs no introduction, crowned by the Propylaia and the Parthenon. But a keen eye is needed to detect them, because leafy, spreading trees allow only fleeting glimpses.

Train 19 draws up to old Monastiraki station. Evi pulls back on the hand brake and taps her foot on the whistle to warn the rail maintenance worker away. "We had a suicide here the other day," she says, as the tunnel to Omonia Square yawns blackly ahead. It was a 73-year-old retired policeman, and despite the emergency brake—a big red button under the windscreen—the metal wheels crushed him. She seems little the worse emotionally for the experience, which isn't surprising when one considers that train drivers have to go through rigorous physical and mental selection at the Greek Air Force Hospital and have eight hours' instruction a day for six months before being allowed to handle a train alone. But drivers are not immune to the risks; sometimes it gets scary. "I was nervous the first time," Evi confides. "I was thinking of all those people I'm responsible for."

The "Columbia" slides slowly forward again with a slight hiss of released brakes. Evi handles the lever with one hand and holds a cigarette in the other. Here the line delves underground for two of the biggest and most populated stations, Omonia and Victoria (named, of course, after Britain's Queen Victoria). The first lap of the tunnel is old, turn of the century. The train drivers tell a poignant story about this tunnel. The engineer who first built it was told the tunnel was no good—so he killed himself. If he only knew that it has lasted a century of constant vibrations, urbanisation, war and earth tremors, and promises to last a lot longer.

Attiki station is where the train drivers change shifts and go to the toilet. Evi steps nimbly across the tracks to the drivers' lounge; as she does, a fellow driver going downtown hoots at her playfully. Between the tracks lie the real ogres of the electric train drivers' profession—the power rails buzzing with 600 volts of direct current, naked and unshielded. A wrong step out of the narrow

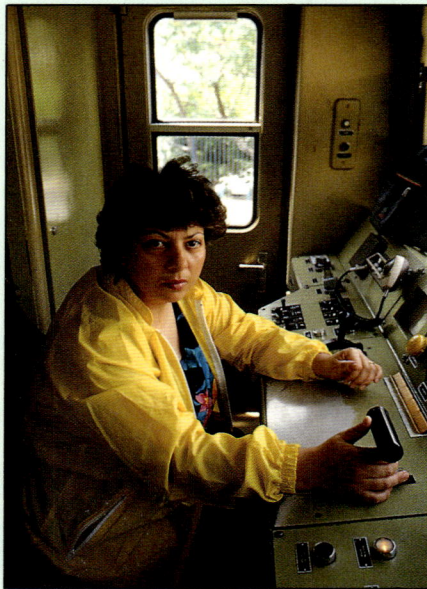

wooden boardwalk, and death is swift. Isn't Evi scared? Actually, no. Characterising the deadly current as if it's the lovable villain in some ancient epic, she says: "It knows us by now." She lifts a dainty pair of high heels over it like it's just an ordinary sliver of metal.

A nation's character comes through in its graffiti, and the multicoloured slogans that cover every square inch of wall space in Patissia, the classic inner-city residential area, revolve around two subjects dear to the heart of the Greek male: politics and football.

A northbound train traveller gets a complete sample at close quarters. Black or blue political slogans ("Kick the rascals out!" "Long live New Democracy!") come from the right wing. Red scrawls ("Workers! What has the government done for you?") are communist-authored, while a few green PASOK signs, probably left over from the last election, support the socialist party of that acronym.

PASOK, by the way, should not be confused with PAOK, which is the football team of Thessaloniki in northern Greece, an arch-rival of Athenian team Panathinaikos, which has the lion's share of graffiti support in this part of town. Even the wall of the Second Cemetery, which extends itself to the right of the line after Patissia, is not immune from spray-paint philosophy.

Evi nudges the control lever forward and Train 19 picks up speed on its way to Perissos station.

The great masses of apartment blocks here give way to more open space; even the occasional cabbage field peeps among the two-storey houses, schools and clothing factories. A familiar logo appears on the left: EMI, the London-based entertainment giant. Here is its Middle East regional office and Greece's oldest recording studios. Built in 1929, these buildings saw the great names of Greek music.

The legendary Sophia Vembo, whose sultry voice cheered the Greek troops on to victory over vastly superior Italian forces in 1940, and whose name is enshrined in the national history and culture, recorded her epochal songs here.

Neon Iraklion, named after the Cretan city Iraklion, is a suburb that's trying to become a little upmarket from its status as a lower middle class stronghold. Luxury flats have been rising along the electric rail line, though the small houses and tiny farming plots of the older inhabitants are still dotted charmingly about.

Though Neon Iraklion is on no-one's tourist map, that's all the more reason why it's worth a look, even a stop-over. Neon Iraklion has good, inexpensive eating places and tons of local colour. An off-the-beaten-track classic.

Irini (Peace) stadium is a modern aluminium-and-plastic structure built to handle overspill from the new Olympic Stadium that appears majestically on the right half of Athens as a backdrop. The name is a strange one, since on football Sundays it's not exactly peaceful, as the train drivers on this line know all too well.

Now the scenery is definitely suburban, and increasing in charm as Train 19 heads for Amaroussion (or Maroussi, as in Henry Miller's novel). Pine woods alternate with the small villas that were built in decades past by well-to-do Athenians. Rococo porticoes, faded window shutters, peeling pink plaster—there is a general air of dusty elegance and languor here. The atmosphere intensifies as the train heads for its final destination of Kifissiá, *the* upper-crust watering hole and residential area.

Evi Chroni gently pulls back the brake, and the doors clatter open. Here in Kifissia the air is clear, the trees green and leafy, the houses elegant and walled and gardened. Small wonder the well-heeled foreign community chose it long ago for its Greek *pieds-à-terre*. Posh pizzerias await the palate, a sophisticated shopping centre awaits the bulging purse, the yuppies are well-dressed and plonked behind the wheels of new cars. Piraeus seems a world away.

It's not Evi's world, either. In a few minutes she will walk to the back of Train 19, take the controls, and lead it back to Piraeus. She will then go home to a modest flat in a quite un-rich section of town and cook for her school-age daughter. Next morning she will get up at five o'clock to drive the commuters to their jobs again.

For the traveller, it has been a tour of Athens the tour operators don't mention, and a lot more rewarding. And all for less than half the price of a *souvlaki*.

They say the sky over Athens and the surrounding sea were once the stuff of poetry—crystal clear, azure blue, diamond bright. That was as little as two decades ago. Even now, there are occasional breezy days when the famous Athenian horizon is as blue as ever and the Saronic Gulf south of the capital flows in shades ranging from aquamarine to rich turquoise. Most days, however, when there is no wind or strong tide to carry the pollution away, the sky over

tan area on the Aegean coast. Greece is more or less keeping pace with introducing European Community pollution control legislation, but there is a long way to go yet in actually containing the damage.

Air pollution in Athens, despite government efforts to control it, is becoming worse. The central business district of the city is hardest hit, and residents often complain of headaches after a foray into the centre. These days, there are more and more emergency

Athens is covered with a drab brown smog that tickles the nose and throat, and the waters close to the Athens-Piraeus megalopolis of nearly four million people teem with bacteria and toxins.

Rush to the suburbs: Pollution has become an issue of concern to most Athenians. Many people have moved out to the suburbs to avoid the worst effects of atmospheric pollution. But from May to October—the swimming season—sea pollution is just as much an issue. Then, local residents often avoid the more polluted beaches south of Athens in favour of cleaner seas north of the metropoli-

pollution alerts, which means more and more people are being treated in local hospitals for pollution-related respiratory and heart problems. People now listen for the regular pollution reports on radio, particularly if they are aged or live in the city centre.

Beginning in the late 1980s, summer pollution, combined with record heatwaves and temperatures that topped 45° Centigrade, was blamed for hundreds of deaths all over Greece, most of them in the concrete canyons of Athens. The people of Athens panicked and vowed to buy air conditioners, or at least fans, before the next summer season.

Until then, conventional wisdom dictated that such modern conveniences create undue draughts, which would surely result in colds, flu or worse. Under pressure of a clear and present greater danger, that ethic began changing, and the old-fashioned Greeks created a unpredicted run on house fans. Air-conditioners, which also enjoyed a sudden sales boom, sold less well than fans only because they cost a lot in relation to the relatively low Greek income. Many hotels

cal engineer: "Athens is not one of the most polluted cities in the world, as some people say, and is far less polluted than Los Angeles." Still, that is only one opinion and there are clearly problems. The biggest offender is photo-chemical pollution, or smog, which is visible but not on the same scale as that of Los Angeles. A noxious brown smog cloud, called *nefos*, forms over the mountain-ringed Athens basin when warm, still weather creates a temperature inversion

that didn't have air-conditioning before have air-conditioning now. Smart tourists arriving in Athens in July, the height of heatwave season, are wise to look for one of the air-conditioned hotels, or head straight for a breezy island where the heat is not as noticeable. Remember that, as the temperature rises, so does the pollution level.

Vehicular emissions create about 86 percent of Athens' air pollution; industry the remainder. According to one leading chemi-

Left and right, motorcycles are an alternative to Athens' 1,200,000 cars.

layer, or barrier of cold air, that traps pollutants in the lower atmosphere.

Nitrogen oxide is the largest, and most dangerous component of Athens' atmospheric pollution. In early 1989, when temperatures were warmer than usual, nitrogen oxide and smoke levels began to exceed emergency levels. The annual summer rush on hospitals by victims of heart and respiratory problems, whose conditions were aggravated by rising pollution levels, began early that year.

In other pollutants, according to the same chemical engineer, Athens scores relatively well. The Attica region has sulphur levels that are under World Health Organisation standards for nine months of the year, and lead levels all year round are under European Community standards.

Vehicular emissions continue to belch from a range of poorly maintained and age-ing buses, cars and taxis, some of them trailing black exhaust in their wake, none of them using lead-free fuel. When driving in the city centre, people try their best to avoid staying behind the big buses—the fumes are sometimes overwhelming. The introduction of cars with pollution-control devices could help the situation, but one expert says most

Prime Minister Andreas Papandreou intro-duced a traffic-reduction system aimed at easing monumental rush hour traffic jams. It allowed cars with licence plates ending in odd numbers into the city centre on odd-numbered days and even-numbered plates into the centre on even-numbered days. These measures made it a little easier to get to work in the morning and a little easier to breathe. But not for long. The city's 800,000 automobiles increased over four years by 400,000; the traffic jams once again became monumental, and the atmospheric "cock-tail" of noxious pollutants became thicker. The government was forced to establish

of the cars used in Greece are too small or too old for the devices to be installed. European Community rules, however, required such devices on new vehicles after 1990.

Industry also contributes its share to the noxious *nefos* and it will be increasingly dif-ficult to obtain permission to establish indus-trial plants around Athens. For now, industry is subject to sporadic checks by the govern-ment pollution monitoring agency known as PERPA. They enforce regulations regarding employers' liability for emission of certain hazardous materials such as asbestos.

In the mid-1980s, the government of

further traffic control measures with far-reaching effect. This time, not only cars, but taxis too were forbidden to enter the city's inner ring, the *daktylio*.

Effected hours were extended from 7 a.m. to 8 p.m. To alleviate the excess pollution created by four rush hours a day, the govern-ment established, during the winter months, continuous working hours in stores. With one fell swoop, the new regulations abol-ished a centuries-old way of Greek life—the traditional three-hour siesta every afternoon, when workers go home to eat and take a lengthy nap. All sorts of traditions had grown up around this time, from the main meal of the day to the preferred hour for *l'amour*. All that had to come to a halt, and both the store owners and their workers were dismayed. A string of shop strikes ensued. But in the meantime, there was no longer a deluge of cars four times a day. Traffic, instead, began to be spread out fairly evenly over the day.

By the end of the same year, taxi drivers had decided they had had enough. They argued that restricting taxis from the city centre every other day was cutting their income in half. The result was a series of taxi strikes and strikes by sympathising bus and

busy they carry multiple riders, i.e. multiple fare-payers, at the same time. Athens taxis are a bargain, costing less then the equivalent of $2 for a six-km ride. As a result, many people who can't afford to own a car, or those with cars not allowed to circulate on a particular day, regularly take taxis to and from work. Taxi drivers were intermittently on strike from the end of 1988 to the spring of 1989. In the end, the government shrank the size of the inner *daktylio*, allowing them to drive a little closer to the centre. The compromise solution may have had a lot to do with public pressure, because whenever there is a taxi strike, people have to resort to

trolley drivers. The strikes played utter havoc with downtown transportation. It even became a little dangerous to venture downtown. In one strike/demonstration action, the taxi drivers used their parked cars to block off the city centre. Police moved in with cranes to remove the taxis, and the 1,500 drivers clashed with riot police.

There are 17,000 taxis in Athens—a huge number by most standards, and most are so

Left, a factory emits deadly *nefos*. **Right**, this partially-obscured sign ("Total Hellas") sums up the pollution problem.

public transport. Taking a combination of bus and trolley, for instance from a northern suburb, can take up to an hour and a half, instead of 30 to 45 minutes by car.

On the seashore, pollution may not be so visible, except on a few beaches close to Athens and the Piraeus-Eléusis industrial zone where some people are crazy enough to swim. Greeks desperate for a summer cooloff have resorted to swimming only metres away from a sulphurous yellow outfall of chemicals from a fertilizer plant at Eléusis and, near Piraeus, all manner of objects have been sighted on the beaches.

An advisor to the Greek Ministry of the Environment says only three to four percent of Greece's 15,000 km of coastline, which equals one-third of all Mediterranean coasts, is unfit for swimming; most of these are near Athens. He denies the Saronic Gulf, which receives most Greek industrial and human waste, is a few years away from eutrification (death), calling it a dynamic system with tremendous absorption capacity. In parallel, a United Nations study of Mediterranean beaches concludes that only 75 to 80 percent of the beaches in Greece, France, Italy and Yugoslavia are safe to swim in.

Greek studies claim the Keratsini Gulf,

$110 million sewage treatment plant, the first for greater Athens. By the mid-1990s, it is expected to be processing 600 cubic metres a day of waste on the islet of Psytalleia, one kilometre off the Athens coast. In the early 1980s, a smaller Athens treatment plant processing 100 cubic metres a day of waste was built at Metamorphoses, using French biological treatment technology, but this solved only a small part of the Athens effluent problem. In tandem, there is a $370-million nationwide plan to build sewage treatment plants in 53 cities around Greece, most of them on or near the coast. A UN study says 85 percent of the pollution enter-

located across the huge Drapetsona industrial area of Piraeus, will undergo a biological "turnover" in another five years, when effluent treatment will not be able to clean the water. At least 500,000 cubic metres a day of effluent, about 80 percent from homes and 20 percent from industry including some highly toxic waste, flows into this little gulf southeast of Athens. Red tides, consisting of gymnodynium and gonyaulax toxic planckton, have washed over the gulf at least twice.

The government's major offensive against the dreaded eutrification of the Keratsini Gulf, and later the Saronic Gulf, is a

ing the Mediterranean comes from land-based factories, domestic sewage and agricultural run-off.

Until the instigation of this programme, there was virtually no sewage treatment in Greece. Only hotels had little proprietary plants to protect adjacent swimming beaches. The biggest hotels also surrounded their swimming areas with nets, but an affluent expert says sewage breaks down into microscopic particles during transit, so nets apparently don't hold much back.

The new system of big sewage treatment plants will replace septic tanks, which are impractical in densely populated areas. In Athens, huge sewage tankers roam the streets of every suburb, occasionally stopping to suction up the contents of a high-rise apartment building's huge septic tank. The new plants will also for the most part eliminate dumping raw waste through outfalls directly into the sea. The main sewer pipeline that leads into the main Athens outfall at Keratsini, where 600 cubic metres of raw sewage is dumped every day into the gulf, is called the "biggest river in Greece."

Of course, the danger from such sea pollution is not only that we swim in it, but also that we eat fish that have grown up in it.

of the fish tested was unfit for human consumption. This is important, because 2,000 metric tons of Mediterranean shellfish are consumed every year. Another UNEP study concludes that pregnant women should radically limit intake of Mediterranean tuna fish and that in some small contaminated areas, fishing may have to be forbidden. Jellyfish which have appeared on a massive scale in the past few years around beaches and fishing grounds are not only a nuisance but also a health hazard. Margaret Papandreou, former wife of Prime Minister Andreas Papandreou, nearly died once after she had an allergic reaction to a jellyfish sting.

According to a study of the United Nations Environment Program, coastal Mediterranean states should start adopting a set of uniform criteria for cleaning up coastal seafood and for measuring the mercury in seafood, and they should develop a plan to deal with the recent mass influx of poisonous jellyfish. The study says that samples of shell fish from 50 places in four Mediterranean countries—Greece, France, Italy and Yugoslavia—revealed that more than 95 percent

Left, swimming is ill-advised near Piraeus. **Right**, siesta has been abolished in winter.

So the waters—and the skies—of modern Athens are a little tarnished these days. Anyone with a good imagination can still see Plato, Aristotle, Socrates strolling through the ancient Agora with a coterie of students *en train*, philosophising away the troubles of their world. But pollution in this day and age can't be philosophised away. It is there, it is a fact, and it is getting worse. New government efforts have begun to combat it. If their efforts succeed, the poets could one day rhapsodise again about the azure blue of the Athenian sky and her brilliantly clear, aquamarine waters.

"Loveliest of what I leave behind is the sunlight, and loveliest after that the shining stars, and the moon's face, but also cucumbers that are ripe, and pears, and apples."
—Praxilla of Sicyon, Fifth century BC.

The Greek heart is a simple affair. It is made of wood, has four legs (one always shorter than the rest) and is covered with oilcloth. Seat four or eight or 12 friends around it, add olives, bread, wine, *feta* and perhaps the sound of the north wind in a yacht's rigging, one *bouzouki*, spontaneous song, and you have the Greek soul.

It is *not* a movable feast, this table set for you in the Mediterranean sun. It is not something you can duplicate in Dublin or Dubrovnik. Greek wine doesn't travel well, and aubergine grown anywhere else (not to speak of "Danish *feta*", the very idea!) tastes like sponge. To sit at a Greek table with Greeks is simply the best gift the country has to offer, but you can take nothing with you when you go, except the odd kilo or two. However, like the pomegranate seeds which brought Persephone back, again and again to Hades, Greek food and its attendant customs may prove addictive.

The "Land of the Olive": The Greeks are obsessed with food. The planning and preparation of meals, the ordering of dinners, the brewing of coffee, the correct service of a "spoon sweet" (a candied fruit in heavy syrup) or liqueur to a guest—all are part of the elaborate gastronomic ritual, almost a religion. From the honey hand-fed to newlyweds (for strength) to the boiled wheat and pomegranate confection parcelled out to family and friends in commemoration of the dead, taking sustenance in Hellas (the "Land of the Olive") is a sort of transubstantiation. What and how you eat *is* what you are.

Perhaps the first word a Greek infant learns is *"Fai!"*, or "Eat!" Visitors may be

Left, to sit at a Greek table with Greeks is the best gift the country can offer. Right, a vase from the well-known restaurant in Mets called Myrtia.

astonished, to see even in Athens, Greek mothers, spoons and bowls in hand, chasing their toddlers around yards or down city streets. Greek children are among the portliest youngsters in the world, force-fed like little French geese. (If you arrive with a child, and a Greek bends down to pinch its cheek, don't panic. This is a simple gauge of how well you are fulfilling your parental duties. Most likely you'll be warned to fatten up your offspring.)

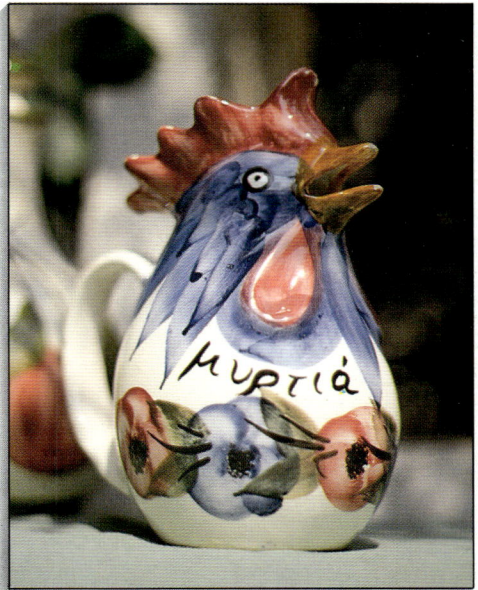

One would expect, then, that breakfast would be a big item on the national menu. Not so. Most Greeks begin the day with a stiff shot of caffeine and a newspaper. The milk shops selling honey and yogurt, eggs and toast (watch it: *tost* is a false cognate in Greek meaning grilled sandwich, usually cheese and mystery-meat), not to speak of wretched Nescafé and tinned milk, sprang up to fill a perceived need of northern Europeans. There is a word for breakfast in Greek (*proïnó*), but no tradition to back it up. There are four words for the types of Greek coffee, however, and they are worth learning. Under no circumstances should you ever refer to any of it as *Turkish* coffee.

Coffee came to Greece from the Middle East. Moslems were its first adherents and called it the "wine of Apollo," "the milk of thinkers and chess players." Today it's just as likely to fuel a political argument, but it's still consumed at one place and one place only: the *kafeneíon*. The coffee houses used to be exclusively male domains, and there are still men-only cafés the female visitor may choose to eschew (obvious by their middle-aged, *tavli*-playing clientèle), but since the 1970s, most *kafeneía* have relaxed this code.

drink the grounds at the bottom of the cup: they're there for another purpose. Some Greek women are adept at reading fortunes in this brown glop, though it's not a project for amateurs.

Breakfast of another sort may be had on the street as, in any season, there are food vendors plying a variety of edible wares. Omni-present are the *koulouria* salespeople, a *koulouri* being Greece's answer to the giant pretzel. Sort of a stretched-out, toasted, sesame seed-covered roll, *koulouria* are delicious dipped in coffee or cocoa. You'll often see commuters buying three and wearing them to work like bracelets.

Making Greek coffee is a minor art. The coffee itself must be finely ground; the small quantity prepared—one, two or three *demitasses*—must be brewed in a *briki*, or long-handled, narrow-throated pot; the froth must rise twice, or thrice. Those suffering from advanced sweet tooth should request a *vareé gleekó*; for light and sweet coffee, specify a *gleekeé vrastó*; sugarless, a *skéto*; medium sweet, a *métrio*.

If you don't announce a preference, you'll generally receive a mediocre *métrio*. If you want a double shot of eye-opener after a night of wine, order a *theepló*. But don't

Also on the street, in season, are roasted chestnuts (tasty on chilly evenings), roasted ears of corn (usually tough and tooth-threatening), sugar-coated, chewy coconut bars, bananas, roasted and salted nuts and, very rarely now, *salepi*, meted out in cups from an urn. *Salepi*, a beverage derived from roots, is now to be found only near the main Athens market on Athinas Street or in Monastiraki. The vendors themselves are sadly a vanishing breed.

Fast food is, lamentably, catching on in Greece, and detestable doughnuts, hamburgers and even fried chicken are invading, all imitations of their western prototypes. Ill-cooked and inedible, they are to be avoided. The original Greek "fast food," however, is still available. *Bougátsa*, a cream or cheese-filled pastry in *fílo* (Greek strudel leaves), *tirópittes* (cheese pies), *spanakópittes* (spinach pies) and *souvlákia* (kebab in *pítta* bread), are all to be had at corner shops located by smell. Yogurt comes in all consistencies; honey may be bought in small containers with pop tops; fruit abounds. In addition, there are bakeries in every neighbourhood, many stocking a remarkable array of munchables.

One bakery on Adrianou Street in Plaka comes along to make up for it. Once the Greeks' main meal of the day, after which they fell into several hours' torpid stupor from 2 to 6 p.m., the *mésimériano* has lost some of its former glory. With the Europeanisation of Greece, midday gluttony has given way: not only are the Greeks of today slimmer, the siesta and the attendant illicit afternoon affair have all but fallen by the wayside. Still, tradition rears its head whenever it can. On weekends and holidays, Greek women slave away in tiny kitchens over steaming stoves to produce multi-course meals for incredibly large gatherings.

A simple Sunday spread: If you're fortunate

features wholegrain bread in breakaway segments, grape must muffins, raisin loaflets, cheese boats, *tirópittes*, cookies, sticky buns and sugarless, chemical-less cartons of juice. There is generally a gaggle of Australians standing out front in summer with paper bags full of baked goodies. Yes, it is perfectly proper to eat on the street.

If there is no breakfast to speak of, lunch

Left, most Greeks do not eat breakfast; fruit is an acceptable alternative. **Right**, the Brazilian Coffee Stores near Syntagma Square is a near-institution.

enough to be invited into a home, expect to start out with a sweet, a homemade liqueur and coffee, followed at a decent interval by lunch, which may consist of several preliminary "salads"—aubergine, yogurt-garlic-and-cucumber, chickpea purée—and then olives, (from the family's home village), bread, meat and potatoes, lots of homemade wine, followed by the hostess's specialty dessert. And that's just a simple Sunday spread. Engagement, feast day or Easter luncheons are sanity-threatening occasions for those possessing reliable bathroom scales back home.

A few words on "Greek table etiquette" might be appropriate here. (If such a book were written, it would be a slim volume, but required reading for philhellenes.)

1) If you are invited out by Greeks, unless they're young and determined socialists, you will *not* be allowed to pay for your meal. You are permitted a weak stab at chipping in, but don't insist. The Greek laws of hospitality predate the Greek rules of cookery, and Archestratus (330 BC) wrote the first cookbook in history.

2) No one has a plate until, perhaps, the main course. Everyone is expected to tuck into the various plates on the table, even

the bottom of a wineglass to the top of someone else's glass: bad form.

5) There are lots of dishes—lamb entrails, fried squid tentacles, grilled brains, even *amelétita* (grilled unmentionables, male)—which are delicious to anyone brave enough to try them. It's considered rude to refuse to eat something others consider a delicacy.

6) It is no longer appropriate to summon waiters by tapping a utensil against a glass.

7) It is still considered appropriate to go into taverna kitchens to survey the pots and to select dinner.

8) Never be in a hurry to order, eat or pay. Would you rush a priest through the liturgy?

people with horrid head-colds.

3) Lovers may be observed feeding one another choice tidbits in Greece. This is perfectly acceptable; an Athenian right of passage. Don't take a taste from the fork of some amorous admirer, however, unless you intend to proceed as you've begun.

4) Wine glasses are never empty, even to half-mast, if the host is doing his duty, so it's often difficult to determine just how much you're consuming until too late. Exercise caution. Greek wine tastes deceptively light. *Oúzo*, *rakí*, *tsípouro* and *tsigouthiá* all hit like hand grenades. Also, do not toast with

Indulge in the art of Zen dining.

9) Don't insult a taverna owner by ordering coffee and sweets. Greece is a highly specialised country. Cooks cook; *kafeneíon* owners make coffee; confectioners… confect? Go down the block after dinner for your *métrio*. And do go to *Floca's* or *Zonar's* for pastry; to *Farouk Hanbali*, at 4 Messinias, Ambelokipi, tel. 692-5853, for Lebanese versions of *baklavá*; and to *High Life*, 43 Akti Poseidonos Pal. Faliron, for Turkish sweets such as *giokgokau*—chicken breast mousse, which is delicious.

10) Do tip, but only a tenth of the bill at

tavernas. A few drachmas just won't do.

Tavernas, you might note, are not restaurants, which are in a (higher, by Greek lights) class by themselves and known as *estiatória*. Why anyone would willingly choose an expensive, stuffy *estiatório* over a taverna is a mystery, but Athenians, who are getting more "EEC" every day, are opting for white tablecloths and stiff tabs with great regularity. Tavernas serve good basic Greek fare as a rule; *estiatória*, for the most part, ape northern Europe.

Time was when the Greek diet was based entirely on "the Mediterranean triad": wheat/bread/pasta, olives/oil, and grapes/

few of them are now slicked up and disguised in wood panelling and wallpaper.

The *Travel Tips* section of this book has a selection of recommended restaurants, with addresses and telephone numbers included. A more comprehensive list can be found in *The Athenian* magazine. For the widest possible selection, however, consult the Greek-language publication called *Athinorama*. Meanwhile, here are a few favourites:

Gerofinikas (The Old Palm) has been situated at 10 Pindarou Street in Kolonaki for over half a century. Specialising in Constantinople-Greek cuisine, this is an elegant place for lunch or dinner. The aubergine and

wine, with some spice and fruit thrown in. Those were the good old days of low cholesterol (still low on oil-rich Crete) and good teeth. Today, you can get just as miserable a *fillet au poivre* in Athens as in, say, Atlanta. The best Greek food may be right around the corner in a more humble venue. There are Greek tavernas and, yes, *estiatória*, that don't seem to change, though more than a

Far left and right, the fish market and the meat market on Athinas Street near Omonia. **Right**, early morning shopping in the markets often ends up on plates in Plaka.

veal, squab, Oriental pilaf with pine nuts and artichoke salad are good choices, as well as seafood, especially the Coquille St Jacques. Chef Araklistianos prepares only a limited number of entrées per day, however, so reserve space—and specialities. Just about anyone who's anyone in Athens ends up here as Gerofinikas is a special haunt of diplomats, politicians, journalists and, of course, spies, all of whom know a good meal when served one.

In Mets, the restaurants *Myrtia* and *Manesis*, at 35 and 3 Markou Mousourou Street respectively, are recommended, especially in summer. Both are Greek in flavour; both have lovely gardens, and *Myrtia* has long been popular with politicians, especially the Papandreou family, but this is no reason to go elsewhere.

Plaka as a place to avoid: Most people head for Plaka when it comes to dining. Invariably they emerge at evening's end disappointed at best, ripped-off and *bouzouki*-bashed at worst. Plaka's only saving grace is its ample opportunities to eat out of doors and watch the passing, eccentric parade. It's not the Mykonian waterfront, but it will do. *O Kostis*, at 18 Kydathineon Street, is friendly and reliable. Nearby *Zafiris*, a very, very old es-

tablishment at 4a Thespidos, is noted for its wild game; *Xynos*, at 4 Angelou Yeronda, with its summer troubadours, is a locals' beloved haunt. Near the Herod Atticus Theatre, *Socrates' Prison*, at 20 Mitseon Street, is a fine place to collapse at the end of a summer festival performance. You may end up eating roast chicken with Martha Graham's corps de ballet.

In Piraeus, though, is probably the city's best-preserved jewel. *Vasilenas*, at 72 Etolikou Street, is a genuinely rare experience, as close an encounter with the eternal Greek (culinary) soul as one can get.

Opened in 1920 by the proprietor's father, *Vasilenas* (originally a grocery store) is today exactly what it always was, a place where the food and the diners and the atmosphere and the song and the wine all come together in a seamless skein.

Winston Churchill signed the "diners' book", as did Tyrone Power, Onassis, René Clair, Elia Kazan, Crown Prince (later King) Paul, Irene Papas and Jeanne Moreau. For some seven decades now, the *table d'hôte* has been set: diners reserve space, arrive, and are served between 16 and 24 courses. (As "Mr George's" father put it so bluntly: "Whatever I serve will be better than whatever you'd order.")

You begin, typically with a bouillabaisse/bisque, fish roe salad, anchovies, olives, Roquefort butter on toast, and then proceed to a Greek salad, baby shrimp in mustard sauce, and a homemade pâté. Sizzling whitebait, crayfish filets, red mullet, lamb fritters, stuffed vine or lettuce leaves, roast chicken and, yes, sweets and fruit follow. The lightly resinated wine is fine; the proportions are formidable; the price can be less than 2,000 drachmas a head.

You may be there three and a half hours. You may never return. You won't quickly forget the experience.

If you are very fortunate, you will be in Greece, on an island, for Orthodox Easter, and you will be invited into a humble home to share in the breaking of the 40 days' fast before the Resurrection. Or, you will go home to dine with a John or a Mary or a Constantine or a Helen on his or her nameday. But wherever you pull chair up to table, don't hesitate to partake.

Attend to the Greek who serves you. Off season, he or she may look into your eyes, and the light of Greek hospitality—*filoxenía*—may kindle. The country is now overrun with visitors and tourism is the biggest of big business here, but the stranger will still find the Greek heart alive and ticking, if he is willing to forgo breakfast *(sic)* at the hotel, and the slicked-up *estiatório* nearby.

Left, George Vasilenas' celebrated restaurant in Piraeus used to be a grocery store. **Right**, wine barrels in Monastiraki.

Herodes Atticus, a Roman citizen born in AD 100, joined the Emperor Hadrian 17 years later at his camp on the Danube, shortly after Hadrian had ascended the throne. Herodes Atticus went on to become one of the greatest rhetoricians of his time and a wealthy administrator. One of his earlier gifts to Athens was to undertake in AD 143 a remodelling of the marble horseshoe-shaped stadium, which became in 1896 the site of the first modern Olympic Games.

In AD 161, Herodes Atticus built his final tribute to Athens: a roofed theatre or *odeon* dedicated to his wife. The theatre, which now bears his name, is an eclectic mixture of Greek and Roman design. It can—and most summer evenings does—hold 5,000 people; dedicated theatre-goers who flock to the ruins to enjoy Greece's premier arts event, the Athens Festival.

The *odeon*, built at the west end of the Stoa of Eumenes, to the south of the Acropolis, is made of Roman materials, bricks and *opus incentrum* (fist-sized stones set in cement). The entrances are barrel-vaulted in Roman fashion but built Greek-style into the hillside instead of on man-made foundations.

Buttresses braced the walls to support the cedar roof. The spectacular façade of the stage was a gracefully arched three-storey structure, ruins which now provide a hauntingly beautiful backdrop for contemporary performances. The orchestra area, lined with green and white Carystus marble, was damaged over the years through fire, and fighting during the Greek War of Independence. Its reconstruction began after World War II and, in 1955, the first performances of the Athens Festival were held.

That same year the purpose of the festival was defined: it would develop domestic talent which could tour abroad and would invite foreign artistic groups to perform works inspired by Greek history, mythology and literature. The first festival had ancient trag-

edy as the central focus. The State Orchestra of Athens gave its premiere outdoor concert that first season, followed by the Philharmonic Mitropoulos, returning to Greece after a long absence.

The proceeds from the two concerts were donated by the government to the Association of the Friends of Music for the construction of the Hall of Music, which was begun in the 1960s. Because of a lack of funds, the magnificiently conceived structure, next to

the American Embassy, was never completed. Work on it has recently resumed.

In addition during that first year the Lyric Opera gave its first open-air concert and the National Theatre performed ancient tragedies, most notably Euripides' *Hecube* starring Katina Paxinou, one of Greece's most notable tragediennes.

Bring a cushion: The enjoyment of a performance in Herod Atticus is enhanced by the graceful setting. But buy your tickets well in advance: some events sell out fast. The lower, more expensive seats have cushioned mats; the steeply raked upper levels do

Left, a dancer from the Dora Stratou Foundation. **Right**, an actress becomes *Electra*.

not. The view is impressive from "the gods" and the acoustics are excellent, but bring padding to sit on and a jumper, since the evening breeze can be surprisingly chilly.

A cross-section of Athenian society flocks to the summer festival. Students and tourists predominate in the less expensive seats but the audience is generally attentive and appreciative. Benefit performances bring out Athens' celebrities who generally arrive at the last moment, making a dramatic entrance as they strut to their seats in the lower levels.

Dimos Vratsanos, head of the Department of Touristic Activities in the National Tourist Organisation, faces a curious dilemma.

but Vratsanos explains: "This only covers the fees of the performers." Tickets are inexpensive—normally the top price is 3,500 drachmas for special events and rock-bottom prices are 500 drachmas for students.

One solution to solve the festival's financial strain is to shorten it, or to increase ticket prices. Vratsanos is more in favour of booking lesser-known quality acts whose fees would be lower. To prove his point, he refers to the Toho Japanese troupes which presented *Medea* in 1983 at the Likavitós (Lycabettus) theatre. The performance attracted all the leading figures in the theatre world but few members of the public. The

The Herod Atticus Theatre's enviable location and excellent acoustics elicit requests from top troupes from all corners of the world to appear at the festival. Yet Vratsanos explains that, under the current guidelines, "it's financially impossible to maintain a festival with the biggest names for such a long period."

Although he praises the festival's many memorable, star-studded occasions, he adds: "I want a cultural democracy but I don't want to be in the red." The National Tourist Organisation recently gave 361 million drachmas (US $2.4 million) to the Athens Festival,

heart-wrenching interpretations by the all-male troupe transcended language barriers. When the troupe once again performed *Medea* in 1984 (this time in Herod Atticus), the word spread and the *odeon* was packed.

Top stars: The demand for big names is hard to resist, however, because right from the start the festival has attracted the best. The highlight in 1957, for instance, was the concert by Maria Callas. Standing in the orchestra of the *odeon*, she gave a moving rendition of selections from her best-known roles. In 1959 Karolos Koun's Art Theatre made its debut in the *odeon* with

Aristophanes' *Ornithos*, which attracted notice because of its innovative direction.

The festival made a further breakthrough in presenting innovative creations in 1963 when Maurice Béjart's modern dance troupe entranced the audience. The enthusiasm for this performance was matched only by that for the return of Margot Fonteyn with her dance partner Rudolf Nureyev, a regular performer at subsequent festivals.

Ancient drama once again regained prominence in 1974 when renowned thespian Manos Katrakis starred in *Oedipus the Tyrant* and Spyros Evangelatos, founder of Amphi Theatre, directed *Electra*. In 1982,

cient drama will now be enacted only in the more suitable classical setting of the Herod Atticus theatre.

One of the most eagerly awaited events in a recent season was the *Axion Esti* oratorio, played by the Athens Symphony Orchestra conducted by composer Mikis Theodorakis. The SRO crowd, dotted with politicians and entertainment figures, was eagerly appreciative of the emotional work, originally scheduled to debut in June 1964 as part of the festival. Owing to Theodorakis's differences with the conservative government, it was not permitted in Herod Atticus and was performed in a small theatre instead. George

the smash hit was the week-long performance by Alvin Ailey's ballet troupe. In 1983, another landmark performance introduced Martha Graham's dance group to Greece.

The Athens Festival organisers have in the past scheduled classical drama performances at the modern theatre of Likavitós, perched on the highest hill of Athens. A recent festival policy, however, has limited performances to modern musical groups; an-

Dalaras, one of the leads who began his career with *rembetika* and popular songs and has performed with Theodorakis since his exile years in Paris in the 1970s, has now developed the range necessary for such a powerful piece.

Grigoris Bithikotsis, the singer who introduced many of Theodorakis's folk songs in the 1960s, was in the festival audience. At the crowd's insistence, he was brought onstage and performed *Lamp Of The Stars*, one of the most loved passages, fulfilling a dream he has held for almost 25 years—of performing this piece in the ancient theatre.

Left, classical drama is performed in the classical Herod Atticus theatre. **Right**, dancers at the Likavitós theatre.

Athens has a great many attractions and charms, but there are times when the heat and congestion of the centre become too much. What then? The only guaranteed escape-route from the torments of the city is the sea, which the Greeks themselves have been relying on for thousands of years.

Taking to the sea, like all escape-routes, is best planned in advance. Although Athens is the sailing capital of the East Mediterranean, with 1,500 professional yachts available for hire, at the height of summer most of the vessels are fully booked. Even the best-equipped yacht brokers of Zea Marina in Piraeus, whose offices overlook a forest of masts, or along the coast at Alimos, Glyfada and Voula, may be unable to meet the requirements of desperate travellers who turn to them in August. If contacted in advance, however, either direct or through overseas agents, the larger brokers can sort through the many yachts on their computers to match a customer's precise whims in terms of type of craft, number of berths, length of charter, and price.

Whale foreskin: There's no end to the choice when it comes to yachts. Those who have studied the country's latter-day myth-makers—the Greek tycoons—may know that Onassis's famous motor yacht *Christina* had barstools covered with white whale foreskin. Meanwhile, the yacht of Onassis's close shipowner rival Stavros Niarchos has provided hanging space for one of the world's finest collections of modern art.

Maybe this last word in opulence is not available for charter, but the top-of-the-range vessels for hire are luxurious enough to attract a growing list of celebrities to Greece for sailing holidays. Other boats, though, are priced so that charterers may end up paying less than if they'd chosen to stay ashore in an average hotel.

Three-quarters of the yachts for hire are pure sailing vessels of up to 55 ft (17 metres)

Left, sailing the seas. **Right**, seafood is best appreciated in the open air.

in length, "bare boats" chartered by yachtsmen who can show some written proof of their sailing experience. Some sailors who come to Greece for their holidays like to choose traditional Greek wooden caiques, strong and attractive vessels which make an interesting change from the standard modern fibreglass yacht. Brokers say prices start at around $130 a day. For those who want to take it easy or who simply wouldn't know one end of a boat from the other, there are

crewed motor yachts and motor-sailers, ranging from budget prices up to around $10,000 a day for something which will sleep 50 people in luxury. Options include hiring a yacht with its own launch for personal waterskiing.

Sailing is attracting more and more people because of the independence it offers, as well as its lack of distractions: there are no golf courses, tennis courts, regimented tours or hotel timetables at sea. Nor is there the remotest danger of being disturbed by phone calls—unless the yacht is chosen deliberately for its communications facilities. In fact, unless the yacht is self-crewed, there's little pressure to do anything except feel the hot Greek sun, enjoy the luxury of a sea breeze and turn to whatever human comforts may have been brought along—books, conversation, chilled beverages.

"The best beach of all is a yacht," according to Bill Lefakinis. As president of the Greek Professional Yachting Association, he is one of the smoothest salesmen for yachting in Greece—yet the claim has a ring of truth to it. Athens is an ideal base because it's not necessary to sail far from the local marinas to find peace and quiet.

The Saronic Gulf has a rich selection of

be able to leave Greece with that facial expression which says "I tamed nature." In July and August, the summer north wind, the *meltemi*, is particularly strong, although it rarely exceeds Force 5 Beaufort in the Saronic, compared with up to Force 6 to 8 further out in the Aegean. While the *meltemi* can be awkward for small yachts, it often dies down in the early evening and so doesn't usually interrupt sleep when at anchor. At other times of the year, the sheltered Saronic has light but changeable winds, so it often seems the wind is blowing in the "wrong" direction and yachts can be becalmed for some time. Brokers say that charterers are

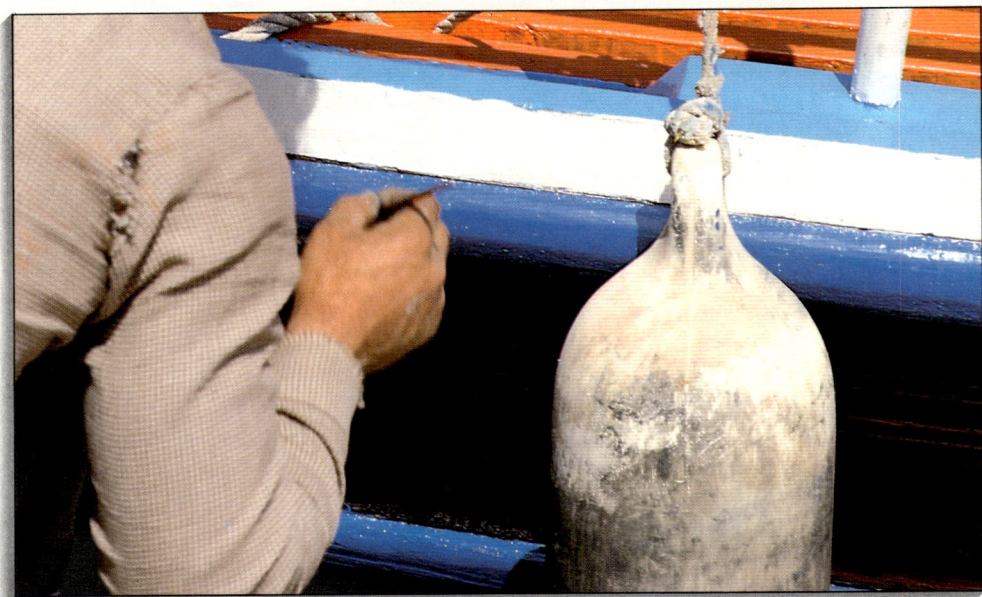

islands at which to call, and many of their best beaches and coves are quite inaccessible without a small boat. For that reason, the chances of finding relatively quiet places for swimming, snorkelling and sunbathing ashore are high. From the practical point of view, the Saronic has no sand banks, coral reefs or dangerous currents and there are plenty of safe moorings just offshore, as well as picturesque coastal and island harbours.

Weather conditions in the region also contribute to a generally safe picture for yachtsmen. However, the winds provide enough of a challenge for the serious sailor to

usually in such a relaxed frame of mind that they often enjoy the unpredictability of being stalled out at sea for an hour or two, or else being kept in harbour for a couple of days by heavy weather.

The romance of sailing is inescapable in Greece during summer, particularly at the end of the day when sunsets are spectacular and the night sky is covered with stars. Like reading Shakespeare's comedies, to be anchored or out at sea at such times leaves you with the feeling of having been in the presence of greatness—perhaps without being able to explain, very articulately, why.

Another delight experienced by many people for the first time when hiring a yacht in Greece is eating sea-urchin. These black spiney creatures gather like sinister mines around rocky inlets. Stepped on, their spines can poison the foot. But if they are collected carefully and cut open, their spongy orange contents are arguably the most delicious of all seafoods. However, urchins are never found in restaurants or on parts of the coast accessible by road.

Many visitors to Greece fall into one of two camps: the Hedonists and the History-lovers. It may seem that sailing in the Saronic would appeal mainly to the former, but this

ingly to life. Storytelling being the traditional form of entertainment at sea as well as a key part of the national character, seafaring Greeks frequently prove to be colourful raconteurs, even poets—and many vacationers finally leave their yacht as experts in Greece's martitime history whether they asked for it or not!

In recent years, Greeks have taken an even more scientific interest in this tradition. The same local boatyards which have constructed many of the pleasure craft in the Aegean today have been called on to build replicas of historic vessels with tools which have changed little over the centuries. The

is not so. To stand at the prow of a yacht and watch the details of a speck-like island slowly come into large focus is to live an experience which has been crucial to Greeks and their visitors, both friends and raiders, for centuries.

Although yacht brokers in Athens can easily provide knowledgeable foreign skippers as crew, having a native Greek on board often brings the link with the past fascinat-

Left, boats come in all shapes and sizes. **Right**, Athens was once described as "the city which makes the beautiful *triremes*".

best-publicised of all is the reconstruction of an ancient Greek *trireme*, the ship which won the naval battle of Salamis against the Persians in 480 BC. According to Aristophanes, Athens was once described simply as "the city which makes the beautiful *triremes*". At "ramming speed", a *trireme* moved fast enough to pull a modern water-skier, though this has not yet been tried out using the reconstruction.

Other, equally-interesting experiments are currently being carried out by the seafaring-conscious Greeks. Reconstructions of a cargo ship of the fourth century BC, of an ancient vessel made of papyrus and of Jason's ship, the *Argo*, have all been made and are being tested on voyages along their historic—or mythical—routes.

Those who sail in Greek waters also emulate the first tourist cruises which, 600 years ago, took religious-minded travellers through the Aegean on their way from western Europe through the port of Venice to the Holy Land. The adventure content of nautical trips was higher in those days, however. Half of the pilgrims never returned home, but fell prey to dangers such as the Plague, shipwrecks and capture or death at the hands of pirates or Turks.

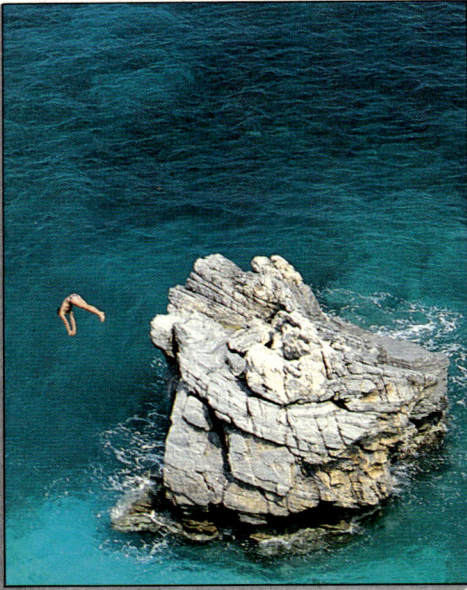

Salamis, though by name Greece's most famous naval site, is not easy to visit, thanks to its role today as the headquarters of the country's navy. Over the years, a number of yachts have been intercepted by Coast Guard patrol boats for straying too close and many tourists on ferries and yachts have had their holiday films confiscated.

However, there are many sites for history buffs within a few hours' sailing of Athens, many of which are best or only approached by sea. Most obvious is the temple which commands the view at Cape Sounion. Even closer is the island of Aegina, where a vessel

can drop anchor close to the hilltop Temple of Aphaía.

Tempting short cut: A little further, there's waterfront Nafplion—the first capital of modern Greece and arguably still the country's most graceful city, and also the Minoan remains at nearby Mycenae. Yachtsmen heading in the direction of the Peloponnese should note that the Corinth Canal, which is the tempting shortcut through to the Ionian Sea, has made its own piece of history by being metre-for-metre the most expensive waterway in the world to transit.

Leaving the historical dimension to one side—although of course it's always present in the salty air of the Saronic Gulf—there are the favourite tourist islands of Hydra and Spetsai. Even closer, less famous islands such as Angistri, near Aegina, nearby Moni which is a nature reserve, or St George's Island, off Cape Sounion, add to the rich choice of destinations. The Saronic provides equally good sailing grounds for those chartering a yacht only for one or two days and for those with time to spare but who prefer a leisurely itinerary of a few hours' sailing followed by anchorage for swimming and sightseeing. Further east of course, lie all the paradise isles of the Aegean.

Because of all these features, Athens has become the sailing centre it is today. It does not hold its position because of the excellence of its marinas or the "clubby" atmosphere awaiting the foreign yachtsman ashore. Frankly, the marina facilities suffer in comparison even with those of next-door neighbour Turkey—a fact that Greece has finally woken up to and for which it is trying to make amends. Greek sailing clubs could also do more to extend a welcoming hand to qualified yachtsmen from overseas, although the main harbours around Athens and the Saronic do have waterfront pubs where a friendly maritime atmosphere is kept alive. Although it's possible to make these complaints about Greece's sailing "infrastructure", its shortcomings do little to spoil the natural joys of sailing the Saronic.

Left, one of the pleasures of sailing the Saronic is finding secluded bays. **Right**, sailing boat motif on the attractive island of Aegina.

BIG
POTTER

SHOP
CLOTHES

BIG SHOP
ARINA
MALL PRICE

KAMATERO

Hassias

Dimokratias

National Road

PETROUPOLI

AGII ANARGIRI

D

NEA LIOSSIA

ANO PATISSIA

National Road Nr.8

HAIDARI

KLONARIDOU

(Athens - Corinth)

PERISTERI

THIMARAKIA

28 Oktovriou-Patission

Akarnon

Iear Odos

EGALEO

Athinon (Kavalas)

Kifissou

Liossion

Lenorman

National Archeological Museum

AGIA VARVARA

El Venizelou

Thivon

Kifissou

Aka

Pa

Stadiou

KORIDALOS

Grigoriou Lambraki (Athens)

Keramikos

Metropolis

Petrou Rali

THISSIO

Acropolis

Ermou

Petrou Rali

NIKEA

TAVROS

PETRALONA

PERAMA

Dimokratias

Salaminas

AGIOS
IOANIS RENDIS

Athens - Piraeus

Vas. Konstandi

Olymp
Stadiu

DRAPETSONA

MOSCHATO

El. Venizelou

Singrou

NEO FALIRO

KALITHEA

NEA
SMIRINI

El. Venizelou

Agiou Dimitriou

Hatzikiriakou

Possidonos

Amfitheas

PIRAEUS

Open-air Theatre

PALEO
FALIRO

AGIO
DIMITRIC

ALIMOS

Allmou

Saronic Gulf

Western Airpo
✈

ELINIK

Possidonos

(Thessaloniki)
Papandreou
Vas Pavlou
Kimis
PEFKI
Irinis
MELISSIA
Pendelis
METAMORFOSSI
Kifissias
Irakliou
IRAKLION
NEA
IONIA
Kapodistriou
Veikou-Onorfoklissias
MAROUSSI
Stadium
Penedelis
VRILISSIA
ISSOS
EA
FILOTHEI
LKIDONA
Vas Georgiou
HALANDRI
Kifissias
ALATSI
AGIA PARASKEVI
ITOS
PSIHIKO
Alexandras
Katehak
Messogion
NEO
PSIHIKO
HOLARGOS
Panoramou
Alimou
Pindou
Venizelou
Mihalakopoulou
PAPAGOS
ZOGRAFOU
Katehaki
KAISARIANI
VIRONAS
Kaisariani-
Monastery
IMITOS
IMITOS
Neomriou 1973
Naston
ILIOUPOLI
G. Papandreou
Argiroupoleos
17
ARGI ROUPOLI

Athens

3 km

iliagmenis
ern
rt

PLACES

Athens, at first sight, can be disconcerting. This chaotic town, choked by traffic-filled streets and surrounded by anonymous suburbs, is difficult to reconcile with the classical past set out in history books.

Athens is best viewed from the top of Likavitós hill, when the city's rough edges are softened by distance. From here a certain symmetry can be observed—the capital lies in a bowl guarded by twin citadels, the Acropolis and Likavitós. Central areas such as Omonia and Monastiraki radiate from the hub of Syntagma (Constitution) Square like spokes from a wheel. Even Plaka, smiled on by the Acropolis, touches the outer reaches of this busy, throbbing centre. If in ancient times all roads led to the Acropolis, it can be said that, as we approach the 21st century, all modern roads lead to Syntagma Square.

What the city may lack in physical charm is compensated for in convenience. Attractions like the Benaki, the Cycladic, the Byzantine and the War Museums, plus the National Art Gallery, fall in a huddle on or near the very same street. Locating them isn't a problem; finding out the name of the street can be. It is called, variously, Vassilisis Sofias, El Venizelou, or Panepistimou. If in doubt, ask for all three.

The best compass points to understanding Athens, however, are the sea and the hills. Piraeus is the gateway to the Aegean, with its island-hopping day trips. The hills provide a number of excursions, from rural monasteries just out of view to the splendid classical site of Delphi. None of this is more than a walk or a day away from the city centre, which says a great deal about a town—rough edges and all.

125

THE ACROPOLIS

Fifteen years under construction, a new temple to the goddess Athena, later to become known as the Parthenon, was opened to the public during the Panathenaic festival of 438 BC. The spectacle it presented then hardly matches the familiar ruin depicted on countless souvenir ashtrays and T-shirts since. It had a tiled roof, for a start, and a wooden ceiling with brightly painted sunken panels.

There was colour everywhere, so much so that some found the overall effect offensive. "We are gilding and adorning our city like a wanton woman," Plutarch complained, "decking her with costly statues and offerings and thousand-talent temples."

The Athenian *acropolis*, a term which simply means the highest part of the city and hence, usually, a natural fortress, had been graced by fortifications and temples for longer than anyone could remember or imagine. Not even Homer, who lived in the eighth century BC and whose *Iliad* describes the war between Mycenae and Troy about 500 years earlier, knew much about the Athens of Mycenaean times, or at any rate he made very few references to it. What he did mention was a Mycenaean palace on the Acropolis, "the Strong House of Erechtheus".

In due course, the new **Erechtheum** with its famous Porch of the Maidens was built roughly where the earlier palace had stood. It, the **Parthenon** and later the **Propylaia** were the principal buildings which, in the Age of Pericles, rose from the ruins of what had been the centrepiece of Athens before the Persian invaders flattened it.

The much earlier Mycenaean traces on the Acropolis are no more than remnants of a wall, not much to show for the origins of truly Greek civilisation, the even older Minoan having been a non-Greek import from Egypt and Asia Minor. What modern visitors mostly see on the Acropolis is a long way down the road of Greek history and is in any case only a small segment of it, a stripped archaeological carcass.

Before and during the Archaic period, which covers roughly 200 years of erratic rehearsal for the glorious fifth century (BC, of course), the Acropolis was a complex of pagan sanctuaries. It went on to flourish as a triumph of Hellenistic and then Roman art, degenerated into a miserable walled town which a 13th-century archbishop said was comparable to living in hell, improved slightly as the headquarters of a string of mediaeval dukes and ended up, at the time of Greek independence, as a run-down Turkish castle.

Its military history includes numerous sieges, massacres and mighty explosions. The skyline variously sprouted pagan statues, church spires, military towers and minarets. Buildings on it have been used as brothels, harems and ammunition dumps. In 1941, a

Left, picture-pretty as always. **Right**, view of the Agora from the *acropolis*.

motorcyclist in military uniform dismounted at the foot of the hill and walked up to plant a swastika.

The present lengthy restoration work on the Acropolis (in the interest of authenticity, perhaps the crane parked in the Parthenon should be included on T-shirts for the time being) is aimed at a specific period in this long and complicated history, and a relatively short one at that. The Classical Age is generally reckoned to have lasted about 150 years, but the hard focus is narrower still—on the 30 years during which Pericles was the dominant figure in Athenian affairs, from 460 to 430 BC. His name will forever be associated with the birth of democracy, architecture, philosophy and the arts, although popular history is inclined to be overgenerous to him and the laurels ought to be distributed more evenly among some of those who preceded and followed.

It is a miracle that any part of the Periclean Acropolis should still be standing after 2,500 years. Ironically, complete destruction can make the detective work of archaeology easier. When the pre-historic Pelagasians first levelled the top of the Acropolis, whatever had been there before would have been preserved under their topsoil. When the next generation of builders came along, they would have saved any of the Pelagasian bits and pieces that looked useful (to them) and ploughed the rest under. Many of the hundreds of Greek city-states were built around natural fortresses, and the Athenian Acropolis would always have been a prime site for human settlement in that part of the country.

There was a time, however, when it was thought that if Athens was to pursue its role as a naval power it would make sense to move the city down to Piraeus. The massive walls which created a secure lifeline between city and port were the ensuing compromise. In any case, demolition and reconstruction is a repetitive cycle and each one, pressed under a protective layer of earth by its successor, becomes an archaeological time capsule.

Although obviously unthinkable, uprooting the Parthenon now would provide clues to the Mycenaean period in Athens about which tantalisingly little is known. As it is, large chunks of the Parthenon are missing. Some were carried away by trophy hunters; others are still there but were subsequently used in something else, if only a hasty barricade thrown up during battle. The decision to concentrate on restoring the Acropolis to its classical format is perfectly understandable, but it has unavoidably meant putting a lid on what lies underneath as well as dismantling some interesting later additions.

Fortunately, many objects related to what happened before and after the classical period are preserved in the **Acropolis** and **National Archaeological Museums**. The best way to see the Acropolis, and the Agora, and the museums for the first time is to join one of the guided tours. The wealth of detail, however, may produce a sensation not unlike the proverbial Chinese meal—wonderful while it is going on but a confusing sense of emptiness almost immediately afterwards.

A Victorian historian observed that the Greeks were not simply "defunct producers of antique curios". In the sepuchral atmosphere in which visitors are shepherded about on the Acropolis (the ropes are an essential precaution against millions of tramping feet per year), it may be difficult to imagine the human drama that was played out on the very same marble slabs. The rest of this chapter, read in conjunction with the book's historical sections, may help to put some flesh back on to the bleached bones of the archaeological carcass.

Celebrated statue: The Egyptian pyramids impress because of the sheer size of the task undertaken with the tools available. The Parthenon is altogether more subtle, although the fact that such a daunting façade contained just two rooms may be considered slightly extravagant. The first, entered from the east (the opposite side after climbing the hill by the normal route), was the **temple** proper, containing a celebrated statue of **Athena**, her skin tones rendered in a layer of ivory and her raiment in gold. The statue was thoughtfully provided with a marble sofa in case it wanted to lie down.

The goddess Athena was worshipped under several guises. The Parthenon was officially the temple of Athena Polias, which acknowledged her role as patroness of the state. Elsewhere she was the distinguished goddess of virginity, as well as of foresight, of horses, of the trumpet, of the workwoman and of the girdle, the last being a reference to armour, not underwear.

Another statue outside the Parthenon was of **Athena Promachos**, "The Champion". Made out of bronze, it stood helmet, shoulders and spear above the buildings and was visible from ships at sea, especially when it reflected the sun. Like many of the

Acropolis statues, this one was later carted off to Constantinople where in 1203 it met an ignominious end at the hands of a drunken mob.

The second chamber in the Parthenon had a separate entrance on the western side. It may have been intended as accommodation for the goddess's handmaidens, but as the hand-maidens existed neither as humans nor as statues the somewhat superfluous living quarters were put to more practical use as a **treasury strongroom**.

It is the attention to detail by the architect, Ictinus, which is astonishing. The floor, long since butchered, rose towards the centre in the imperceptible gradient of 1 in 450. Paradoxically, it was in order to preserve the illusion of straight lines that there is hardly a straight line or right-angle anywhere. The two rows of columns which form the **colonnade** slope inwards a fraction, but in the interest of harmony the inner row slightly less so. The difference in the angle is less than 1 percent.

The Parthenon once held a celebrated statue of Athena.

The taper of the columns would have been distorted by strong backlight, so they were given a faint swelling in the middle to counter that effect. Corner columns were made slightly thicker than their neighbours because they caught more light. The back of figures carved in high relief were invisible in normal circumstances, yet they were finished to much the same meticulous standard as front and sides.

Was it all absolutely necessary? Would anyone notice or, for that matter, care? The answer, perhaps, was that people might not be able to appreciate the finesse, but the gods would.

New ground: One of the great attractions on opening day would have been the **frieze** which ran high and uninterrupted around 524 ft (160 metres) of the inner wall of the colonnade. Sculpture was normally about gods, prancing horses, heroes slaying monsters and so on, and while there was plenty of that on the pediments and metopes of the Parthenon, the inner frieze broke new

ground in depicting common citizens.

One of the conspicuous features of classical Greek architecture was the result of the seemingly mundane invention of the **roofing tile**. Tiles made sloping roofs possible, and sculptors made the most of the triangle (or pediment) created at either end where the sloping roofs met.

There were about 30,000 citizens living in Athens when the Parthenon opened (plus rather more slaves and resident aliens), and many of them would have fraternised with craftsmen working on the site under the master sculptor, Phidias. They must have scrutinised the frieze for familiar faces because there was a scandal when they thought they recognised not only Pericles but the sculptor himself on the shield that was part of Athena's statue. Phidias's arrogance was compounded by the suspicion that he had helped himself to some of the gold that was supposed to have decorated the statue. The wretched sculptor, who had spent

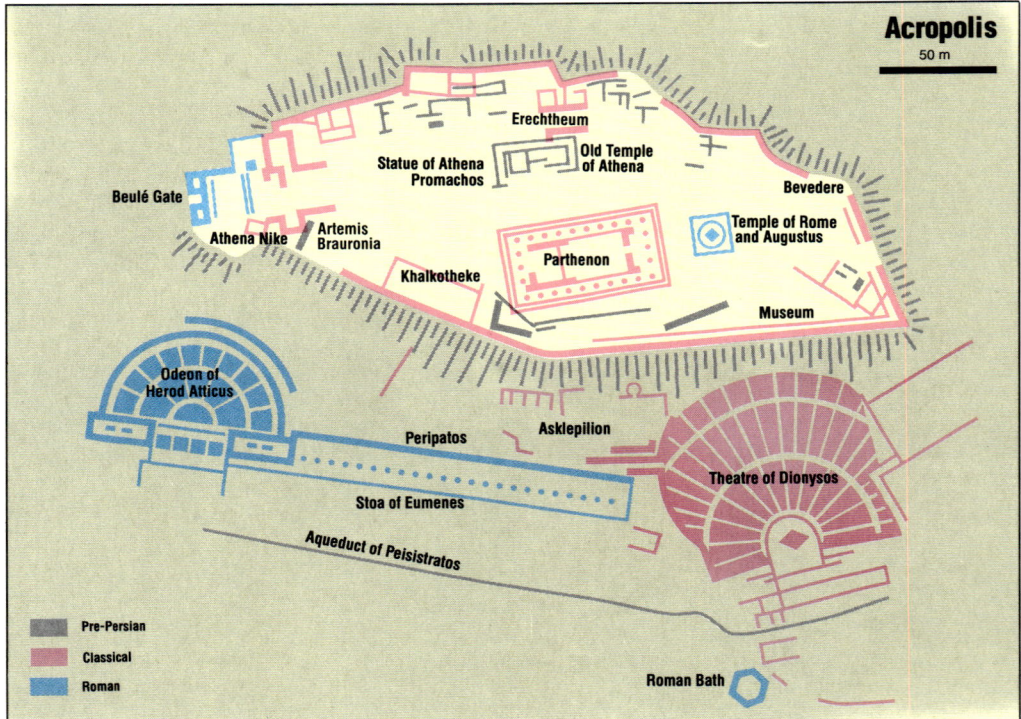

Acropolis
50 m

Erechtheum

Statue of Athena
Promachos

Old Temple
of Athena

Beulé Gate

Belvedere

Athena Nike

Artemis
Brauronia

Temple of Rome
and Augustus

Khalkotheke

Parthenon

Museum

Odeon of
Herod Atticus

Peripatos

Asklepilion

Theatre of Dionysos

Stoa of Eumenes

Aqueduct of Peisistratos

Pre-Persian
Classical
Roman

Roman Bath

the better part of his career on the Parthenon and had gone to the trouble, for instance, of canting the figures on the frieze so that they could be better seen by viewers at ground level, was drummed out of town forthwith.

The theme of the frieze was the highlight of the same Panathenaic festival which the vindictive visitors were themselves engaged in. Every fourth year, the population formed a procession which made its way up and along the Acropolis to present Athena with one of her badges of office, a saffron robe. She and her divine companions were included in the frieze too. Instead of the usual godlike mannerisms, they were lounging about in casual disarray, chatting among themselves while waiting for the procession to arrive.

Gods and mortals appeared to be on easy terms with one another. One of the young knights was calmly holding up the procession while he tied a bootlace. The frieze was a message of well-being and camaraderie: the gods were good to

Cast of a votive relief *circa* 500 BC.

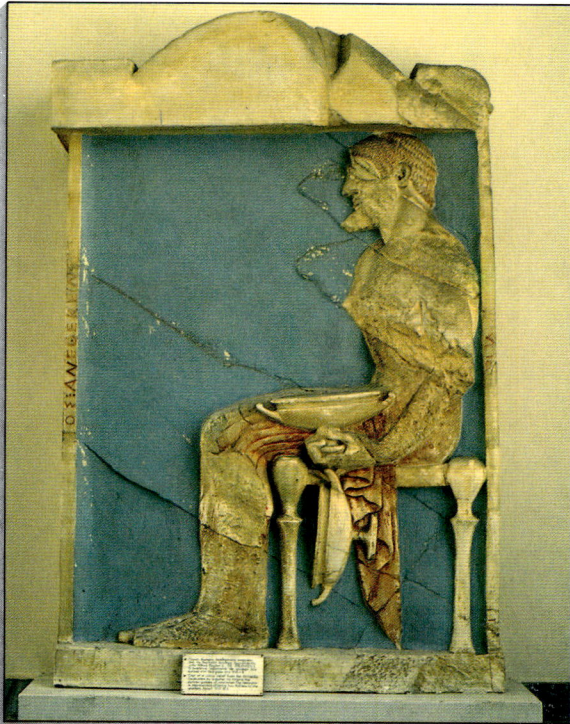

Athens and Athens was good to them.

At the beginning of the fifth century BC, Athens was still recovering from two Persian invasions in quick succession. The population had fled and Athens was razed in their absence. Rebuilding the houses in and around the Agora was obviously the first priority when the residents returned, and some consideration was given to leaving the wreckage on the Acropolis just where it was as a war memorial.

In spite of the almost total destruction, Athens, capital of Attica, recovered quickly and indeed prospered because of the leading role it had taken in the eventual defeat of the Persians. Until the war unexceptional among hundreds of independent Greek city-states, Attica was unexpectedly catapulted to the forefront. The state finances, previously dependent on olive oil exports and a silver mine, were flush with money which the lesser states had agreed to contribute to a common defence fund. Athens had no qualms about diverting the money for self-aggrandisement, although some of the contributors were heard to grumble about high-handedness.

Among the ruins left on the Acropolis after the Persian withdrawal were the **foundations** and a few battered columns of what had been planned as a new temple to Athena. As divine intervention had clearly saved the city from the barbarian onslaught, the people felt obliged to repay their debt to the gods on the grandest possible scale. The existing plans were scrapped and new ones drawn up. In the absence of a common enemy such as the Persians, the Greek states were bound to start warring with one another again: a magnificent Parthenon would not only appease the gods but also show the potential opposition what they were up against. Show them it might, cow them it did not—the Peloponnesian War, which pitched Athens against Sparta in a general mêlée of internecine fighting, was not long in coming.

The design and construction of the Parthenon was going to be a big job, so the more modest Temple of Athena Nike (or "Wingless Victory") was planned as a stop-gap. As matters turned out, the design by Callicrates, who worked also on the Parthenon, ran into difficulties and the little temple took longer than its bigger neighbour.

The victory theme involved giving Athena's statue in the temple a pair of wings. According to Pausanius, who visited Athens in the second century AD and wrote a book about it (a translation by Peter Levi is published by Penguin Classics in two paperback volumes), the Athenians were worried about these wings and removed them in case she flew away.

The spot chosen for the **Temple of Athena Nike**, a promontory on the southwestern corner of the Acropolis, was a natural vantage point. It was especially appropriate because it overlooked the island of **Salamis**, where the Athenian fleet had success-fully trapped the Persians, and it also had popular connections with another famous victory, albeit one with an unhappy ending.

In prehistoric times, the story goes, Athens had to send annual tribute in the form of child sacrifices to King Minos at Knossos in Crete. Theseus, son of the then king of Athens, Aegeus, went off to Crete to put an end to this vile practice. He left under black sails but promised his father that, if successful, he would return under white ones. He was successful—it is the tale of his entering the labyrinth and slaying the appalling Minotaur with the help of the beautiful princess Ariadne—but he forgot to change the sails. His father, waiting anxiously on the strategic rock, assumed the worst and threw himself off, thereby drowning in and lending his name to the Aegean Sea. (The story ignores the awkward fact that the distressed king would have crashed on to dry land, the water being some kilometres distant.)

An artist sketches the Caryatid porch.

The Periclean plans for the Acropolis included two more buildings. The new **Erechtheum**, replacing one destroyed by the Persians, was a kind of museum, and it presented special problems for the architect because it had to include a number of immovable sacred objects, such as a snake-pit, a rock which Poseidon once struck with his trident, an olive tree, and a salt-water well.

Athenian religious belief was then in a state of upheaval. It retained elements of earlier aniconic fetishism—the worship of inanimate objects, including trees and rocks—and was struggling with the difficult precepts of the Pythagorean Orphic faith. This was the same Pythagoras whose sharp mathematical brain worked out the implications of the right-angled triangle. His mind seemed to cloud over when dealing with religious belief; followers were under instructions never to eat beans, a commandment which was apparently unconcerned with flatulence.

The olive tree enclosed in the Erech-theum was supposedly Athena's gift, the origin of Attica's olive oil industry. Like the much later petroleum variety, olive oil was the principal fuel (no coal in Greece) and not merely a salad dressing. The salt-water well puzzled Pausanius because it emitted the sound of waves when the wind blew south. Work on the Erechtheum ceased during the Peloponnesian War and was only resumed afterwards to provide work for the unemployed. Its most famous feature is the **Caryatid porch** supported on the heads of six pretty maidens.

The largest building project on the Acropolis, designed by Mnesicles in the same period, would have occupied the whole west side of the Acropolis if it had not run into difficulties with priests in charge of the precinct of **Artemis Brauronia** on the Acropolis. Their cult required young girls to imitate a bear walking on its hind legs and also to do a lot of running about and dancing in the nude. Pausanias was mystified and not a little cynical about the cult, although it had official status and no Athenian girl was supposed to marry unless she had participated. Perciles hoped to overcome the religious objections, but in the end the **Propylaia** was limited to what had once been intended as the central section alone.

The Propylaia replaced an older gateway built in the time of the tyrant Cimon and, even in its truncated form, it is probably the most impressive of the buildings erected by the Greeks for secular purposes. It incorporated a **picture gallery** with frescoed walls and a famous ceiling. The building was usually commandeered as the residence of whoever ruled Athens, and as such it was forever being modified to serve particular needs.

In the third century AD, the Romans added a gate which modern visitors pass through on their approach. It was filled in and forgotten when the Acropolis reverted to a military role and, of course, the defenders wanted to make entry as difficult as possible. During the

The Caryatid porch is the most famous feature of the Erechtheum.

Byzantine period, when the Parthenon was converted into the **Church of Our Lady of Athens**, the Propylaia was home to Archbishop Michael Acominatos. The pious cleric "was moved to tears at the sight of the destroyed walls, the empty streets, and the ragged, badly-fed people". It was he who compared the 30 years he spent in 13th-century Athens to life in hell and regretted what his term of office had done to him. "I too have fallen into barbarism," he moaned.

Post-Periclean alterations: By the early 15th century, the Venetian Duke of Athens, Antonio Acciajuoli, was in residence. He added a second storey, battlements and, opposite the Temple of Athena Nike, a square tower 27 metres high. The tower survived until 1874 and would still be there but for the policy of purging the Acropolis of post-Periclean alterations.

The Turkish occupants of the Propylaia made the fatal mistake of storing gunpowder in one of the rooms. It was struck by lightning. Two columns collapsed and the pasha and his family were killed, although the walls withstood the explosion remarkably well. Funnelled skywards, the blast made a fiery rocket out of the contents of the building including, one imagines, the pasha and his family. His successor installed his harem in the Erechtheum.

Whether as a result of the Propylaia explosion or not, the Turks then stored powder in the Parthenon with a similar combustible outcome. In 1687 a Venetian force under General Francesco Morosini was trying to wrest the Acropolis from the Turks, who dismantled the Athena Nike temple to make space for a gun battery. The Venetians mounted their guns on **Filopappou Hill** (where Socrates swallowed the hemlock) and pounded what was left of the Propylaia after its recent tragedy.

The gunnery officer, Count de San Felice, was described as "a fool with absolutely no idea of the art of artillery". One of his men with the unconvincing

Below, a view of Likavitós. **Right**, from the south *metope*, now in the British Museum.

LOSING THEIR MARBLES

The crux of the dispute over the "Elgin Marbles" is that much of the sculpture which once adorned the Acropolis is no longer in Greece but in the British Museum in London. The sculpture in question includes pediments, metopes and the celebrated frieze from the Parthenon as well as some of the Caryatids, the maidens who held the Erechtheum porch on their heads. Greeks, notably the former actress and Minister of Culture, Melina Mercouri, have petitioned the British government endlessly for their return because the sculpture is "a symbol of our nationhood and an integral part of a unique work of art".

The official British line is that the marbles belong to the museum trustees, not to the government, and that the trustees are prevented by an Act of 1753 from disposing of original works. The implicit point in the British defence is that if the great museums of the world, not excluding Greek ones, were required to repatriate all non-indigenous items, they would be left looking threadbare.

The historical facts of the matter are that Greece, as such, did not exist when the British ambassador to Constantinople, Lord Elgin, negotiated the right to remove a number of objects of Greek antiquity. "Greece" in 1799 was nothing more than an undefined province of the Ottoman empire and there were no Greek authorities with whom Lord Elgin could have dealt with, even if he had wanted to. The relevant power was Turkey, and the Turkish sultan gave his permission. The Greeks concede that permission was sought and granted but simultaneously insist that the British ambassador, who assembled 500 workmen and 37 ships for the task, took far more than he was entitled to. They have accused him of bribing Turkish officials to turn a blind eye.

Lord Elgin's defenders say that his conduct was absolutely proper. He was certainly no treasure hunter; indeed, the operation cost £75,000 of his own money, a colossal sum in those days, and he recouped less than half when the sculpture was passed to the museum trustees. Lord Elgin, they say, rescued for posterity vital parts of Greek civilisation which the Greeks themselves were incapable of preserving.

Most of the pieces were lying on the ground where they had fallen after an explosion 150 years before. If they had been left unattended any longer, there was every likelihood that, when danger threatened, they would be thrown together as a defensive barricade or subjected to some other destructive abuse. The Acropolis had a long history of whatever stood there being recycled as convenient building material.

As things turned out, over-zealous restoration of the Acropolis after Greek independence in 1834 saw many of the marble slabs which Lord Elgin left behind hacked about to fit some ill-conceived scheme. Butchered pieces are an irreparable loss to the dedicated team of archaeologists who are now attempting to reconstruct an intricate jigsaw on sensible principles. Battered and defaced as they were long before they came into the British Museum's possession, the Elgin Marbles are nevertheless singularly better preserved than anything that stayed behind, largely because of the dreadful pollution which afflicts modern Athens. Copies of the sculpture held in the museum have been made available to the restorers. The Greeks have acknowledged that the originals, if they were returned, could not resume their original positions but would have to go into a museum. "In that case," the British reply, "what's wrong with *our* museum?"

British archaeologists have immense respect for, and work closely with, their Greek counterparts. Most of the heat is generated in political circles, and emotions can cloud the issue. A Greek politician can always raise a popular cheer with a belligerent demand for the immediate return of the marbles. A British hardliner, on the other hand, may be tempted to say that modern Greek governments have not yet demonstrated conclusively that they can be trusted with them. After all, it is said, as recently as 1987 the government was proposing to build a chemical factory which would have belched corrosive waste all over Delphi, a site even more ancient and almost as important as the Parthenon.

Venetian name of Schwarz nevertheless scored a direct hit on the Parthenon powder room. Three hundred Turks were killed and the houses which had been erected among the historic buildings burned for 48 hours.

Morosini and his men were not finished yet. As soon as the Turks withdrew from the Acropolis, they moved in to collect some souvenirs. They attempted to prise the sculpture off the western pediment—and dropped it.

As an act of vandalism, Morosini's pales in Greek eyes next to the effort mounted by the British ambassador to Constantinople, Lord Elgin. At the turn of the 19th century, he carried away a treasure house of Greek antiquity, including half of the frieze depicting the Panathenaic procession. Elgin believed he was saving the marbles for posterity, but the Greeks put a different interpretation on the operation and have campaigned hard to secure their return.

The War of Independence (1821-32) revived European interest in classical Greece. Athens was an unlovely mess when the Turks finally withdrew, a town with a population of little more than 4,000. Volunteers assumed the responsibility of restoring the Acropolis to its pristine, Periclean condition. Pieces of the Temple of Athena Nike, displaced by the Turkish artillery, were found and reassembled. The forgotten Roman gate below the Propylaia was uncovered in 1852 by the French archaeologist Beulé, by whose name it has since been known.

Gateway to history: The **Beulé gate** was one of the exceptions to the general rule that any structure not belonging to the Classical Age had to go. The urgent enthusiasm with which this policy was implemented hindered later efforts. In spite of centuries of pilfering, a large proportion of the Periclean building material was still on the Acropolis, albeit where explosions had deposited it or incorporated in some later edifice. With sufficient expertise and patience, these pieces could have been identified and put back where they originally belonged. Instead, marble blocks which had been fashioned to meet Ictinus's exacting standards were broken up to fill gaps in some pet project of the moment.

Fortunately, a more considered and responsible policy now prevails, and the aim of the present restoration programme is to reassemble the jigsaw. New pieces are manufactured where they are absolutely necessary—reinforcing clamps are made of titanium, which does not corrode—but there is no intention of fully winding the clock back 2,500 years.

It would be futile to put a new roof on the Erechtheum, for example, because no one really knows what the original looked like. It remains to be seen whether the restorers will resort to the splash of bright paint which, while authentic enough, would undoubtedly cause yet another round of jibes about giving the Acropolis the face of a wanton woman.

Left, boy with goat, from the Acropolis Museum. Right, all roads lead to the Acropolis.

PLAKA

Plaka has always been the heart of Athens. Like all Gaul, it is divided into three parts, running from the **Anafiotika**, the whitewashed 19th-century village clinging to the side of the Acropolis's northeastern slope— just beneath the Long Rocks to **Ano** (Upper) **Plaka**, which stretches down to Adrianou (Hadrian's Street), to **Kato Plaka**, where the quarter levels off into the city, with Filellinon and the Acropolis on the west. Plaka is a distinct entity, as Greek as Athens can be.

Now protected by the Greek government, Plaka is rapidly being restored to much of the colour and elegance of the last century. And although in many cases the restoration work seems to conform more to the 20th-century notion of what the 18th and 19th centuries were all about, Plaka is a much more pleasant place to be today than it was

two decades ago, when the quarter had become a 120-decibel nexus of sordid bars, *boîtes* and discos. Pedestrian walks have replaced formerly frantic thoroughfares like Adrianou and Kidathineon Streets, and the traffic in the streets is mostly two-legged.

Plaka's thousand or so buildings date mostly from the 19th century. Very few survived the era of Turkish occupation, though there are some houses left standing which are being renovated and are under government protection.

The origin of the area's name is disputed. Popularly, the district is known as the area surrounding the **Church of the Transformation** on Kidathineon Street. (This church—the primary place of worship in Plaka—is just off Nikis Street and was erected by Turkish converts to Christianity, and restored by the Russian community in 1834.) Of recent origin, it is believed that the name Plaka was derived from *plakas*, an ancient word for a joke being played, or from a large stone slab found in the area of the Church of St George of Alexandria near Thespidos Street. But another school of thought supports Plaka's being a bastardisation of the Albanian *pliaka*, meaning "old". Albanian residents called this quarter "Pliaka Athena".

No. 96 Adrianou Street, purportedly built by members of the Benizelos family, was erected during the Turkish era and is one of Plaka's oldest extant buildings. Most pre-revolutionary houses were levelled during the door-to-door fighting in 1827, but the Benizelos house survived with its courtyard, graceful arches, well and olive press. Once divided precisely in half by two heirs, even the well of the house was split: water was a major problem in Athens, then as now, and especially in arid Plaka.

Richard Church's house, at 5 Scholiou, is also an 18th-century survivor, once used by the Turks as a police precinct headquarters. Church, at one point commander-In-chief of the Greek Revolutionary Forces, lived here, as did historian George Finlay, who restored this distinctive dwelling with its walls of small stones, tiny windows and a tall chimney.

Greeks, Turks, Franks, Arvanites (or Albanians), and Ethiopian slaves have populated Plaka, and the current population is far less exotic than those of centuries past. In 1841, Hans Christian Andersen met with some of the descendants of Ethiopian residents, the precursors of today's Anaphiotes.

As Monastiraki, and Plaka, its stepchild, constitute two of the city's soapbox areas, it is not unusual to encounter colourful figures declaiming poetry, predicting the world's end, performing readings, or simply singing.

Fterou, the omnipresent featherduster pedlar, whose call may be heard, like the peacock's, from a great distance, is usually about, selling dusters and fracturing heroic verse. Athanasios Diakos's quatrain on the occasion of his execution by the Turks can be translated roughly thus:

*See what season Death has picked
To take me,
Now that all the branches are blooming
And the hills, green.*

Fterou's rendition is fortunately somewhat gayer:

*See what season Death has picked
To take me,
Now that leave has been granted the sailors
And soldier-boys.*

Characters much more eccentric than Fterou go their sundry ways in Plaka, entertaining a tolerant ambulatory audience. Yiannis, the khaki-clad troubador, may appear at your table to play an off-key ballad on his miniature guitar. His singing is often superb; his strumming is not.

Various segments of the quarter carry their own names still which reflect the character of former inhabitants. One area hugging the foot of the Acropolis—or *Kastro*, as locals have termed it—is called Yerladha. This name,

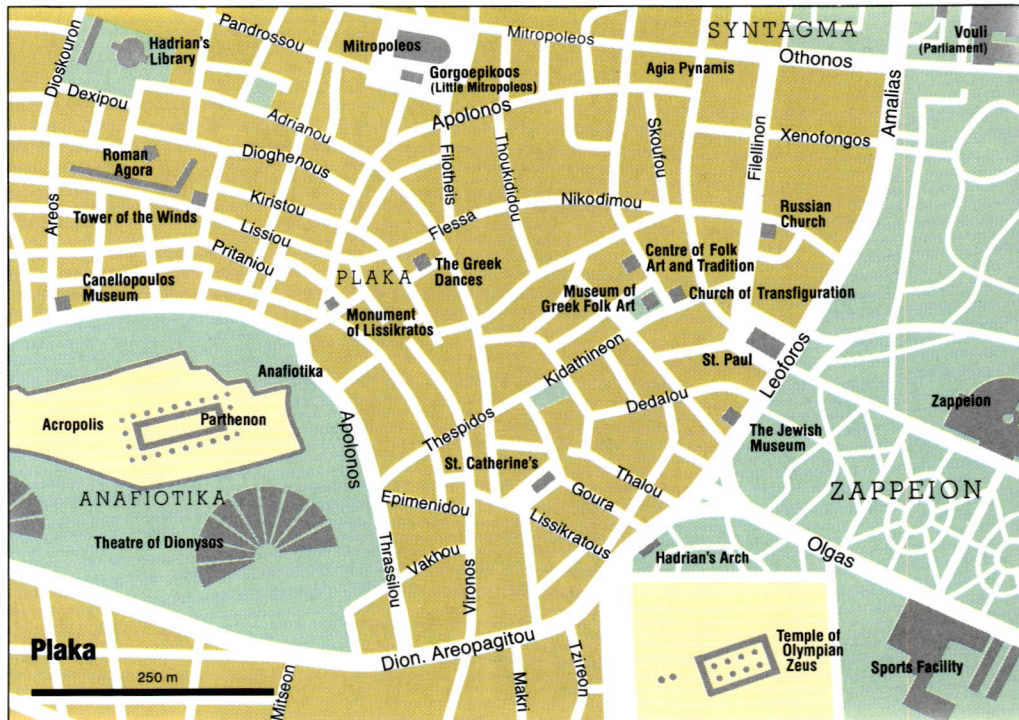

Plaka

250 m

meaningless in Greek, derives from the word *guirlande*, or garland, an appropriate epithet for the Acropolis's slightly fallen halo. **Upper Plaka**, later called Rizokastro (Place-built-at-the-foot-of-the-castle), is immortalised in a popular street song:

You Nereid of Rizokastro,
I haven't seen eyes like yours before.
Going up and down the stairs,
I've lost a lot of weight.

When Athens became the Greek capital in 1834, the city expanded according to a calculated plan towards Syntagma and Omonia. Large public buildings were erected in the deserted area and drew the population away from "The Rock", yet Plaka stubbornly remained the focus of activity a decade after hostilities ended.

Home to many of the young capital's first families, whose mansions still grace the area in various hues of pastel plaster, Plaka had many firsts. The first High School of Athens was located on Adrianou Street. In 1837, Athens' first University opened at No. 5 Tholos Street. The city's first police precinct has always been located in the quarter.

The city grew and the rich moved to greener pastures. Plaka's decline began. Preserved in its present state due to building restrictions, and thus spared the apartment-block syndrome that hit Athens like a plague of concrete after World War II, Plaka retained its character in spite of the sleazy 1960s and 70s. Now with a government policy fostering renovation and money moving back in, Plaka has once again an exciting neoclassical future.

Exotic people-watching: This is nice area for ambulatory visitors interested in unusual small museums, stray antiquities, good Greek and authentic exotic food and people-watching. Take a walk with a map. The street plan becomes scrambled here and there, a labyrinth which Plaka always has been and it is hoped always will be. Two rules apply to those in doubt: uphill is the Acropolis: downhill are Monastiraki,

An ouzo and wine shop on one of the pedestrian thoroughfares.

the Cathedral and Syntagma Square.

The **Paul and Alexandra Canellopoulos Museum** on the corner of Theorias and Panos Streets is uphill from the Tower of the Winds in two neo-classical mansions frosted with "acroteria", those familiar scrolled ceramic roof ornaments which echo the classical marble prototypes. The Canellopoulos is noted for its fine icons, but its collection is eclectic.

The first and second floors house pre-Christian antiquities—Prehistoric, Neolithic, early Cycladic, Minoan, Mycenean, etc. Not all the objects are Greek: some are from Luristan, Egypt and Mesopotamia.

Hellenistic jewellery, sixth-century BC helmets, an exquisite black-figure drinking cup of the "little master" class (sixth-century BC) and the matchless icons from both the School of Constantinople and the Macedonian Painting School, plus Coptic textiles, and statuettes round out this remarkable family collection. A second-century

painted portrait of a *Woman from Fayoum* is worth seeking out.

On the corner of Pritaniou, moving around the curve of the Acropolis, you will find the 11th or 12th-century Byzantine church of **St Nicholas the Rangavas**. This basilica, built perhaps on a much earlier Christian site is a lovely gingerbread edifice of stone and brick. Its walls include fragments of ancient columns and capitals. The saint's epithet is unusual: "*Rangavas*" can mean either "prodigal, dishevelled, rowdy young man" or "Leviathan". This Nicholas may have been either, a wayward youth who mended his ways—or a whale of a man!

White-washed village: Walking clockwise round the path which circles the Acropolis will bring you to the highest part of Plaka. The Anafiotika, the whitewashed 19th-century jumble of houses tenaciously anchored on the slope is a village of its own, with an interesting history.

Occupied in Neolithic times, the area

Plaka is Athens' most colourful district.

144

of **the Anafiotika** (which means "village of the people from Anafi") was abandoned in classical times when the Delphic oracle proclaimed the site holy ground. During the Peloponnesian War, however, when Attica was beseiged, refugees flooded into Athens and sought refuge in the sheltering caves under the Long Rocks. Later, Ethiopian slaves sealed off the caves with walls.

A law dating from 1834 prohibited building in the area but impoverished Greeks, faced with public building restrictions, have always reacted with ingenuity. In the 1830s, stonemasons and master craftsmen from all over the Aegean islands flocked to Athens because of the building boom, and though these skilled islanders erected beautiful mansions for wealthy Athenians, they found buying land, let alone a house, impossible on their wages. The makeshift village they threw up near Kaningos Square was soon overrun by the burgeoning city.

Finally, two enterprising craftsmen from Anafi, a Cycladic island near Santorini, turned to the steep eastern slope of the Acropolis. Under the pretence of building a church, overnight they put together two houses for their respective families.

Notified of the deed by the inhabitants of Rizokastro, the police came up to inspect but were faced with a *fait accompli*. After that the Anafiotika grew like a honeycomb. At first it was only Anafiot emigrants, then others drifted in. It was and is a clannish area, as picturesque as a Cycladic island.

The residents restored the half-ruined **Church of St George of the Rocks** and **St Simeon** and brought to the latter a miracle-working icon of Our Lady of the Reeds.

Downhill is a landmark square at the junction of Lissikratous, Epimenidou and Vironos Streets. Here is the graceful **Choregic** (musical competition) **Monument of Lissikratos**, justly famous for its Corinthian capitals and its almost capricious delicacy of design. This "ivory tower" bears the inscription: "Lyssikratos of Kikyna, son of Lysitheides, was choregos, the tribe of Akamantis won the victory with a chorus of boys: Theon played the flute; Lysiades of Athens trained the chorus; Evainetos was archon." This was the equivalent of a platinum record in 334 BC.

Competing for attention in this same square is all that remains of the **Capuchin Monastery** founded in 1658 by French friars of that order, one of whom, Father Francis, first introduced tomatoes to Athens. Father Simon, the superior, bought the Lissikratos Monument in 1669 and the monastery stood till 1821, with the monument itself serving as a friar's cell. It was here, too, inside the hollow drum, that Lord Byron purportedly composed segments of *Childe Harold* in 1810–11.

A favourite café on the corner is known as "Dirty Corner" to a group of expatriates associated with the arts.

Still in Ano Plaka, in the square

Puppets are a permanent fixture in many shop windows.

formed by Chaeefontos, Lissikratous and Galananou Streets with a little garden and fronted by two ancient columns, stands **St Catherine's Church**, granted to the Monastery of Mt Sinai during the time of the Patriach Bartholomew, between 1765 and 1782.

Open-air dances: At 8 Scholeiou Street off Adrianou is **The Greek Dances-Dora Stratou Foundation**, housed in a four-storey renovated mansion. Dora Stratou devoted her life, which ended in 1988, to noting and preserving traditional Greek dance. She created a dance troupe, which performs in the open air theatre behind Filopappou Hill in summer. In the building are some 3,000 traditional Greek costumes, a collection of jewellery and a library of recordings and reference books on Greek dance and costume. Regular classes are held at the Scholeiou building and lectures on the dance and related topics are offered by noted scholars.

Two other museums of note in Kato Plaka are the **Centre of Folk Art and Tradition**, on Angeliki Hadzimihali Street, and the **Museum of Greek Folk Art**, at 17 Kidathineon Street.

"The Hadzimihali" is in the mansion of the late folklorist, who, like Dora Stratou, devoted her life to rescuing the traditions of Greek folk culture from oblivion. Both the Stratou and the Angeliki Hadzimihalis collections are monuments to the vanishing heritage of Greek village life. Temporary and exciting exhibitions are scheduled continuously at the centre and many focus on the costumes of a particular Greek region. Weaving, embroidery, tools, woodwork, shelters and even decorated breads are included as documents of a traditional heritage.

The Museum of Greek Folk Art, a stone's throw away, also houses an impressive collection of embroideries, hand-loomed fabrics, wooden spoons and kitchen utensils, costumes, metal work and wood carving, ceramics, shadow puppets from the *Karagiozis* theatres, naïve art and stone reliefs dat-

A nice area for ambulatory visitors.

ing from 1650 right to the present day.

On the edge of Plaka at 36 Leoforos Amalias, on the third floor of a building with one of those lovely crazy wood-and-wrought iron lifts from Paris, is the **Jewish Museum of Greece**. Founded in 1977 to collect, preserve and publicise the surviving heritage of Greece's Jews, this inspirational museum includes religious and ceremonial artefacts, costumes and embroideries, old photos and documents.

A working synagogue is also located on the premises, removed *in toto* from Patras. The history of Greek Jewry stretches back unbroken to before the third century BC, but 87 percent of the population was wiped out in World War II. Today there remain only 5,000 Jews in the whole of Greece. The museum also runs a small gift shop and the Friends of the Jewish Museum publish a newsletter.

First Gothic building: At the corner of Filellinon and Leoforos Amalias stands **St Paul's** active Anglican Church, founded on Easter Monday, 1838, when it lay on the very edge of a devastated city. Designed by Henry Wadsworth Acland, this first Gothic building in Athens originally stood in a large, ornate garden.

A slab just inside the entrance which commemorates the death of one George Stubbs and two merchant navy officers who died in 1685, is the oldest British monument in Athens. The simple interior is highlighted by stained glass windows depicting Saints Paul, Andrew, Stephen and Lawrence; plus Joshua and Caleb, and the Life of David. Recently restored, St Paul's turned 150 years old in 1988.

In the next block is the so-called **Russian Church of St Nicodemus**. Probably built between AD 1000 and 1025, it was part of a monastery within Athens' ancient walls. The monastery was destroyed in the 1701 earthquake. Ceded to the Russian Orthodox Community in 1852, the church was eventually restored and is today the largest medieval structure in the city. The belfry and bell were gifts of Czar Alexander II in the 17th century. The German artist Thiersch painted the fascinating interior wall paintings.

Another muralist is responsible for modern works throughout Plaka. In fact, wandering up the quarter's taverna—and nightclub-studded streets, such as Mnissikleous and Lyssiou, you will see naïve painter George Savekis' work, both on exterior walls and on canvases indoors.

This Plaka old-timer has a studio at **14 Thespidos Street**, and has left his mark on the district with large-scale studies of turn-of-the-century night life, the *manghes* (a sub-culture of men with their own particular code of dress, honour and fighting), and peripatetic musicians. Lively and colourful, Savekis' work reminds present-day Plaka residents and visitors alike of what life used to be like in these narrow user-friendly streets before the days of electric lights and amplifiers.

Dance classes are held in the mansion housing the Dora Stratou Foundation.

AROUND SYNTAGMA SQUARE

The hub of Athens is the open area called **Syntagma**, or **Constitution Square**. Here is the centre of all activity, from the functioning of government (serious business) to the ogling of ladies' legs (even more serious business), and all degrees in between. Cultural activity may go on around the corner near the University, and archaeological around the Acropolis, but Syntagma Square is where all the world must pass in order to cross the city. Around this green oasis roars traffic, angry traffic and angrier traffic (except when everybody leaves town at Easter and Christmas, and on election days—then Syntagma Square is truly peaceful).

In the centre of the Square is a circular fountain surrounded by shade trees, benches and five outdoor cafés, where occasionally buskers and acrobats perform. Athenians sit and sip small coffees and look at foreigners looking at Athenians: people-watching is a favourite occupation of Greeks. At the western edge, a tiny kiosk offers tickets for certain concerts.

On the west side of the square are bus and trolley stops, banks offering exchange services, and both the **National (Ethniki) Bank** and the **General Bank** which offer National Tourist Organisation brochures and information. There are four more sidewalk cafés here, the oldest being **Papaspirou**, and another row of people-watchers.

The north side is a row of luxury hotels, notably the N.J.U. Meridien, the now-abandoned King George, the Grande Bretagne and at the beginning of Leoforos Vassilisis Sophias (also known as El. Venizelou), the Astir Palace Hotel.

The square is often a gathering point for demonstrations about everything from tax protests to election rallies—which means traffic comes to a complete halt, buses are re-routed and it is generally accepted that transport chaos reigns. The **House of Parliament**, a large lemon-coloured structure, occupies the high ground. It was built to be the Palace, but after the second of two serious fires, it was judged in 1935 to be unfit for royal occupation, and turned over to the *Vouli* or Parliament.

In front of the building is the **Tomb of the Unknown Soldier**, where visiting dignitaries lay wreaths, and on major holidays, officials bury its marble step in flowers. The bas-relief of a dying soldier is modelled on a sculpture from the Temple of Apháia in Aegina; the bronze shields on the wall represent the victorious battles in which Greek soldiers have fought since 1821. El Alamein, Crete and Korea might be names recognisable to English-speakers.

Keeping watch over the tomb are a pair of the élite soldiers called *Evzones*, an honour guard which changes every hour. On Sundays and holidays these men wear the uniform of the Revolutionary mountain fighters, short white

Left, flower vendor by Parliament. **Right**, the *foustanella* of each soldier consists of 400 pleats.

foustanella—a cotton kilt with 400 pleats—and white stockings, embroidered velvet jacket and heel-less red shoes with pompoms, called *tsarouhi*. On weekdays they wear a tan tunic in summer, navy blue in winter, but still perform their elaborate goose-step choreography as they change positions, accompanied on Sundays at 11a.m. by a company parade and band. These dedicated chaps should not be taken as merely decorative: they are in fact highly trained special troops, albeit with extra fine legs. In the area in front of their little shelters, tourists feed flocks of pigeons, while a seller of shiny balloons adds a dash of colour, as do the flags displayed along Amalias Avenue, to honour whomever may be currently visiting the Prime Minister.

The south side of the square is lined with airline offices and fur shops, and one rather interesting but slightly expensive auction house. The street is named for Othonos (Otho), the first king of modern Greece.

In the beginning: It was only after the War of Independence in 1834 that this area was developed. In prehistory, it was another one of the ancient cemeteries outside the city walls, as was discovered during street repairs in the late 1950s. Nearby was Apollo's Garden of the Muses, which gave the name "Square of the Muses" to the space on the town plans of the 1830s. Here Aristotle lectured his students as they walked, earning the nickname the "Ramblers"—the Peripatetics.

The War of Independence bankrupted most Greeks: in 1832, **Ermou Street** was a wide dirt road lined with a few huts. Property vacated by the Turks was going for a song, often to the repatriated. Yet the rebuilding of Athens was strangely desultory. Only 160 houses had gone up, and deliveries of window glass and wood were few and far between.

At the time, Athens was ruled by King Otho, the teenage son of King Louis I of Bavaria. King Louis' large-

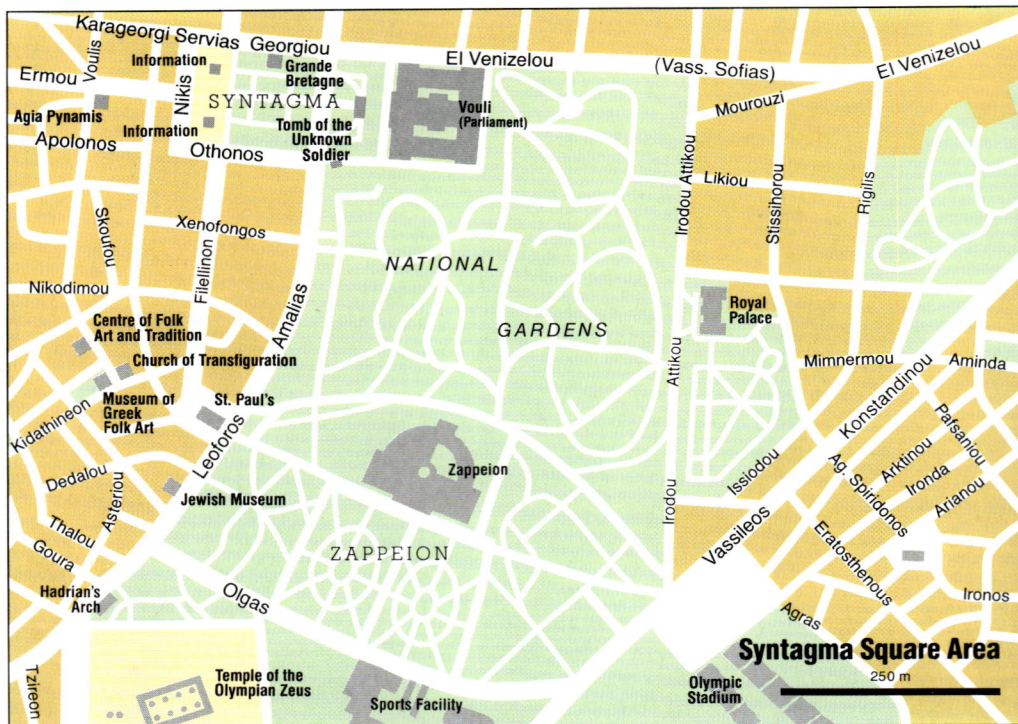

Syntagma Square Area

250 m

scale planning of Munich created that city's graceful, classical style. Louis announced that Athens would rise again, in the "shade of the Acropolis", a new city to be raised on the ruins of the ancient, and the glory of the classical world restored. Forget Constantinople: Athens was the capital of the Kingdom of Greece. Property prices soared.

It might have worked better to build a new city in an underdeveloped area instead of superimposing the plans on top of an old and war-torn village, but architects and designers rallied to the task. From Munich came the expatriate Greek Cleanthes and his colleague Schaubert, no doubt licking their lips at this golden opportunity. Classical influence and modern comfort! A royal palace! Parks and squares and gardens! What vast improvements on the ancient world, as seen from Munich!

Athenians objected strenuously. Expansive boulevards are all very well in foreign parts, they said, but we'll be fried on those big flat baking sheets! It's all too big, too wide. Our little streets are going to look like slums in contrast. Where is our shade? Where are our shops to be? They were, perhaps, accustomed to mazes of streets with plenty of hiding places.

There was dissension. The Regent sighed, and called on Klenze, another Munich architect, to sort out the mess. His revised plan was adopted on the same day in 1834 that Athens was declared the official capital of Greece.

Athenians, ever political, made an issue of it. The plans were altered. The green parks vanished. Streets that were meant to be wider became narrower instead. Stoas that looked elegant on paper ended as crooked alleys. The old narrow streets in the centre still crisscross the wide avenues, making a web of little lanes that causes traffic control headaches—and accommodate hundreds of tiny shops.

The king and his new queen, Amalia, took up residence in the Papagarripoulos house, near **Klafthmonos Square**,

Hemingway called *Evzones* "fighting men in ballet skirts".

while they waited for the palace to be completed. In January 1840, the king threw a party for his builders on the day he laid the cornerstone, at which 50 roast lambs and 4,000 bottles of wine were consumed.

By 1842 the **Royal Palace** was standing ready on the high ground of Perivolaki (Little Garden) Square, where Queen Amalia had been planting trees and flowers. The building has been described as hideous, dignified, clumsy, austere, ugly and a fine example of neo-classical architecture. King Louis professed himself satisfied that it was sufficiently imposing to impress the people, which was what what one wants of a Royal Palace.

The Grande Bretagne: The houses of the general public were small and mean compared to the fine public buildings or the houses of the wealthy. A Mr Demitriou applied for permission to build a mansion under the windows of the palace. Since the design was an elegant affair by Theofil Hansen, already a

well-known name in the new Greek architecture, His Highness was pleased. Besides, it was a good location for extra guest rooms, which the king required for state visitors. So many stayed there that it was called the "Petit Palais".

For a brief while after the owner died, it was occupied by the French Archaeological Institute. Later, it was bought by a royal cook who had gone to Paris, become a master chef and wanted to run a hotel. Now dubbed the **Grande Bretagne**, the building was described by a guest as "among the greatest hotels of Europe, for its charming position, imposing building, well-ventilated rooms, exceptionally good cuisine and architectural regularity". Until the 20th century, however, there was only one bathroom—in the basement!

In 1924 and again in 1930 the Grande Bretagne was enlarged, in harmony with the original design. During World War II it served in turn as headquarters for Greek, German and British officers. The building seems to be lucky: at one

The green avenues of the National Gardens offer an illusion of privacy.

point, Greek soldiers mined it to blow up the Germans, but the task was unsuccessful. In 1944, during the Civil War, Communists lobbed a grenade at Winston Churchill who was inside conferring with the government: they missed.

The Grande Bretagne, the first European hotel to install air conditioning, was entirely rebuilt in 1956 still based on the Hansen design—but this time with bathrooms.

Leafy romance: As the Royal Palace neared completion, Queen Amalia determined on an exotic **Royal Garden** nearby. Almost 40 acres were set aside, and the Frenchmen Barauld was imported to make the plans. Soon the workers found themselves excavating a lost Roman site, and it was decided to leave the antiquities in place. A mosaic floor, tumbled columns and fragments of marble lend romance to the gardens even today.

Thousands of plants were laboriously brought in by cart from Italy and many parts of Greece. As usual, water was a serious problem; then a sixth-century BC aqueduct was found under the wilting shrubbery, which serves as a basis for the present watering system. Water now flows through channels throughout the gardens, occasionally passing through ponds where ducks, goldfish and turtles disport themselves.

The biggest duck pond is near a little **zoo** close to the centre of the gardens. The animals on exhibit are mostly birds: you may see an arrogant peacock giving a fantail pigeon an inferiority complex. A few ill-caged deer, goats, wolves, and a pair of lions have also been housed here. There are hundreds of stray cats, fed by local animal lovers.

Of course, these gardens were for the use of the royal entourage, not open to the public. It wasn't until 1923 that the park was decreed the **National Gardens**, and today many still call it the Royal Garden. A pavilion once used by the Court has become a **Botanical Museum**, and a few metres away is the cool stone house of the **Children's Lib-**

The gardens are watered by a system based on a sixth-century BC aqueduct.

rary—books and games in English, Greek and French. Note that on the doors of these structures are opening hours written in chalk, which might as well be water: in general, they are likely to be open in the mornings till about 2 p.m. and closed Mondays.

The gardens make ingenious use of space, with little paths that wander among the leaves of 500 different varieties of plants under a canopy of trees. They open into flower circles where perhaps an ancient stone seat has been joined by wooden benches, or on to steps which lead under a rose arbour. You are meant to get lost in it, and it is easy to do, especially since all those leaves create an oxygen supply that can make a smog-breather quite dizzy. The green avenues offer the illusion of privacy while birdsong fills the air. The park is open from dawn until dusk.

In the back of the palace is a **coffee shop** serving ice-cream, drinks and snacks. Its street exit is on **Irodou Attikou**, one of the most expensive and exclusive residential streets in Athens. Just after the greenhouse and caretakers' area is the barracks of the *Evzone* troops from which they emerge to march around the Palace to their stations. Opposite, also guarded by the picturesque *Evzones*, is the **President's House**, which housed King Constantine after the fires in the palace, until his expulsion in 1967.

The Zappeion: Between the National Gardens and the Temple of Zeus is the smaller park area called the **Zappeion**. It was a barley field when the Royal Gardens were designed, and only later was this area developed by the brothers Zappas: the handsome **exhibition hall**, designed by Hansen in the 1840s, was finally built in 1874–78. Both the hall and the wide walks are used for exhibitions of books, camping gear, and furnishings. In the winter months, children provide a colourful spectacle in their carnival costumes.

Next to the building is a pagoda-like structure with bright golden yellow walls and red tiled roofs. This is the popular **Aigli Cafeteria**, which offers not only refreshment but entertainment. Behind it is the **Aigli outdoor cinema**. If the cabaret at the café is too loud, however, the sound of the film is drowned out and you have to depend on Greek sub-titles to follow the plot.

On Amalias Avenue is the **Oasis Café** with pretty lanterns and a fine view of the world strolling by.

Little paths and squares lead from the building to a large children's playground, where unaccompanied adults are not admitted. The entrance is from Leoforos Olgas, where the buses line up for the coast. On the corner of Olgas and Amalias Avenues stands a ridiculous **statue of Lord Byron** being beaten over the head, or perhaps having his hair brushed, by *Ellas* (Greece).

Although the gardens close at dusk, the Zappeion is always open. If you choose to prowl in the shrubbery after dark, however, you are likely to meet other prowlers.

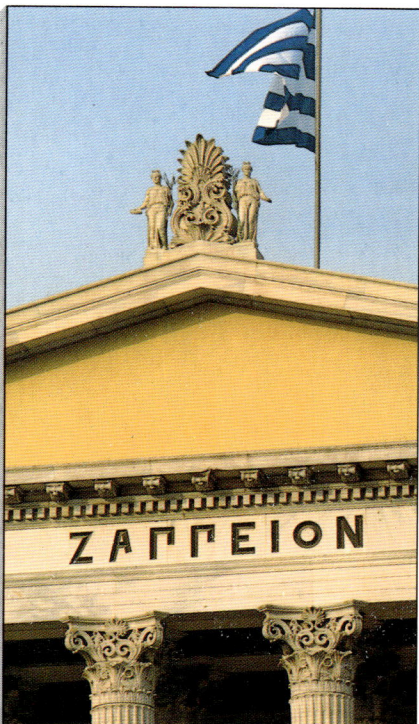

Left and right, the Zappeion was once a barley field.

SYNTAGMA TO MONASTIRAKI

The streets running west from Syntagma are major shopping thoroughfares, each with its own flavour. Athens has its own distinctive shopping patterns, left over from the old days of the guilds. Whole streets are devoted to pots and pans or bridal wear or church supplies. This is not always as convenient as a generalised shopping area but, on the other hand, it certainly facilitates comparisons.

Karageorgi Servias (which becomes **Perikleous**) has expensive tourist traps near the square and then waxes Greek as it proceeds. Costume jewellery, hosiery and haberdashery, trimmings and laces predominate. A side street, **Leka**, is full of Ionnina silversmiths. Hungry shoppers may stop off at the **Ariston** at 10 Voulis Street. Since 1910, people have been queueing up here for *tyropitas* (cheese pies).

Ermou Street at Syntagma displays up-market women's clothes, imported fabrics and fine shoes. Towards the little church of **Kapnikarea**, prices and quality take a plunge. On Ermou, too, are bridal shops and children's wear and the large household store, **Diamantis**.

The **Kapnikarea church** is caught in the traffic of Ermou Street, which divides to encircle it. Louis I of Bavaria preserved this 11th-century structure from demolition. Its name is an enigma: was the founder called Kapnikarias, or was he a "hearth-tax gatherer"? A letter from an Athenian woman in 1703 mentions the monk Kapinakas who may have given the church his name. Restored by the University, the cruciform Kapnikarea, with its **chapel of Saint Barbara** on the north side, is the city's best preserved Byzantine church.

Beyond the church, Ermou is mostly cheap fabrics and *souvlaki* shops until it reaches Monastiraki.

Mitropoleos, above the cathedral, is the furriers' street. Below are fabric, rug and souvenir shops, not to speak of long-standing *souvlaki* shops. Peering out between the legs of the Ministry of Education building on Mitropoleos Street near Voulis is the tiny Turkish-era **Church of Holy Strength**, or **Agia Dynamis**, a cell of the monastery of Pendelis. This little gem could have just as easily been called Holy Dynamite, as it was here that the master ammunition maker, Mastropavlis, manufactured cartridges for the Greek rebels. The bullets were smuggled out in laundry baskets by one Kyria Manolaina Biliari. Inside are traces of a wall painting by Athens' own Saint Filothei.

A few minutes' walk west, all light is temporarily blocked by the **Mitropoleos**, Athens' cathedral. Not since the Parthenon has big equalled beautiful in the realm of Athenian ecclesiastical architecture. The tiny human-sized **Agias Dynamis** is a Lilliputian treasure. The cathedral is large, conceived by four successive (but not so very, one might say, successful) architects, and consists of cannibalised masonry from some 70 older basilicas. Children use the ramps to the velvet-hung cathedral doors for skateboard practice; right wing demonstrators make better political use of the heel-catching textured marble in the square.

Theofil Hansen, the architect who also designed the University, drew up the original plans for "King Otho's cathedral" which was to be erected on the site of the present Church of St Denis. However, Hansen's great structure—a beautiful synthesis of Gothic/Romanesque/Byzantine/Renaissance which now exists only on paper—was never to be. The present cathedral site was selected over the Panepistimou Street location. Hansen departed, another architect's plan was begun and a cornerstone was laid at Christmas, 1842. Then work was stopped the next spring when the officials disagreed and the money ran out, naturally. The structure you see today, the result of a sort of let's-make-it-more-Byzantine architectural competition, was dedicated in May 1862. Known to one and all as The Cathedral, the church is actually the Church of the Annunciation.

Playing dimunitive Beauty to the great Beast next door is the Gorgoepikoos or Agios Eleftherios, also known as the **Small Mitropolis**. Cowering under the great church's armpit, it seems to be turning its face away in disgust. This church is the creation of an anonymous 12th-century Athenian architect who may have attended services in the church inside the Parthenon. The church of Gorgoepikoos ("Virgin Swift to Hear") and Agios Eleftherios ("Liberator"), may have been sacred to women in childbirth or perhaps the private chapel of the archbishop of Athens. It is constructed entirely of Pendelic marble no longer white, interspersed with heraldic animal relief elements which may be of Sassenid Persian origin. The frieze of the church illustrates the Attica calendar and the signs of the zodiac. This plaque was probably removed from the ruins of the Hellenistic temple of Serapis and Isis, once located close by. A few yards beyond the cathedral is an excellent **Post Office** with unusually obliging personnel.

Oasis of calm: The sheer sensory overload of shopping may give the uninitiated a headache. If so, it's time to head for the little square where the **Center of Hellenic Tradition** offers an oasis of cool calm, entered through a small stoa which passes between 36 Pandroasu and 59 Mitropoleos. Sip your Greek coffee in the first-floor café, **Beautiful Greece**, and gaze out of the window through climbing poinsettia plants at the side of the Parthenon. Here too are excellent copies of traditional textiles, marbles, woodcrafts and jewellery. The sales people are unobtrusive—a far cry from the streets below.

Icon seekers should give Monastiraki a miss. South of the cathedral is a warren of streets selling ecclesiastical gar-

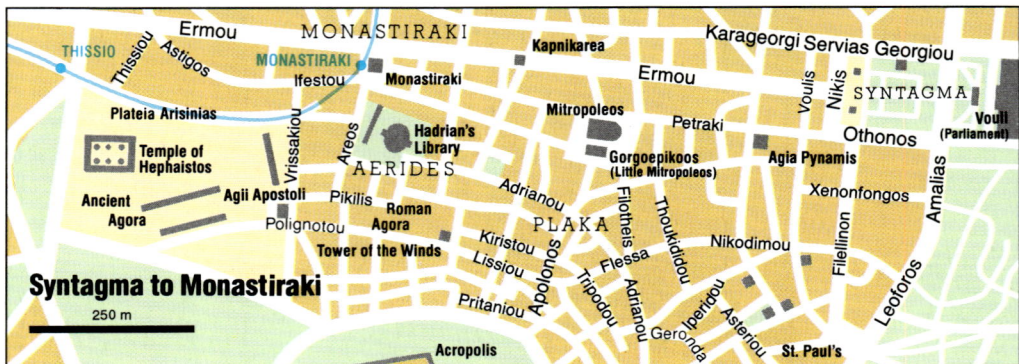

Syntagma to Monastiraki
250 m

ments and supplies, icons, pectoral crosses, votive offerings, candelabra etc. Agia Filotheis Street houses the **Palace of the Archbishop** and the **Church of St Andrew**. Apolonos and Navarchou Nikodimou Streets are lined with icon painters, some actually at work at easels in shop windows.

The area of Aerides: Above Monastiraki Square is **Aerides**, a colourful quarter named for the **Tower of the Winds** which ends Eolou Street (also spelled Aiolou Street).

The Tower of the Winds, Aerides, is also known as the *Horologio* (Clock) of Andronicus of Kyrrhos. It is basically a water-clock, a marble octagonal building on three steps. Each face marks a cardinal direction and shows a carving of the appropriate wind.

This structure is more complex than it looks. A reservoir of water dropped measured doses into a semicircular cistern outside the wall; there was a sundial on each of the eight sides. The water probably came from the Klepsydra

Spring on the Acropolis. The sides are perfectly aligned as to direction, and could serve as a compass. There was a weathervane on the peak, shaped like a sea god. Rumour has it that Julius Caesar gave the tower to Athens as a planetarium. During the Turkish era, the odd little building was used as a bijou dance hall by Dervishes, a sect which whirls for God. Old pictures show an astonishing amount of interior space being used for the ceremonies.

The north face shows Boreas, the God of the North Wind, blowing into a shell; northeast, grouchy old Kaikias throws hailstones, or possibly pine cones, from his shield; on the east, young Apeliotes displays a harvest of fruit and flowers; on the southeast, Euros threatens a gale; Notos, the South Wind, is emptying water on the world from an urn; southwest, Lips is blowing a ship's stern as western Zephyros throws flowers in the air; northwestern Skiros is busy drying up the waters left by the South Wind. In fact, a south wind in Athens often brings

Tower of the Winds: each face marks a cardinal direction.

dry dust from Africa rather than rain, but perhaps before the modern drought it was different.

Brush past gypsy women touting authentic hand-operated machine-made lace tablecloths and you will find yourself at **Agoras Square**, where among the baskets, a *tamata* shop on the corner will sell you an icon of almost any saint, with or without tin or base metal coating, with or without votive light, electric or oil. Above the Aerides area are the **Church of the Archangels** (Tachiarchi) and the beautiful old houses of Plaka.

Aerides to Monastiraki: Between the Tower of the Winds and Monastiraki Square are the **Roman ruins**. Just beside Aerides is the **Roman Agora**. This was a covered market with a colonnade and a double porch over the gate. Occasionally in summer it is furnished with chairs and a stage, and used for concerts or plays. The architrave is inscribed with a dedication to Athena Archegetis and explains that it was funded by Julius and Augustus Caesar. It was probably built between 17 BC and AD 2. On the north side of the doorway is an edict of Hadrian regarding taxes on oil sales. Inside the wall were rows of shops, some of which have been excavated, and inscriptions giving the names of the shopkeepers were found on the floors and columns. In a corner are the remains of the **Fetihye (Victory) Mosque**. Just inside the **Gate** are the remains of a giant public toilet, first-century AD.

One of the main streets of the quarter is **Adrianou**, which does not run straight but wanders around the edges of the excavations. It can be confusing. Along Adrianou are shops selling hand-beaten copper and brass, and behind the site rows of basket sellers offer everything from chairs to pencil holders. Some interesting hods and baskets have been created from crushed old tyres.

A small street called **Areos** runs from Monastiraki Square past the Mosque and the adjacent wall of the **Stoa** (or forecourt) **of Hadrian's Library**, and

The architrave in the Roman Agora was funded by the Caesars.

into Adrianou at the south side of the site. The wall of the Stoa is well preserved. A small church was once built on to it and only a bit of mosaic remains.

The Library must have been a charming place to visit, laid out with a cloistered arcade around a pool and garden. Three sides of this large building survive. In the east wall were five rooms: the central one housed the books on shelves in the large niche and the four smaller ones which flank it. In 410 Governor Herculius built what was probably a lecture hall over the end of the pool—nine ft (three metres) of wall still stand. This was converted into a church of the Virgin in Byzantine times.

Monastiraki Square: Monastiraki is many things. It's a small, circular square-in-a-loop fed by seven busy shopping streets. It's the "Little Monastery", the Pantanassa or **Church of the Dormition of the Virgin**; the suffix "*aki*" of Monastir shows a diminutive form of the word. It's also an idea. "Going to Monastiraki" for both the

Athenian and the visitor means entering Athens' seemingly eternal agora, flea market, souk, bazaar or *yusurum*, a Turkish word meaning "place-where-you-can-find-everything".

The capital's mercantile heartland has always been located here and, despite the renovation and beautification programme instituted by the City Fathers, the area is likely to resist attempts to lift its face. They intend to pave and plant the square, and it is hoped this will reduce the traffic, but it may be but a pious prayer. No amount of Western peroxide can ever obliterate Monastiraki's Oriental roots.

The square was in medieval times a convent belonging to the **Church of the Theotokos** (Pantanassa or Virgin Mary), the tiny structure now under restoration in the centre of the square. Its age is not certain, but may be 10th-century: its foundations may be even older. The ground level has risen since its time, so it is entered down a short flight of steps. The convent made a

Kittens find unlikely hiding places in Athens.

unique coarse cloth, *aba*, cared for the needy, and survived on its out-of-town olive groves. These assets gradually faded away after Independence and the church decayed. The building has undergone a series of amputations to allow for excavation of antiquities and the building of the electric railway. In 1907 the basilica was garishly redecorated and plastered, and asphalt was laid in the square. Weavers and nuns are long vanished.

The square has been called Hadrian's (because of the Library), the Square of the Lower Fountain, when it was a Turkish Bazaar, and in the heyday of the horse, "Carriage Square", because it was from here that one engaged transport to the port of Piraeus. The building of the railway to Piraeus stopped all that, and the **"Monastirion" station** is now the one most used by tourists.

The junction of Mitropoleos, Ermou, Athinas, Miaouli, Ifestou, Areos, and Pardrossou Streets is now a tangle of traffic, vendors selling coconuts and seasonal fruit and nuts, an occasional acrobat, mime or busker, the banner misleadingly announcing "Entrance to the Flea Market", a shop selling herbs and occult paraphernalia (between an icon shop and a shop selling chains), almost always a great cloud of dust, and plenty of sound and fury.

On one corner stands the only complete relic of the Turkish occupation, **the Mosque** built by the Athenian Moslem Tzisterakis in 1759, who made himself unpopular with the local Greeks by pulverising a column from the Temple of Olympian Zeus to make whitewash. The building, with dome and pillared loggia, has survived since 1759, *sans* minaret, functioning at one time or another as prison, barracks, warehouse, military band music room and a museum of folk art. The collection is temporarily in the Museum of Folk Art in Plaka while repairs of earthquake damage suffered in 1981 are completed.

Most visitors are less interested in the mosques (though the door of the **Men-**

dresse Seminary is still standing in the Roman Agora, and one can also see the remains of the **Fetihye Mosque**) and the antiquities up the street—most of which are closed to the public—than they are in jostling on the pavements of **Pandrossou** and **Ifestou** and **Adrianou**, their cross streets and mini-stoas. Here passers-by are invited very urgently to come in and look at real Greek whatever-we-are-selling—even if the labels say "Made in Hong Kong". In fact, many items are made in Greece.

The **Church of the Holy Apostles**, Agii Apostoli, stands beneath the Acropolis, west of the Tower of the Winds, at the edge of the ancient Agora. Built on top of a second-century AD *nymphaeum*, the church originally had four niches and a narthex. Founded between 1000 and 1025, this was the first of Athens' important churches.

Monastiraki as bazaar: From Monastiraki Square west, Ermou Street completely loses its memory of those *soigné* shops up at Syntagma, and becomes a

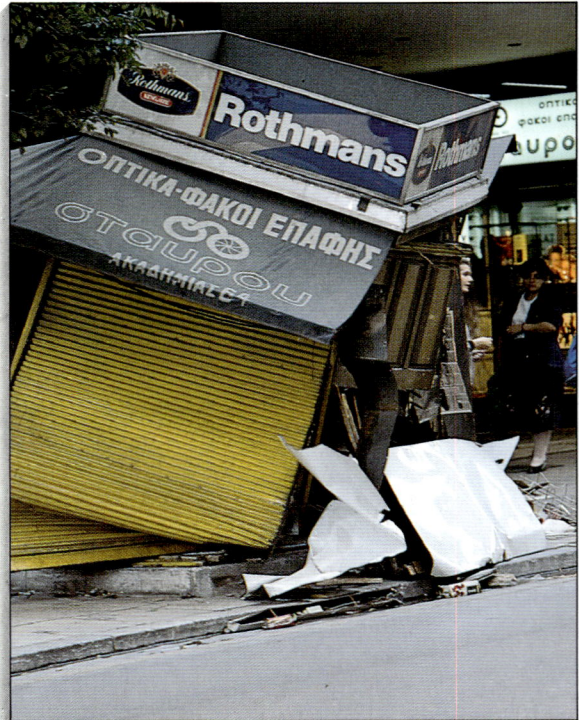

Closed for business.

turmoil of wire fencing shops, ironware, office furniture and hardware. In the few streets between Ermou and the ancient Agora—presently dug over for repair, hopefully not "restoration"—is all that remains of the real **bazaar**.

In **Normanou** is an old restaurant open at lunch-time serving traditional workers' fare. Very Greek. Lots of brain-building garlic. In **Dexipou** and **Areos Streets**, both behind glass shop windows and spread on the pavement, or squirrelled away down steep steps, you will find anything your heart desires and much that it doesn't.

One shop on Areos Street, which sports a sign proclaiming "We Mail Anything Anywhere" contains: ships' lanterns, *kelim* rugs, British helmets, working (though antediluvian) typewriters, Mickey Mouse slippers, china dolls' heads, horseshoes, naïve oil paintings, imitation victrolas with morning-glory trumpets, purloined diaries, mortars and pestles, 19th-century undergarments and a portrait of Franklin Delano Roosevelt on tin.

Plunge deeper into the market, into **Ifestou**, which is always festooned with bright banners of cloth hanging above eye level, furniture, brass and copper ware, tourist cassettes and souvenirs, and wall-to-wall humanity.

Dolls in Greek costumes, furs, marble, onyx and alabaster, metalwork…you could go crazy here. It is wise to do some comparison shopping however; bargaining can only go so far. Check quality and prices in several different places, and beware of attractive cotton clothes where seams have not been securely finished. You won't find any pre-shrunk labels: ask if things will shrink, and get a larger size if necessary. Some ceramics are neither dishwasher nor detergent proof: ask about washing. Most shopkeepers will tell you fairly, if you don't make your question a challenge. Make room for him to save face.

Basement shops like the Nasiotis family book-and-periodical shop at 24 Ifestou, in a tiny stoa, are mind-bog-

Walking to work.

gling. Here are some 200,000 volumes and issues which will turn even non-readers into weak-kneed capitalists. If the conjunction of *Forever Amber*, the *1944 Harvard University Catalogue* and *What Eisenhower Thinks* doesn't lure a shopper down the steps, perhaps the books on *rembetika* (Greek blues songs) and picture postcards of Golgotha, possibly from AD 33, will do the trick. Nasiotis *père* sold books from a hand-wheeled cart between 1927 and 1949, and only later established less transitory digs. This is the story of most of the older Monastiraki merchants, some of whom are still working the pavements in push-carts painted pistachio green.

The picturesque persons squatting on the pavements with boxes of jewellery or paintings are probably tourists.

The centre of the real **Flea Market** is **Plateia Avisinias** (Abyssinia), where in fact every morning junk dealers trundle in with loads of furniture and oddments and a brisk trade is held in *palaiodzidika*—old stuff. Permanent shops line this little square, offering old iron, furniture galore and even pot-bellied stoves. These shops have resisted all efforts to refurbish the square. In spite of fire and earthquake, they reappear like mushrooms after rain. Once this was the place to hunt for interesting antiques; it's much harder these days to find anything of real value. The vendors are hip. You may be better off at one of the **auction rooms**—there's one on Ermou Street. On Sundays most of the shops are closed, and then the fun begins. It is always commercial chaos, but on Sundays from the station to the square, the streets are full of carts selling all sorts of merchandise old and new, often at good prices, just as often at outrageous ones. This is a morning for bargaining. Some vendors are almost disappointed when deprived of a good haggle, others just smirk and pocket the unexpected windfall.

In **Pandrossou Street**, the shops have become a little more up-market.

The place to buy dolls in Greek costume, victrolas, marble…

Craftsmen and quality jewellers offer their wares, and gold jewellery may be a bargain. Woven mats and rugs, *flokati* rugs and handbags, ceramics and leather shops crowd each other.

At the intersection of **Pandrossou with Kyrikeou Street** is a flight of steps, on which are spread colourful handwoven woollens from the mountain village of Metsovo. Après-ski booties are a nice buy. On the opposite corner is one of the area's oldest and most respected antique dealers.

Between 1928 and 1939 **Hadrian's Street** regained its original name. It runs, with the deviation around Hadrian's library, from Hadrian's Arch in Leoforas Amalias to Thissio. From just above Monastiraki, follow it along the edge of the Stoa of Attalos and the Agora excavations. In the first block are several women's shoe shops of varying qualities and usually low prices.

The **Church of St Philip** probably dates from the 11th century but was rebuilt in 1806 after it was destroyed in the War of Independence. According to legend, St Philip the Apostle once lived in Athens, and became annoyed while preaching to the secretary to the Chief Priest of Jerusalem. Even saints tire of aggravation, it seems, and the story has it that on the site of the church, Philip caused the earth to open up and swallow his nemesis.

Second-hand clothes dealers lurk in the shade of the tree nearby, in the little square where the newsagent sells the *Athens News*, the English-language paper. The restaurant is acceptable.

The entrance to the Agora site is often blocked by the itinerant *salepi* seller, peddling his beverage derived from the roots of orchids, from an oriental brass and chrome container. A policeman attempts to move him along, but the locals protest, "Leave the fellow alone, he's not doing any harm!" The policeman eventually ambles off shrugging, "*Ti na kanoume?*" which means, "What can one do?", a much-heard phrase.

A few steps along Adrianou, you will

...kelim rugs, British helmets, or 19th-century underwear.

find an *ouzerie* for refreshment in the shade of the pines. There is a new excavation opposite, the **Stoa** for which the Stoic philosophers were named.

A maze called Psiri: On the other side of Ermou Street, west of Athinas Street, is a rather grubby, ancient maze called **Psiri**, in antiquity a place of iron workers and ceramicists. There are still iron workers, but mostly the trade is now leather and plastic—shoemakers, handbags, buckles and trimmings. **No. 11 Ag. Theklas** was the address of the Makris family with whom Lord Byron stayed on his first visit to Athens in 1809. Teresa, the daughter of the house, was the subject of his *Maid of Athens*.

It is surprising that with the War of Independence just over, only a few squares or streets were named for the revolutionaries. But **Psiri Square** is officially the Square of Iroon, (the Heroes), and is coming up in the world, for among the rusty old iron salvagers and shoddy plastic have bloomed a "Meat Boutique" and a croissant shop, looking proud but uneasy. In the days of the *manghes*, the area was off-limits to police, and before 1910 this was the Square of the Bachelors.

At the bottom of Ermou Street, at the edge of Psiri, is the church of **Agii Assomaton,** the Bodyless Archangels. This small square accommodates an intersection of many streets.

If you would like to visit the **Synagogue**, turn your back on the Acropolis, bear left on Agion Assomaton Street for just a few steps and turn into Melidoni Street, which is startlingly quiet, on the edge of the greenery of **Keramikos**, the ancient and very beautiful cemetary. The funerary monuments—sphinxes, a prancing bull, scenes of farewell— were erected by wealthy Athenian families of the fifth and fourth centuries BC. The Synagogue is a charming building to the left of the cemetary.

Northwest of Keramikos near Odos Pireos is **Eleftherias** which is the bus terminal for lines to Daphní and Eléusis. Nearby is the **Municipal Art Gallery**.

Monastiraki masks.

SATURDAY NIGHT AT THE MOVIES

For many visitors, one of the delights of a stay in Athens is going to the outdoor movies. After a hard day at the Acropolis, what could be better than sinking into a chair under a romantic full moon and watching, probably not for the first time, *Casablanca* or *The 39 Steps*?

The atmosphere is appropriately relaxed. Whole families attend, usually seated on sagging lawn chairs, and snack bars serve soft drinks, beer, crackers and chips. Some, such as the Amarylis in Aghia Paraskevi, operate as cinematic *ouzeries* where one can sit at a little table, nibble on *mezedes* and sip an *ouzo*.

Fortunately for foreign viewers, Greeks prefer subtitles to dubbing so only original-language films are screened. The volume must be reduced at late screenings because of complaints from neighbours in the vicinity of the cinemas, causing foreigners without a knowledge of Greek to resort to lip-reading. No new films are released for viewing during the summer; hits from the previous season and classics are screened instead. It is doubtful whether any other European city except Paris offers the chance to attend so many retrospectives of venerable directors.

A decade ago, American films were often screened in Greece as much as a year later than in the US, and European releases were delayed for many months. Athens is now one of the first European cities to receive copies of foreign films, often months before they play in London.

But in the past few years, this form of entertainment has lost popularity and owners of both indoor and outdoor cinemas are in the throes of a crisis. The seriousness of this situation can best be gauged by looking at statistics. In 1968, in the heyday of Greek movie houses, cinema admissions totalled 138 million while only 20 years later, they were less than 17 million.

According to Christos Karavias, president of the Panhellenic Federation of Film Exhibitors, factors contributing to the drastic decline include an increase in admission prices, the popularity of video recorders, and changes in shop hours. Television broadcasts of football and basketball games are devastating to cinema business. According to one cinema owner, "Every time the championship team Aris appears on TV, we might as well close up for the evening."

Owners of a number of first-run cinemas have been forced to close their theatres and it is expected other defeated entrepreneurs will follow suit. Not long ago, there were almost 200 indoor cinemas, now reduced to slightly more than 100.

The proliferation of mindless buffoonery and blood-and-guts shenanigans on video cassettes has however, had its positive effects on programming in indoor cinemas. Experimentation has tapped an audience hungry for sophisticated, thought-provoking films as a viable alternative.

The Last Emperor and *The Incredible Lightness of Being*, both long, somewhat intellectual films, were big hits in Athens, whereas a few years back distributors might not have risked booking them in a city known for its fondness for romantic comedies and adventures. Until recently, American and British independent films never made it to Greece but now many of them attract large audiences and have had successful extended runs.

Pandelis Mitropoulos, head of Prooptiki distribution, predicts, "We now have 45,000 to 50,000 seats in cinemas in the Athens area. Fairly soon, we will have only 15,000 seats in 25 cinemas, five to eight of them deluxe houses and the other multiplexes." Refurbishment is vital.

Other owners and leasers of cinemas are aware that improvement in cinemas, including the renovation of furnishings and installing Dolby stereo, is the only way to stay in business. Spentzos Films invested US$350,000 in completely renovating the historic Ideal Cinema near Omonia. The classical showpiece, installed with a massive screen, Dolby stereo and plush seats imported from France, is doing remarkable business compared to pre-renovation days. Other rehabilitated central cinemas are doing as well as in previous years and a couple have double and quintupled business, compared to at least a 40 percent drop from the previous year in unimproved houses.

Maybe Hitchcock will rise again, after all.

SYNTAGMA
TO OMONIA

Between **Syntagma** (Constitution) **Square** and **Omonia** (Concord) **Square** is European Athens, in contrast to the quintessentially Greek Plaka, and Oriental Monastiraki. The central part of the capital between Syntagma and Omonia was laid out by the architects who came with the Bavarian king and queen. (Steeped in a classical education, Herr Eduard Schaubert and his colleagues leapt at the chance to embody their own German variations on Greek themes in the city of their origin.)

The centre of the classical world was the Acropolis. The new palace at Omonia would be at the end of a great avenue which would lie between them—now **Athinas Street**—and a third boulevard would go to the Olympic Stadium, all to be generously supplied with green parks and squares. After the plan was changed to place the palace at Syn-

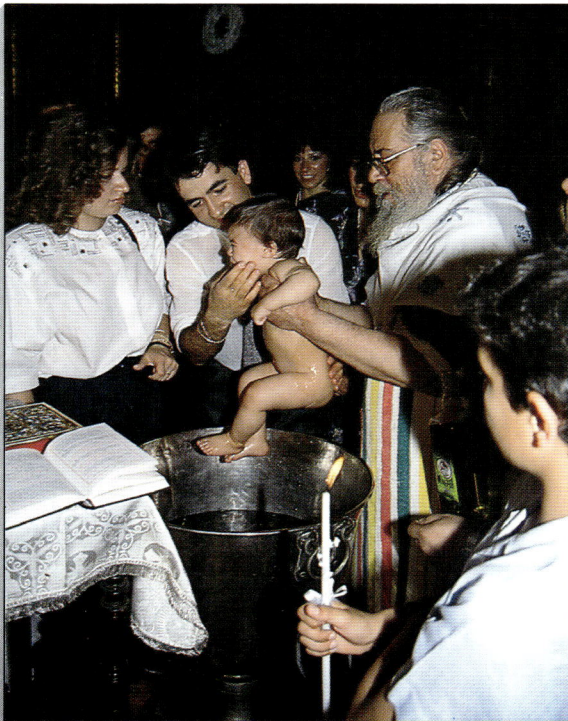

tagma because of disagreements among the officials and architects, there wasn't enough money to do much with Omonia. (This explanation applies to all the unsolved problems of this city from antiquity to tomorrow morning.) So the area which displays wide avenues suggesting the boulevards of Paris, instead of winding little streets for donkeys and *hoi polloi*, is that which is bounded by the Zappeion, Syntagma and Omonia. Stadiou Street never reached the stadium after all, and stops at Syntagma.

Streets of Confusion: Street names between Syntagma and Omonia are confusing to those who read signs more often than lips. **Leoforos Eleftheriou Venizelou** is known here as **Panepistamou**, or **University Street**; **Stadiou** is really **Churchill Street**, though no one calls it that; and if you ask for **Roosevelt Street**, you'll draw a blank—locals know it as **Akadimias**.

In 1834 Athens contained 5,000 souls. Today the population has soared to over four million, who drive a million cars and more than 70,000 motorcycles. In an effort to put a silencer on the middle city, many streets have been turned into pedestrian malls. The cross of paved streets formed by **Voukourestiou** and **Valaoritou** has become one of the city's poshest shopping districts. Jewellers ornament Voukourestiou, clothing boutiques line Valaoritou. Between Kriezoutou and Amerikis on Panepistimou are Greece's two foremost gold shops, **Lalaounis** and **Zolotas**. In the stoa at number 10 is Athens' legend of an *ouzerie*, **Apotsos**.

South on Voukourestiou, pedestrians are replaced by sleek black limousines available for hire, and their grooms. In the same block is the **Aristokraton**, famous *confiserie* with lovely chocolate truffles, and opposite, among theatres and the Pallas Cinema, is the **Brazilian Coffee Stores**, dating from 1932, on the edge of the stoa containing the Parcel Post Office and the Athens Festival Box Office.

Amerikis Street contains four theatres, the only *rembetika* (music) club in central Athens, the YWCA, the Athenaeum concert hall, and two English language bookshops.

Stadiou, Akadimias and Panepistimou Streets are lined with buildings, the least of which is adorned with plaster columns and cornices, and the fanciest of which are the three **Temples of Learning** in Panepistimou Street. These dramatic monuments to erudition were designed by the Hansen brothers in the decades after Independence. Hans Christian Hansen, the elder, spent 17 years in Greece painting antiquities and working with the planners of the new city. He designed **the University** with the graceful fountain in its courtyard and circular staircase. Behind the row of columns in its porch are colourful frescoes of classical subjects, often illuminated at night. At the top of the stairs is a dazzling lecture hall, with a brilliant, painted ceiling and a portrait frieze behind a crystal-paned door. University precincts are an inviolate sanctuary for students: the police are not allowed to interfere on university property, so the approach is usually blocked by young persons protesting about something, hunger strikers, and jewellery pedlars. The backs of the buildings are layered with political posters and artistic graffiti.

The University's decorative motifs are echoed inside the other buildings: Theofil Hansen, the younger brother, designed the **Academy** which is flanked by two wings decorated with coloured friezes and a pair of tall columns adorned by statues of Apollo and Athena. Socrates and Plato seated before it assure us of its intellectual authority. Theofil's simple, stately **National Library** on the left houses books in all languages. Inside, however, one feels one should have brought along one's quill and silver ink-bottle for taking notes among all the oak panelling and dusty pillars.

On the east corner of Panepistimou is a grey-and-red chunk of terminal Ro-

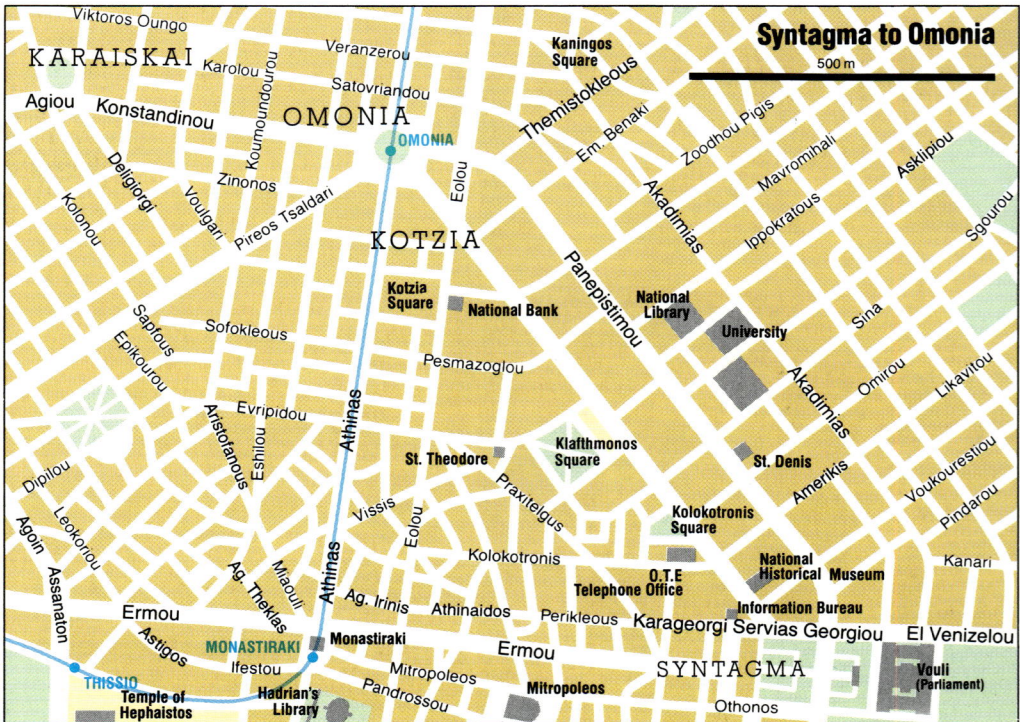

Syntagma to Omonia

500 m

man neo-classicism: the public **Eye Hospital** of 1845 designed by H. C. Hansen. Further towards Syntagma looms the imposing, iron-fenced Roman Catholic **Church of St Denis**—Agios Dionysios the Areopagite, patron saint of Athens.

Behind the three Edifices of Learning is Akadimias, and the jammed open-air bus terminal for many city lines, crowded, noisy and stinking with fumes. On the opposite side of Akadimias is the **Cultural Center of Athens**, which was originally the City Hospital. Its size gives an idea of what needs were foreseen for the town population of 1840! Now, lessons are offered in all the arts and crafts, computer science, chess, mental health, and exercise, in various centres around town—all free to the public. Furthermore, the Cultural Center sponsors lectures, theatrical performances, photography and poetry competitions, films and seminars.

In the basement is the tiny, charming **Theatrical Museum**, with reproductions of the dressing rooms used by famous Greek actors in their best-known roles, a poster collection and research library.

Now the City Fathers have decreed that the area surrounding these buildings is to be a Cultural Precinct. Accordingly, the **Palamas Building**, presently painted an eye-catching bordello pink, is used for exhibitions and lectures.

Between the University and Stadiou Street is Korai Street, a new pedestrian walk with benches and plants, and occasional exhibitions of sculpture.

To the south, on Stadiou Street, is **Klafthmonos Square**, a small, shady, green park with benches, a restaurant and a coffee shop. Officially, this is the **Square of 25th March**, because here Greece celebrated her first Independence Day in 1821. Since 1879, the square has been called the **Square of Wailing and Weeping**. There was a café frequented by dismissed civil servants and other unemployed men who noisily lamented—wailed and wept—

A Temple of Learning in Panepistimou Street.

their fates when they were made redundant by changes of government.

On Stadiou are booths selling monthly bus tickets, and during the Athens Festival in summer, others offer tickets to performances. Facing the Square on Paparigopoulou Street are two striking buildings, the simpler of which is the **Museum of the City of Athens**. This was the temporary dwelling of the teenaged King Otho and Queen Amalia while they were waiting for the builders to finish the palace—which took seven years. It is still furnished in Regency style, with a simple, tasteful Throne Room. The damask-upholstered throne itself looks like a parlour chair, and what might be taken for wallpaper is actually hand-painted plaster, reproducing the original decoration which can still be seen in the frieze at the top of the stairs. Downstairs there is a model of Athens in 1842, where it is quite clear that Panepistimou was occupied only by the University, two houses and the Royal Stables, and

Akadimias was an academic question. The adjoining and more elaborate house is to shelter art works of the period.

In the corner of **Klafthmonos Square** there is a pile of ancient cut blocks of stone: these are remnants of the original **city walls** built by Themistocles in 490 BC and in the under-basement of 6 Dragatsaniou Street is a carefully preserved piece of the same wall, among the electric repair shops.

A contemporary of the Kapnikarea, the **Church of Saint Theodore**, the Holy Horsemen—or possibly foot soldiers—is located behind Kalfthmonos. Dating from the 11th century it was rebuilt of stone and brick with Cufic ornament a century later.

At 2 Christiou Lada off Stadiou is the **Eleftherios Venizelos Memorial Collection** devoted to the statesman who was on-and-off Prime Minister from 1898-1935, through the Russian Revolution, the Balkan Crises, World War I, the war with Turkey and the exchange of populations, finally falling to the Metaxas government. Around the corner is the Parnassos Lecture and Concert hall. At 15 Stadiou is the central office of the **OTE telephone company** from where you may call abroad.

Pass the Church of St George Karystos (1845) and come to the square where a bronze Kolotronis on horseback—"The Old Man of the Morea" and hero of the Revolution—guards the **National Historical Museum**. The inscription engraved on the pedestal reads: "Ride on through the ages, brave General, showing people everywhere that slaves can be freed". Nearby is a new construction of mud and cactus plants, purporting to be a timepiece and readable only from the third storey of adjacent buildings.

The Museum was the original House of Parliament. In 1905, Theodore Deliyannis, three times prime minister, was assassinated on the steps. Now it holds costumes, books and prints, laid out to show the history of the newborn Greek nation. Right next to it is a charm-

Detail from one of the area's elegant buildings.

ing outdoor café hidden among flowering shrubs, and seeming much further from the traffic than it is.

Just outside the formally designed Cultural Precinct is the **Melathron Ilion,** the Palace of Ilium built in 1878 for Heinrich Schliemann, the German pastor's son who unearthed Troy and the treasures of Mycenae. It was designed by Ernst Ziller, who also built the Presidential Palace and other public and private buildings, and excavated the Stadium. **The Schliemann House** is becoming a **Numismatic Museum**, unless, of course, the officials find themselves in disagreement.

The oldest square in Athens used to mark the northern city limits, beyond which point Athenian strollers would not stroll of an evening. **Omonia Square** was originally called simply the Northern Edge. Its present name derives from an oath of concord (*omonia*) taken by two rival political groups—brigands, actually—the mountain men and the plainsmen, who favoured

Omonia: the oldest square in Athens.

bloody confrontations in the years following Otho's deposition in 1857. During the reign of King George I, the square was the city's social centre, redesigned to be a cool oasis, with fountains, palms and charming little hotels where the Army band played light opera music among the trees and gaslights.

In the 20th century the square declined from a leisure park to a series of low-life cafés, and by the 1970s it had become a traffic-ridden, hot, dusty, tawdry market-place with "sleazy-come, sleazy-go" shops on the ground floors of once-pretty buildings. Eight major arteries debouch into the roundabout from which it is easy to be swept into the wrong street.

The old fountains have been changed recently, and a monument made of stacked sheets of fractured glass occupies the place of honour. It is meant to symbolise an Olympic runner. There are new palm trees. The **Bretania Kafeneion** offers some of the best yogurt in Athens. There is also a large pharmacy,

Bakakos, which has just about every medication available in Greece.

Underground is the large **metro station**, with watch shops, a post office, banks, and the endless staccato of passionate discussion by groups of interested men. Escalators sometimes work.

The kiosks of Omonia sell foreign newspapers and magazines, books, as well as the usual tobacco and sweets. Some display magazines that would bring blushes to the cheek of a married mistress, let alone a maiden aunt.

Northeast of the square is the department store, Minion, which occupies several buildings, and **Kaningos Square**, named for George Canning, Prime Minister of England at the time of Greek Independence. It is a major bus and trolley stop. Good *souvlaki* is to be found on the corner of Gladstones and Kaningos Streets, in a tiny no-traffic square with a wee fountain and benches.

Around Omonia are many hotels. Most are registered with the Greek National Tourist Organisation formally classified according to the NTOG's own mysterious specification as A or B or C or D: but some doors do not lead into family hotels. You can tell these by the ladies in the lobbies wearing their daughters' clothes, and the simple cash desks which serve as "Reception". Payment is by the hour.

Also around Omonia are many government buildings, gentlemen desiring the company of ladies, ladies desiring the company of gentlemen, others, and chaps discussing politics, inevitably. These are evident from the intensity of the debate, the waving newspapers and the gathering crowds. Circling the square—a geometric possibility in modern Greece—one reaches **Agiou Konstandinou Street**. In an arcade off this avenue, past the **National Theatre**, is a café where itinerant gypsy musicians congregate in a sort of musical labour exchange. The place is identifiable by the sounds of clarinets, violins, and small drums or *tambourlakia*, and by the singers in floor-length gold lamé

who stop in after work in the early hours of the morning.

Omonia to Monastiraki: From Omonia there are several routes which may be followed toward the Acropolis and Monastiraki. **Athinas Street** is the main artery directly to the square.

Along Athinas Street are glass cases in the street, manned by the *serafidhes*, men who sell socks, watches, coins and jewellery. Then one comes upon the uninspired **Town Hall** (Dimarchion), a feeble version of the classical ideal. But charming National Bank buildings in yellow and white front **Kotzia Square**. At present this square is merely an excavation of a mysterious mud city, perhaps, or tunnels made by square moles. The plan was to construct an underground car park here, but the digging, as so often happens in Athens, unearthed an ancient burial ground, and all construction halted while the archaeologists got out their little scrapers and brushes. Sadly, they found nothing of great importance.

Between the two National Bank buildings on one side of the square is **Sofokleous Street**, and the **Stock Exchange** opposite the naughty Rivoli cinema. Founded in 1876, the Stock Exchange engages in trading between 10 a.m. and 2 p.m. on weekdays. Only 32 individuals are allowed to become members; brokers and traders jam the central floor, all shouting at once since the system is aptly called "open outcry". Tiny dark offices line this Greek Wall Street and these little holes in the wall house the simple desks and busy phones of Athens' zillionaires.

Farther down Athinas Street is the **Central Market** (1879). The handsome arched building contains the very nitty-gritty meat market, not for the squeamish or sensitive, since the carcasses, heads and innards are proudly displayed for the customers. The central section holds the fish market where fresh and frozen squid, octopus, cod, and live crabs, as well as pigs' heads and trotters are on sale daily. In the fish market is a tiny *ouzerie* for shoppers and salesmen, overseen by the price control police from a balcony. Built into the outside walls of this edifice are sausage shops and cheese shops and coffee grinders. There are entrances to the market on all four sides.

Athenians in the know come at three in the morning to the **Monastiri taverna** inside the market to eat *patsas*, a soup made of hooves, horns and entrails. Well, it tastes great. But the crowd occasionally gets rowdy inside.

Opposite is the **produce market** with fruit and vegetable stands, presently squashed into the middle of the road while a new design, including an underground car park, is slowly and messily being constructed.

At the back of the vegetable market are shops selling olives from huge barrels and bulk olive oil, along with loose grain and pulses.

Every picture tells a story…

Aside from the tiny, busy little church of **Agia Kyriaki** just down from the market, only hardware aficionados are likely to enjoy a stroll down Athinas to Monastiraki Square. It is quieter on Eolou Street, which parallels Athinas on the far side of the market, mostly traffic-free and lined with clothing shops. Just below Evripidou Street and the market is the modern church of **Panayia Chrysospiliotissa**, Our Lady of the Golden Cave, formerly Our Lady of the Golden Castle. Here there was an ancient church housing an icon of the Virgin found on the Acropolis. It happened that when this icon was returned to the Acropolis, it miraculously homed itself back to the church. The church fathers thereupon decided to build an edifice more worthy of this icon. An unusual kiosk by the church sells icons, medallions and votive plaques in addition to sweets and tobacco.

Further down Eolou, one reaches the **Church of Agias Irinis**, which was the Cathedral of Athens at the time of King Otho, and the small garden centre in its courtyard. At the foot of Eolou is the Tower of the Winds.

STOP

STOP

28

TOTAL

Sper Softex

...ΤΙ ΤΟ ΑΚΡΙΒΕΣ
...ΜΟ ΤΟΥ ΕΙΣΙΤΗΡΙΟΥ

...ΕΝ ΘΑ ΘΕΛΑΤΕ ΝΑ ΜΠΛΕ
...ΑΡΕΣΤΕΣ ΠΕΡΙΠΕΤΕΙΕΣ ......

...ΕΣΙΣ ΤΑ ΑΤΟΜΑ
...ΠΟΥ ΧΡΕΙΑΖΟΝΤΑΙ ΒΟΗΘΕΙΑ

Sound

FAIR m

KOLONAKI TO EXARHIA

Kolonaki is an area of distinguished museums and elegant shops. The **Museum of Cycladic and Ancient Art** at 4 Neofítou Doúka is one of the finest in Athens. Its fame is partly owed to the unrivalled first-floor collection of early (third millennium BC) Cycladic idols, whose interest to 20th-century artists is immediately apparent. The stark, white marble figurines were dismissed by earlier critics as barbaric, but both Picasso and Modigliani were admirers. The precise use of these eerie and powerful mannequins, including one five ft (1.4 metres) high, is still disputed; from their frequent discovery in graves it is variously surmised that they were spirit-world guides for the deceased, or stylised effigies, or substitutes for human sacrifice.

Much of the second floor is devoted to a vivid collection of classical painted bowls. Highlights include Hercules throttling the Nemean lion, Eos unsuccessfully seducing Cephalos and three merry-makers who anticipate Brueghel by two millennia. The museum considers the latter the floor's prize exhibit; on the reverse side of the urn two men in *himatia* (cloaks) converse while a third looks on. A lanced figure on a horse on another exhibit is a dead ringer for Don Quixote; horses are actually raced on items further along.

Consultation of the labelling reveals that the most exquisite items date from the fifth century BC; not for nothing was this period dubbed the "Golden Age", with work of a century before or after perceptibly less refined. Still, there is not one inferior exhibit in the museum; to top it off there's a shop, a snack bar, and a quiet courtyard with tables and a fountain.

The **Benaki Museum**, on the corner of Vass. Sofías and Koumbari Street might better be called the "Middle Eastern Museum"; its founder Emmanuel Benaki was a wealthy Alexandrian cotton merchant, and the collection is accordingly biased toward all things Levantine. An initial jumble of gold, bronze, and terracotta antiquities is barely labelled, but this is not missed; just beyond them Coptic and Ottoman textiles excel among Egyptian and early Christian artefacts. Similarly self-explanatory is a vast array of pottery and glass—Roman and Byzantine; Iznik, Canakkale, and Kutahya ware (the best outside Turkey); Damascene and Cairene—plus a reconstructed Egyptian reception hall complete with mosaics and fountain.

In the strictly Greek wings and basement, the labelling improves as required. Embroidery from around the Aegean is well represented, as are clasps, belts, and jewellery. Memorable exhibits include coral-encrusted items from Saphrambolis (Safranbolu) and gold from Asia Minor and the islands. The second floor houses period paintings and engravings, plus historical

memorabilia relating to various national uprisings and leaders.

Last but not least comes a penthouse café, blessed with an outdoor terrace overlooking the National Gardens, and the museum store with quality reproductions, cards and recordings of folk music. On Sunday mornings at 11a.m. the café-terrace is the place to watch the best military parade in town as the *Evzones* march to their barracks opposite the museum.

Beyond the two museums, **Kolonáki Square** (officially Platia Filikis Eterias) is the haunt of high-rolling and xenomaniac Greeks. This is one of the most sophisticated neighbourhoods in Athens. Imported foodstuffs, designer clothing, and even a couple of embassies hold sway in the immediate vicinity; the **British Council** is here too at number 17, with weekly film showings and a good library.

Up Patriarhou Ioakim are some of the most expensive cafés in town, and the prices of luxury goods on pedestrianised Tsakálof will knock your socks off. Find the *kolonáki* (little classical column) on the southwest side of the square, hiding under a tree as if ashamed of its Greekness.

Just north, **Dexamení** plaza supports pleasant cafés above and below a covered water depot begun by Hadrian. This, and a shady square next to the huge church on Skoufá, are the only other public spaces of note in Kolonaki. Villas at the corner of Fokilidhou and Pindarou below Dexamení are reputedly the most expensive in Greece.

The urban planning think-tank of Doxiades Associates is housed at 24 Stratigou Sindesmou, a block northwest. Asked to prepare a study to solve the Athenian urban crisis, they came up with drastic proposals: a new airport on Makrónissos, a remodelled ferry port at Lavrion, a bridge linking them, and several tunnels through Mt. Imitos, among other unlikely strategies. The report was politely allowed to gather dust. Another airport at Spáta, under sporadic

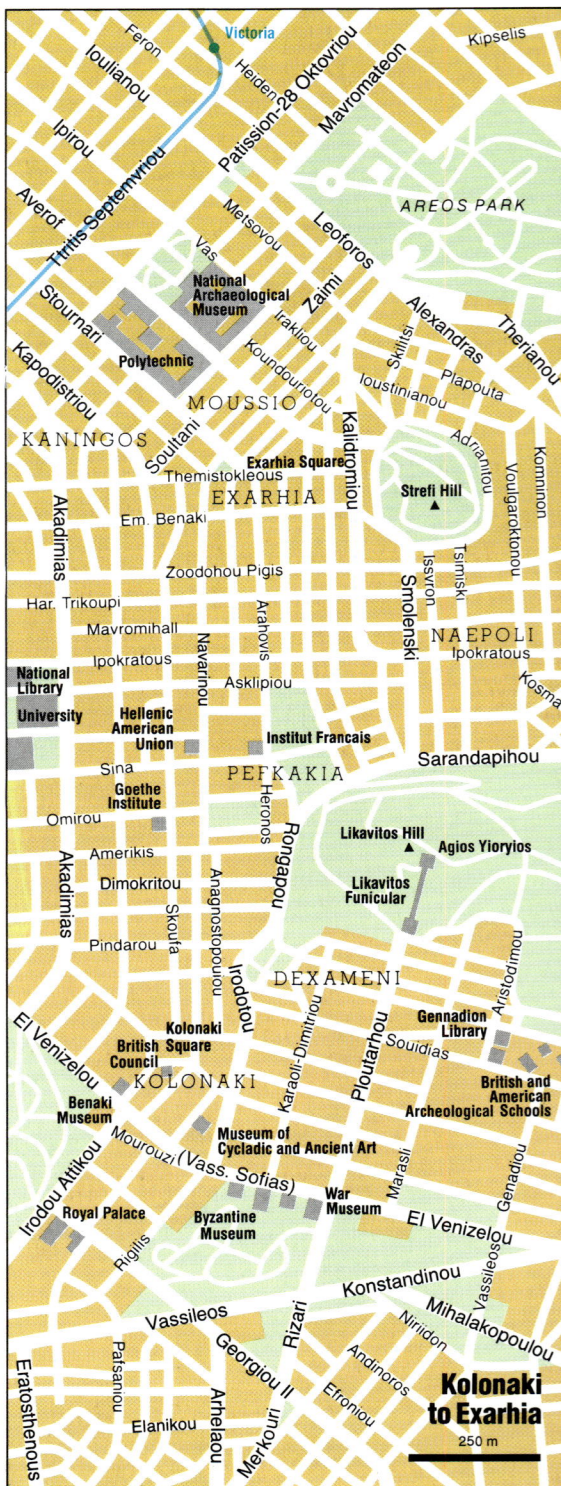

Kolonaki
to Exarhia

250 m

182

construction since the junta, is at last nearing completion.

Athenian stair-streets reach their apotheosis beyond Dexameni as they scale the slopes of **Likavitós**, the city's highest and most popular hill. Slightly to one side, at the very edge of Kolonaki, the **British** and **American Schools of Archaeology**, and the excellent **Gennadion Library** (selling good Edward Lear reproductions) each hide in patches of landscaping. On Athens' highest street, Hoïda, the zoned limit is four storeys, and offers wonderful views down the steep San Francisco-style streets over much of Athens and all the way out to sea.

The easiest way to cover the last stretch is by **funicular** from the corner of Ploutarhou and Doras Distria which runs several times daily throughout the year, though there are plenty of paths up through the shrubbery if you don't mind tripping over amorous couples with nowhere else to go at night, or the prophylactic evidence of such trysts the next day. The summit is graced by the white chapel of **Agios Yióryios**, plus a few very pricey cafés capitalising on the magnificent view—Athens at its finest—best observed near sunset as the city lights up for miles far below.

A few hundred metres northeast, tucked behind Likavitós' secondary peak, is the **Likavitós Theatre**, hosting fringe events during the Athens Festival, and sporadic jazz/dance performances in warmer months. Keeping it company down the far side of the hill on Nikifórou Ouranoú is the **Half Note** jazz club, which moved here recently after many years of hosting name acts in Illissia. Directly below Agios Yióryios, **Pefkákia** park is an extension of Likavitós and makes for a pleasant walk down toward Exarhia.

Leaving Kolonaki from lower down, along such streets as Solonós, Skoufá (later Navarinou), and Tsakálof (then Didótou), it becomes apparent that the intellectual and artistic life around the university and law school extends up

The view from Likavitós funicular.

through this area. A concentration of publishers and book stores (mostly Greek language) hark back to the medieval tradition of specialised trade-streets. Various national cultural institutes cluster here too: the **Goethe Institute** at 16 Omírou, the **Institut Français** at 29 Sina, the **Hellenic American Union** at 22 Massalías.

Closer to Likavitós, art galleries and photo shops are thick on the ground, as are musical instrument dealers and record stores. **Pop 11**, on the corner of Tsakálof and Pindárou, is a city institution, which has information and/or tickets for a wide variety of events and once even pressed its own line of *rembetika* records. Times have changed; the *rembetika* bin is almost empty now and the emphasis is on jazz, blues, and modern rock discs.

Son of Plaka: If you ever wondered where Plaka's loud bars disappeared to, wonder no more; they resurfaced in **Exarhia**, some 50 square blocks just south of Aréos Park. Ten years ago there were perhaps two "pubs"; now there must be 100. Exarhia's triangular "square" is frequented by idling students from the nearby Polytechnic; Arahóvis Street is packed with bistros and clubs, as are Themistokléous and Kallidromíou.

Despite rumours of "anarchists" vandalising and terrorising people or buildings, and their obvious grafitti, night-time reality is relatively tame and disturbances that do take place tend to be the settling of private scores. Even disorderly drunkenness is rare; the clubs' purpose is to socialise, with students buying a limited number of quite expensive drinks. Supernumerary *souvlaki* joints nearby are more in line with scholastic budgets.

Dominating Exarhia to the northeast is **Stréfi hill**, last of the central Athenian knobs and, along with Aréos Park, a final noteworthy green space. It's ingeniously landscaped, with arches, terraces, and walls in "mock castle" style.

At Stréfi's base, on the district's

Exarhia is the haunt of students.

western fringe, stands the **Politehníon** (Polytechnic), its walls today festooned with posters for every conceivable event or cause, the streets surrounding it dense with recently-opened computer and graphics retailers.

In 1973 months of student demonstrations culminated during November in a barricaded occupation of the premises. As numerous citizens mobilised in support, smuggling in supplies, the military regime showed its true nature. On 17 November, tanks broke down the gates, while sharpshooters fired down into the courtyard, leaving still-visible bullet holes on columns and steps. The number who died remains in dispute, particularly since rumour had many buried anonymously in mass graves. However, it is indisputable that the outrage engendered was instrumental in the collapse of the junta just eight short months later.

The nation's debt to the students is acknowledged by streets called **Iróön Politehníou** (Heroes of the Polytech-

Both Kolonaki and Exarhia abound in restaurants.

nic) in many sizeable Greek towns, and by an annual 17 November march on the US Embassy. Recently the procession has degenerated into a carnival, with *souvlaki* and popcorn for sale at the start, and the nominally apolitical "anarchists" have taken to staging an anti-march of their own.

Just north of Exarhia looms the **National Archaeological Museum**, which requires a great deal of stamina to cope with its badly organised, mislabelled, and ill-lit displays. But this is a reflection on the gallery designers, not the original artists. If your time or patience is short, dodge the crowds to glimpse the following highlights.

The **Mycenean hall**, with its gold mask of Agamemnon and a myriad of minutely-decorated daggers, rings, seals, and vessels, is a perennial favourite. Cycladic art treasures not found in the Kolonaki museum, particularly the famous lyre player, can be seen here in the adjacent Cycladic art room.

The balance of the ground floor is mostly reserved for sculpture, which gets more interesting at and beyond Room 15, dominated by a bronze god (either Zeus or Poseidon) in the act of throwing a trident or thunderbolt; the lack of the implement hampers positive identification. The bronze jockey in Room 21, gesturing and with face contorted, affords a striking contrast with the god's Olympian calm of two centuries before.

The **Minoan** frescoes are upstairs, dating from the 15th century BC. Entire rooms from the site of Akrotiri on Santorini have been reconstructed, with period furniture ringed by walls decorated with flowers, monkeys, boxers and presumably noble ladies. (The swallows-in-spring painting caught the imagination of film-set designers and features in more than one exotic epic set in the Himalayas.)

The frescoes are said to be on their way back to Santorini, however, so it might be an idea to see them as soon as possible.

METS AND PANGRATI

These desirable neighbourhoods extend southeast of Plaka, the Zappeion, and the National Gardens, beyond two Roman antiquities and the dried-up course of the river Ilissos.

The incongruous bulk of **Hadrian's Arch**, gateway to this area, today presides over the most chaotic stretch of Leoforos Amalias. The Roman emperor Hadrian endowed post-Hellenistic Athens with numerous monuments and foundations during his second-century AD reign, and this arch was intended to separate the classical town from imperial doings. Accordingly, the northeast side of the arch is inscribed (in Greek): "This is Athens, city of Theseus", while the opposite side reads "This is the city of Hadrian, not of Theseus". As such, it's not strictly reliable, since there are plenty of Roman-era structures in the Plaka.

But without doubt the most impressive Roman relic in Athens—the **Temple of Olympian Zeus**—does lurk just beyond. Dedicated by Hadrian in AD 131 seven centuries after its foundations had been laid, it was the largest temple in ancient Greece; today, only 15 of the original 104 Corinthian columns remain.

Whatever the temple's condition, its precincts have always been publically esteemed, if not quite as initially intended. In Byzantine times a stylite perched on one of the surviving architraves; during Ottoman rule Moslems would pray for rain to Allah, syncretised with Zeus Ombrios in his role of thunder god; and until the early 1960s the milkmen of Athens held their annual festival here.

Bordering the archaeological site to the east is a wide dirt walkway leading down and south to the only remaining uncapped/filled section of the **river Ilissos**, though its normally dry bed soon disappears into a tunnel beneath Kalirois Boulevard. It's hard to believe that this was the burbling river, fed by still-active springs at Kaisarianí, that so delighted Socrates and his entourage.

One fork of the path ends by the chapel of **Agia Fotini**, just below Arditou Street; built over an ancient shrine of the nymphs, with fountain and benches in a sunken courtyard, it's a surprisingly quiet refuge only a few metres from the traffic overhead.

East of the path, towards the apex of the triangle completed by Leoforos Olgas and Arditou, are various facilities of the **Lawn Tennis Club** and the **National Gymnastic Club**, unfortunately all off-limits to non-members. So you may as well run the gauntlet of high-speed traffic on Arditou and cross over to **Mets**.

Before World War I this district was known as Yefíria (Bridges), after those used to cross the then-flowing Ilissos. The current French name comes from a pro-Entente café in business here after 1914 (the royal family was pro-German and a mini-civil war ensued before Greece's entry on the allied side in 1917). After the war the neighbourhood became an artists' quarter, then became rather frowsy during the Depression, but its evolution has now come full circle and Mets is again one of the more exclusive quarters of the city.

The area is small—a rough square some seven blocks on a side—but seems larger, especially when hoofing it up one of many stair-streets. Sadly, rediscovery has come at a price. Most of the old houses which persisted here until the 1960s have been replaced by buildings which, while low-rise and relatively tasteful, are still modern. Land values and rent are currently such that no full-time artist can afford to live here. For a glimpse back in time, find dirt-surfaced **Kefalou Street** (above the Gymnastic Club), narrowest of all Athenian thoroughfares, where a row of abandoned neo-classical houses awaits the next jump in real estate prices and the wrecker's ball.

Márkou Moussoúrou street, forming the arbitrary northeastern boundary of Mets, is home to upmarket restaurants and bars. Most notorious (and, basking in its repute, unmarked) is **Myrtia** at number 35. This walled compound was "discovered" by Major Ládas, actually one of the most brutal and feared junta "colonels", and has been the haunt of the power élite ever since. The food is not the quality you'd expect for the steep price, and the main distinctions, besides the clientèle, are a doorman and caterwauling summer *chanteuses* in the back garden.

Noise of a different sort was once heard on **Nikiforou Theotóki**, a tiny street just one block north. From here, and Arditos hill just above, ELAS forces bombarded British headquarters at Syntagma during December 1944. The leftist guerrillas were eventually forced to pull back, but not without fierce resistance. Most houses here have been tidied up as part of the local gentrification, but not so long ago all

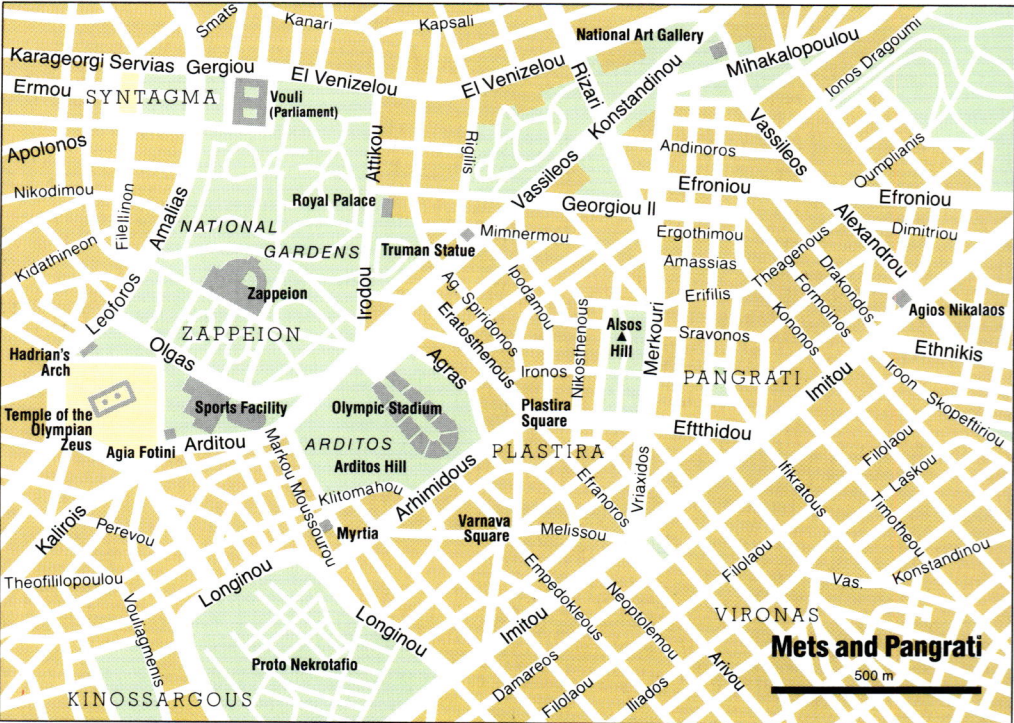

Mets and Pangrati

500 m

were as bullet-scarred as number 14.

Arditos hill proper is not so famous as other Athenian peaks, but it is certainly the most forested, and in the interest of protecting the thick pine groves from summer pyromania, you can no longer get in. Cradled in Arditos' northwest-facing flank is the **Olympic Stadium**, originally built in 330 BC for the Panathenaic Games, adapted by the Romans for their spectacles, and refurbished handsomely by Herodes Atticus. The convenient ready-cut slabs from the 60,000 marble seats were systematically pilfered by Byzantine and medieval builders, but in 1896 the stadium was restored to its present form for the first modern Olympiad.

When good Metsians—or any other worthy Athenians—die, they haven't far to go to heaven, by way of the **Proto Nekrotafio** (First Cemetery). Imagine a blend of Washington's Arlington, Paris's Père Lachaise, and London's Highgate cemeteries without, respectively, honour guards, hippies at Jim Morrison's grave, or dangling moss, and you'll have an idea of this tract's place in Greek society.

The only approach is along **Anapafseos (Eternal Rest) Street**, essentially the western edge of Mets, climbing a slight grade past shops devoted to funerary arts. In addition to florists and marble-monument carvers, there are storefronts displaying sample ceramicized memorial portraits. Images of departed luminaries—poet Seferis, city planner Constantine Doxiádes, actor Mános Katrákis, novelist Ilías Venézis—are conveniently viewable in different windows, should you fail to find their actual graves.

Immediately inside the main gate, grandiose mausoleums of the greatest Hellenes and philhellenes—Emmanuel Benaki, Yiórgos Avéroff, Kolokotrónis among others—confront you, but these neo-classical shrines soon yield to more intimate family graves. The most famous of these, and high in popular affections, is the **Kimomeni** (Sleeping

Most of Mets is mercifully low-rise.

Maiden) by the sculptor Halepas, a wonderful pre-Raphaelite, post-Romantic effigy on the Afendakis family plot, some 300 metres inside on the right. Although the 18-year-old girl idealised has been gone a century and more, there are still likely to be fresh red carnations in her lap. Conversely, 1930s-era dictator Ioannis Metaxas, though dying in an odour of sanctity after defying the Italians, has a simple, almost anonymous slab-tomb in the centre-rear section—perhaps to protect it from politically-minded vandals.

If death is no respecter of persons, neither are Athenians respecters of death in the usual sense, and the Proto Nekrotafio is considered a legitimate arena for the Greek flair for competition, dubious taste, and more benign public family life. Plots have long since been exhausted, and as they filled in the 1960s they could theoretically change hands for one million drachmas ($34,000 back then).

Those who did not come from "good" families with existing tombs, might—and still may—be buried in lesser cemeteries, exhumed as is Greek Orthodox custom after three years, and their bones deposited in the huge ossuary just to the left of the gate. If serial numbers are to be trusted, more than 9,000 skeletons are boxed within—a fantastic example of posthumous social climbing.

With every *nefos*-aggravated heat wave the elderly and infirm succumb rapidly, and, given delays in burial and inadequate refrigeration, the resulting aroma engenders much public discussion on the advisability of embalming or cremation. The church doggedly defends its conventions and threatens to excommunicate dissenters, but finally everyone forgets the whole thing until the next summer.

More cheerfully, the relatives of the deceased treat graveside visits as a dignified weekend excursion, picnicking, sweeping and changing bouquets, and leaving *kóllyva* (boiled wheat and other seeds—a very ancient custom) on the

When worthy Athenians die they go to heaven via Proto Nekrotafio cemetary.

tombs and handing it out to passers-by. Outsiders are also welcome to treat the peaceful, cypress-planted, and evocative grounds as a park, as long as they are unobtrusive.

Just above the highest corner of the cemetery, at its junction with Márkou Moussoúrou, Arhimídous Street squeezes through a rocky defile, as good a place as any to call the start of the area of **Pangrati**. One block along, at the corner of Dompóli, perches the **Athens Centre**, one of several intercultural and language-learning institutes in the city.

But Arhimidous's real attraction is its **Friday street market**, taking place in the four blocks west of Platia Plastira. Mostly produce, fish, nuts, and eggs are on offer, but also houseplants and trees, throw-rugs and kitchen utensils. Go early in the day, since it's all history by 2 p.m. The biggest winter sellers are bananas, even at 400 drachmas a kilo; Greeks are still starved for them after nearly 20 years without. Early in the

junta period import was banned. This, it is claimed, was to benefit Greece's lone banana plantation on Crete, owned by a crony of Colonel Patakós. Even after the restoration of democracy it took until 1988 to have the embargo lifted.

Platia Varnava, with its benches, fountain, and shrubbery in the centre, is one successful example of the early 1980s "greening" of Athens. The longest-lived and most popular of several good tavernas around it is **Vellis'**, which has served the same exceedingly brief but popular menu (dinner only) for as long as anyone can remember; a greater contrast to Myrtia can scarcely be imagined.

Between Varnava and Imitou Streets sterile apartment blocks vie with increasingly rare turn-of-the-century houses or walled gardens. Just northwest of Platia Pangratiou (dull in itself) sprawls the green and fertile **Alsos** (Grove) of Pangrati, exactly what its name implies, spilling down a hillside to stop at the edge of Spírou Merkouri.

Street markets abound in Athens; Pangrati's is on Friday mornings.

The park provides a welcome respite from the city heat, and is a haunt of local Athenians during the summer. This busy artery lies at the bottom of a "valley", the slopes of east Pangrati rising on the far side. There's a seven-storey height limit in most of Athens, and here that's equalled — just one of several differences between this district and Mets. Another is the stolidly bourgeois atmosphere; by now Imitou is a flashy shopping strip with neon restaurants and movie houses.

Several steep blocks east of Merkouri are two Greek rarities: a relatively handsome modern church (**Agios Nikólaos**), and a huge **housing estate** across the way. The ideal of home ownership, even if it's a dark cubbyhole in a high-rise, is deeply engrained in the Greek psyche, and the development's rarity is a reminder of how seldom this solution was resorted to, even in the wake of the Asia Minor disaster.

Heading west again, the hill above the Alsos proves a rather dull twin of the one opposite, but descend the far side toward yet another vale threaded by Eratosthenous Street, and some Mets-like character reappears: stair-streets, low-rises, and even the odd neo-classical house. At the top end of Eratosthenous, the grand, old-fashioned **Kafenion Ellas**, with a pergola-ed terrace, provides a focus for **Platia Plastira**. At the opposite end is Vassileos Konstandinou, the northwestern boundary of Pangrati.

On the corner of Rigilis and Vassileos Konstandinou stands the **Truman statue**, controversial since its erection in 1965 by a conservative Greek-American group. Truman's doctrine justifying US intervention in the 1947–49 civil war is excerpted on an adjacent wall. An initial attempt by domestic leftists to topple the image took place under the colonels; the bomb was discovered, but a policeman was blown to bits while defusing it, and Harry was left at a slight tilt. Only recently was the former president re-stored to his pedestal; there's often a permanent guard to prevent reprises.

The **National Art Gallery** at the end of Vassileos Konstandinou marks the northern tip of Pangrati. On the first floor, the left-hand gallery contains a large collection of the works of Nikos Hatzikyriákos-Ghíkas (Ghika), one of the few Greek painters with an international following. The opposite wing is devoted to temporary exhibits, and the mezzanine has a small group of rare canvases by early 20th-century muralist **Theóphilos** of Lesvos.

Second floor left is taken up by modern oils; the centre by assorted late 19th-century maritime scenes; and the right sections by a mixture of religious works, engagingly camp revolutionary themes (one Delacroix), and portraits of the post-independence nobility. All diverting, but with the exception of the Ghika wing, it is fair to say that the most enduring art in Greece has always been folk art, emanating from an historically rural culture.

Below, an elegant doorway. Right, Mets and Pangrati attract bright characters.

OTHER NEIGHBOURHOODS

Filopappou hill lies just behind the Acropolis, a tumbling expanse of greenery surrounded by desirable neighbourhoods. Plaka's tourist honky-tonk spills over to some extent into Makrigiáni, but crossing Hatzichrístou this ceases. It's difficult to tell where the district of **Veïkou** ends and **Koukáki** begins, but lately their namesake squares are better defined by pedestrianised streets, Drákou and Olimpíou respectively, abutting them.

While the latter plaza is slightly livelier, each has a concentration of tavernas, *psistariés* (grills), bakeries, and milk/ice-cream shops in the nearby blocks. This is not Exarhia or even Pangrati by any means, but solidly family-oriented; food runs out and sidewalks roll up by 11 p.m.

The lowest streets parallel to Singrou are crammed with spare-parts dealers,

Left, a locality to watch out for. Below, a woman, a corner, and a road sign.

the flip-side of the glitzy car dealers out front; but the higher you climb up the grade toward Filopappou, the quieter and more desirable the area. Look up into second-floor windows—Filoppapou street is a relatively homogeneous stretch of neo-classical houses—and you're likely to see self-employed professionals, the *côte garde* if not the vanguard of Athenian yuppies, bent over drafting boards. Both neighbourhoods have become popular and expensive recently, with foreigners also beginning to move in. As you stroll around the south tip of Filopappou hill, where steep streets are pressed up against the slope by the Kaliróis expressway (still concealing the Ilissos stream beneath), Koukáki blends imperceptibly into **Ano Petrálona**.

On foot you will arrive near the maze of refugee-era alleys between Kalisthénous and Apoloníou, with a tunnel under the latter to a villagey church ringed by vegetable patches. (Just above lies the **Dora Stratou theatre**, where folk dances are performed every night in season.)

In the low-slung houses, each room originally housed a family, with several sharing a water tap, a privy, and a courtyard. As refugees became wealthier and some moved on, these shacks were amalgamated into single-family dwellings by those left behind.

Alternatively, you can ride the number 9 trolley to **Ano Petrálona Square**. This seems anticlimactic, with a tiny, dilapidated archaeological zone in one corner and little other semblance of life. But walk a few blocks north and Petralona's character asserts itself: working class and blessedly low-rise, with a good mix of neo-classical and 1920s buildings.

Tavernas in particular are excellent and unpretentious. Not necessarily the best, but the most famous, is **Askimópapo** (The Ugly Duckling), just north of the shanty zone. During Andreas Papandreou's first term, Pasok honchos used to come here to slum with "the people"; now the locals have reclaimed it and a half-dozen other eateries along Dimofóndos Street.

Another cluster of old houses at the north end of Dimofóndos has escaped the concrete contractors. The terrain imposes its own height limits, regardless of official edict, making it not worth a developer's time to demolish this enclave. However, most refugee houses weren't built to last; their packed earth walls crumble at finger-touch. That, and wood worm, will soon see to the buildings that remain.

Trails lead up to the **Hill of the Muses** and a 19th-century observatory, whimsically capped by a figure of Arion riding his dolphin. Urban airglow has rendered the telescope useless, and the grounds are usually locked, but from the smaller, higher auxiliary dome you've a five-star, unconventional view of the Acropolis, without the crowds.

Continuing southeast along the ridge, you pass traces of ancient walls (the *diatíhisma*) and the **Hill of the Pynx**, used in classical Athens for frequent citizens' meetings. All issues except criminal cases and banishment could once be discussed; today the partly restored arena hosts (on summer nights) the rather forgettable Acropolis sound-and-light show.

At a shallow pass, site of a gate in the ancient ramparts, huddles the ninth-century Byzantine church of **Agios Dhimítrios Lomvardiáris**. This is a popular weekend promenade spot, and you can have a coffee nearby; the front entrance to the Dora Stratou theatre is also adjacent.

From here it's a short, pleasant ascent, via a web of paths through a semi-wilderness of conifers and low shrubs, to the truncated **Filopappou monument** near the summit. The Roman senator-donor is portrayed in a frieze driving his chariot, but people come here chiefly for the views.

The hill itself has had a rather chequered career. Northeast of the peak some cavities in the cliff are known, with

The Hilton Hotel is situated on Athens' most confusing street.

more poetic licence than truth, as **Socrates' Prison**. During the 1687 Venetian siege of the Turkish-held Acropolis, a Swedish artilleryman named Akerhjelm fired from up top the shot that blew the roof off the Parthenon; in 1967 the colonels parked tanks below. More lightheartedly, people still fly kites from Filopappou on the first Monday of Lent, and the trendies of Koukaki jog diligently and walk their dogs through the greenery.

AROUND AMBELOKIPI: Years ago the authorities attempted to rename Panepistimou Street in honour of early 20th-century prime minister Venizelos; the tag never stuck, and now they have transferred the moniker to one of the city's longest streets. The street is called Panepistimou, El. Venizelou or Vassilisis Sofias, depending on which map you read or who you may be talking to. It runs all the way from Syntagma Square past the Hilton Hotel to Ambelokipi near the American Embassy.

Heading east from the National Gardens, the first point of interest on the right is the very pretty **Byzantine Museum**. The icon collection is housed in the two newly-restored side wings of a 19th-century compound, with an attractive courtyard in the middle. The rear building contains marble ornamentation such as column capitals, plinths, and animal figures, as well as a reconstructed basilica.

Barely 200 metres away squats the **War Museum**, the lone "cultural" foundation of the junta. Weaponry and methods of warfare from Neolithic to Ottoman times are intelligently presented, but as more modern times are approached, the exhibits degenerate to sheer militarism.

What the avenue is really about is hospitals and embassies, and these alternate for most of its length. Predating (and perhaps prompting) the re-naming of the street is the **Venizelos statue**, looking rather like Lenin, in a vast grassy area near the Naval Hospital. This was an army base from 1920 until

The Byzantine Museum on the street with three names.

1922, then it became a refugee camp.

Right next door to the US Embassy lies another long-standing joke, in all senses: **The Hall of the Friends of Music**, half-completed for more than a decade. The auditorium is being finished at last, much to the relief of music lovers everywhere.

Sofias/Venizelou continues past the **Athens Tower**, the city's tallest skyscraper (27 storeys), and ends at **Ambelokipi** junction. These streets are more interesting by night, when several cinemas and good music clubs come alive.

KIFISSIA: This suburb, five miles (eight km) from downtown Athens, has always been a place of refuge. Ancient writers praised its amply watered groves which are filled with birds—oddities in barren Attica. **Mount Pendéli** to the east blocks morning sunlight, but in compensation sunsets are spectacular, and the springs surging forth from the mountain's base created the oasis and indirectly provided its name—Kifissia, a water nymph.

Under the Ottomans, Kifissia was a village of some 1,500 inhabitants, half Christian, half Muslim, again unusual during an era when the Turks rarely settled in rural areas. After independence, Greeks gradually started taking advantage of its virtues. During the 1860s aristocratic Athenians began spending the relatively cool summers here. Then, as now, the road journey up was harrowing. Today it's possible to arrive by metro.

By 1900, Kifissia had acquired international fame, partly because it had the only hotels of adequate standard in Attica. The wealthiest families also built exotic villas in various pseudo/hybrid (and occasionally genuine Greek) styles. Between the world wars the community continued to flourish; politicians Eleftherios Venizelos and George Papandreou endowed many schools, and the Asia Minor disaster caused only a ripple here, with some villa owners graciously making their premises available to refugees.

Abundant water irrigated many market and ornamental gardens; development was also fostered by the Mouhlidis family, former landscapers to the sultan. Thus began Athens' flower market, and Kifissia is still renowned for its many plant nurseries. The elegant **Alsos** (Grove) in Káto Kifissia is another result of this horticultural tradition. The prominent botanist Costas Goulimis worked in Kifissia, and a young assistant, the botanical painter Níki Goulandrís, eventually started the Natural History Museum with her husband in 1964.

In keeping with this theme, eminent conductor Dimítris Mitrópoulos staged a performance of Beethoven's Pastoral Symphony here in 1937. But this was perhaps the high point of "Belle Epoque" culture, and the era ended abruptly. At 3 a.m. on 28 October 1940, the Italian envoy Grazzi delivered his country's ultimatum to Greek dictator Ioannis Metaxas at his recently purchased villa on Kefallinías Street.

Exhibit from Kifissia's Natural History Museum.

198

Metaxas' apocryphal *okhi* (no) reply precipitated Greece's entering World War II on the Allied side. During the Nazi occupation Kifissia suffered as did the rest of the nation, though here the damage was mostly to buildings.

Today it's a town of 55,000 people, with only shadows of former glories; the famous *plátanos* (plane tree) of Káto Kifissia's central square, near the metro station, succumbed years ago to the ravages of paving, pruning, and traffic. One of the few relics of past days are the horse-drawn carriages which wait to take visitors for a spin.

Tatoïou Street, a long, south-north artery, boasts various surviving villas, with good examples at numbers 10, 29, 31, 33, 38, 40, 50, and 56. The last of the luxury hotels is the **Cecil**, on the corner of Xenías and Hariláou Trikoúpi; 19th century prime minister Trikoúpis had his own premises at 13 Benaki, while Benaki himself (he of the museum) had digs at number 42 of the same street.

The Pesmazóglou family stayed at number 25 of their namesake street, which sports several other fine residences. One of the most ornate is the Yiorgánda/Kolokotróni mansion at 7 Kolokotróni, while the simplest, and perhaps the first, villa is Trikoúpis' political rival Deliyánnis', at 19 Levíhou.

It is difficult to date the remaining structures precisely, since the hall of records in nearby Maroússi burnt down during World War II. One method used by current owners is to examine spare roof tiles found in basements; daily newspapers were used to keep them from adhering to the molds and often legible pages remain stuck on the undersides.

The one villa to which you are guaranteed admission is at 13 Levíhou, now the **Goulandrís Natural History Museum**. Exhibits feature Greek birds and butterflies as well as more exotic species such as the monk seal and sea turtle. There's also a café and a good shop selling publications and wildlife-related souvenirs.

Kifissia has been a place of refuge since ancient times.

PIRAEUS

Most tourists, even those who retain a sentimental image of Piraeus's earthy cafés and waterfront inspired by the film *Never On Sunday*, never get a chance to explore this seaside city. Guidebooks tend to regard Piraeus as Athens' untidy, noisy port through which travellers are obliged to pass on the way to the islands. They caution that Piraeus is devoid of charm and there is no reason to spend any time in the area, unless one is dining in the touristy harbour of Mikrolimano.

On the contrary, Piraeus is well worth at least a day trip to explore its three harbours, its museums and charming quayside restaurants. A lively flea market operates on Sunday and international troupes perform at the Veakio open-air theatre in summer. People overwhelmed by the noise and pollution of landlocked Athens, worsened during the hotter months, might find staying in Piraeus, especially by the sea, a pleasant respite. Frequent buses, an electric train or taxis can get you into Athens in about half an hour.

Warlike people: Piraeus has a rich history, although few of its monuments remain. Of the tribes which appeared on Piraeus's shores, the first to settle were the Minyans, a warlike seafaring people. They worshipped the goddess Artemis Munychia, whose temple was on the hill now known as **Kastella**. The church **Prophet Elijah** stands on the site today. Another remnant of prehistoric civilisation is the **Serangeion** or **Pareskevas' Cave**, behind Votsalakia Beach below Kastella.

The original houses near the cave had been turned into baths during Roman times. After World War II, the cave was converted into a small club which featured the famous performers of the day. The cave can be explored but one needs rubber-soled shoes and a torch.

The first port of Athens was Phaleron,

not Piraeus, and it was from here that Theseus left on his journey to Crete. In the Golden Age of the fifth century BC, Piraeus replaced Phaleron as Athens' naval base. Themistocles persuaded the Athenians to use Piraeus for their new fleet and the shipyard owners of Piraeus returned the favour by building about 100 galleys a year for the fleet.

Piraeus quickly developed into a progressive trade centre. Women were allowed to sell foodstuffs in the market and the temples were open to foreigners as well as to Greeks. Piraeus was fortified at the same time and the *Makra Teixoi* (Long Walls) extending from the base of Munychis (modern-day Kastella) to Athens were built soon after 400 BC. About 450 BC, the architect Hippodemus of Miletus created a unique city plan for Piraeus based on a gridiron, which became one of the great achievements of the Golden Age.

The Spartans' annihilation of the Athenian fleet in 405 BC resulted in the capture of Piraeus, and General Lysander ordered the fortifications destroyed. The Athenian leader Conon rebuilt them and the Long Walls in 393 BC but Athens was on the decline and the walls fell into ruin. In 85 BC, the Roman general Lucius Cornelius Sulls razed Piraeus and destroyed the harbours. Following this destruction, Piraeus was considered insignificant and became virtually uninhabited.

In the Middle Ages, Piraeus was known as Porto Leone, a reference to the imposing 10-ft (three-metre) marble lion which had guarded the harbour entrance since classical times.

In 1688, Venetian general Francesco Morosini, not content with having blown up a major portion of the Parthenon, decided to confiscate the lion and take it home to Venice as a souvenir.

Modern times: Two early petitions to settle in Piraeus came from the islanders of Hydra fleeing from an epidemic in 1792, and from the people of Psars in 1825, after the holocaust by the Turks. Both petitions were turned down.

In 1834, the Greek government began a reconstruction of Piraeus. Stamatis Cleanthes and Edwardo Schaubert, the architects who created the Athenian city plan made one for Piraeus as well. The first settlers were 106 refugees who had emigrated to Syros from Hios after an island massacre during the War of Independence. They came to Piraeus in 1835, just one year after Athens had become the capital of the new state. Piraeus was nothing more than a wilderness with the ruined monastery of St Spyridon as the sole edifice.

The government offered land on favourable terms in the hope that they would service the needs of the new capital. The immigrants, who settled around the harbour, dreamed of creating a "New Hios." Their keen grasp of mercantile and industrial development established Piraeus as an independent commercial town rather than merely an Athenian satellite.

Piraeus absorbed many further immigrations beginning with the Hydriots in 1837, followed by Cretans during the rebellion of 1866-69, Peloponnesians in various movements during the second half of the 19th century and refugees from Asia Minor in 1922. The population rapidly increased from 2,400 inhabitants in 1840 to 10,000 in 1870. By 1920, Piraeus had a population of 130,000, a number which almost doubled after the "great catastrophe" of Asia Minor. The figure has now levelled off at slightly less than 200,000, according to a recent census.

Industrialisation began with the Hydriots; the first factory was founded in 1847. By the turn of the century there were 76 steam-powered factories, or one-third of the total in Greece, earning Piraeus the international label "the Greek Manchester."

Piraeus's cultural life developed in tandem with its economic growth. The splendid Municipal Theatre was built in the 1880s. The town's reputation as a literary centre flourished when *Apollo* magazine was launched in 1892 and

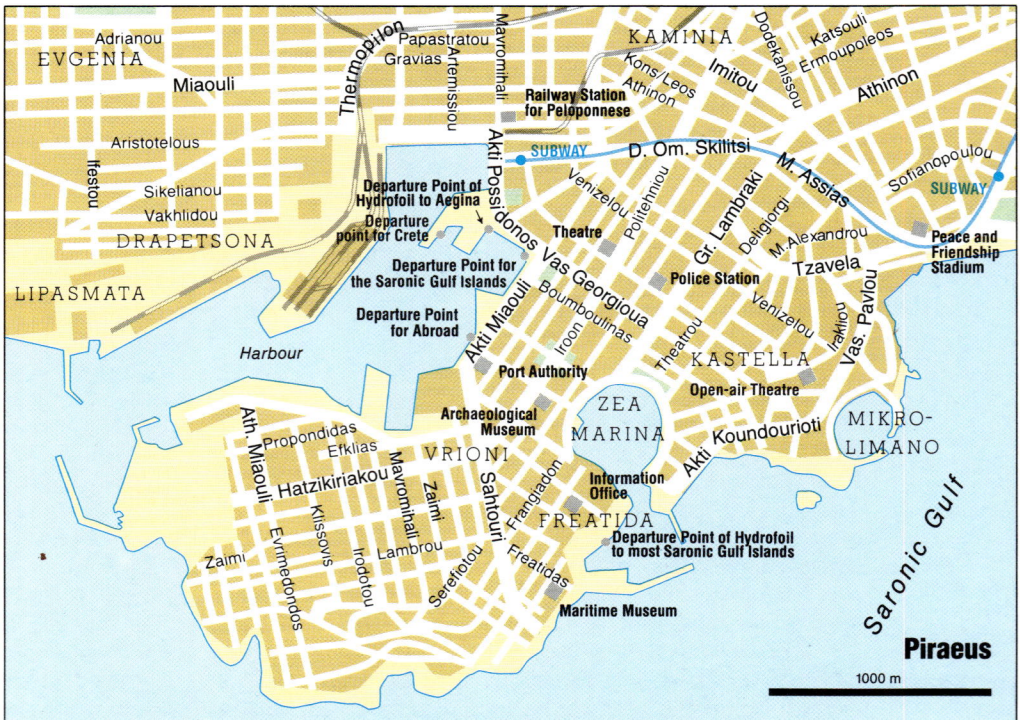

Piraeus

1000 m

was enhanced by the debut of *Our Magazine*, the first modern Greek literary publication which printed articles written by well-known Athenians.

Of more importance to a large segment of the population was the establishment of **Olympiakos** in 1925, a football (soccer) team to rival Panathinaikos of Athens. Olympiakos is still one of the most popular teams in Greece, and inspires fervent loyalty.

Unfortunately, after 1900, the pro-Athenian trend among the upper class became more pronounced. Writers were lured into the capital by publishing houses and daily newspapers. By the 1920s, Piraeus was relegated to the economic sphere, while Athens became the cultural centre.

Piraeus became increasingly unfashionable between the two world wars. Social and cultural life stagnated; it was home to mostly the working and lower middle class. During the 1930s, the *rembetic* society, a fringe subculture with its own life style, dress and music,

came to symbolise Piraeus itself. The port was bombed extensively during the war, a fate Athens escaped, and much was rebuilt.

From 1951 to 1971, Piraeus's population decreased by three percent while the population of Athens increased by 55 percent. Even worse, during the junta years the municipality embarked on an ill-advised campaign to modernise Piraeus. Many of the city's historic buildings were destroyed and replaced by tasteless monstrosities. At the same time, the charming wooden *periptera* (kiosks) were demolished and ugly corrugated metal boxes erected.

Piraeus has now become known as a banking and insurance centre but even more, its identity is linked to the sea and the shipping trade. The current worldwide shipping crisis has put a strain on the economy. Those dependent on the world's largest merchant fleet and many of the 600 or so shipping offices have been feeling the pinch.

A sense of community pride has been

Never on Sunday revisited: Melina Mercouri and friends.

REMBETIKA

The port of Piraeus was the focal point of *rembetika*, an earthy form of urban folk music often compared to the blues. The derivation of the word rembetika is unclear but may come from the Turkish word "*rembet*", which means outlaw or outsider. The first rembetika songs date from the 1800s and until 1920 these melancholy laments of poverty, loneliness, death and lost love were sung exclusively by the lower classes.

Rembetika was given a boost in popularity after 1922, when Greece was inundated with about one and half million refugees from Turkey in the population exchange following the "Great Disaster" in Smyrna. The homeless, many of them upper middle class business people who had been reduced to poverty, piled off the boats in Piraeus and were most often forced to live in substandard housing or worse still, sleep in railway stations or backyards.

Most refugees were struggling to survive in an inhospitable environment and had little time for leisure pursuits. After regaining stability, the new residents revived their Anatolian-flavoured rembetika, given true poignancy through recent hardships. The immigrants also revolutionised the night life of Athens and Piraeus by introducing mixed socialising in night spots, until that time frequented by men only, plus a smattering of prostitutes and unconventional women, the female counterpart of rembetists known as *derbederisses*.

The colourful "rembetists" were a subculture of nonconformists living on the fringe of society. They had their own style of dress which included tailored English-style suits, shiny pointed shoes and Borsalino hats. They also spoke an exceptionally rich *argot* (slang).

In the evenings these bohemians gathered in the *tekes* (hash dens) and lulled away sorrows by smoking and playing their evocative music. Hashish was legal in Turkey in the 1920s and although laws were on the books forbidding its use in Greece, they weren't enforced until the Metaxas dictatorship came to power in 1936.

The most popular rembetika instruments are the *bouzouki* (plucked stringed instrument) and *baglama* (a baby *bouzouki*). In the 1930s "classical" period of rembetika, the *bouzouki* was usually played solo with a guitar or *baglama* accompaniment. Later a second *bouzouki* was added as well as an accordian and piano, or a *santouri* (struck dulcimer) or *kanoni* (zither). Orchestras kept getting bigger until the 1960s, after the best of rembetika music had already been composed, and instruments were doubled and electrified, often with drums and an electric organ added. The end result was an ear-splitting commercialisation of the original musical form.

One cannot speak of the songs of rembetika without mentioning the dances which are an inseparable part of the music, and a powerful form of self-expression. The intense solitary *zeybekiko* and tightly synchronised *hasapiko*, done by two or three people, are the two main rembetic dances. The more sensual *tsifteteli* (belly dance) and the couple dance *karsilama* were imported from Anatolia and are less widespread.

Some rembetic songs end with a hope for better days, but for most rembetists, these happier times never came. Some of them became *manges*, defiant rebels who drank heavily in the cafés and whose wide sashes often hid weapons which they used in their frequent fights. *Manges*, a bother for authorities, were frequently jailed.

Many rembetists died of starvation during World War II and those who survived had to adjust to a new way of life. Musicians who continued to perform in Greece had to adapt to large orchestras playing an electrified form of rembetika still popular today.

Rembetika was once eschewed by the middle and upper classes as lowbrow. Suppressed by the totalitarian Metaxas government in 1936, it was until recently disdained by leftists because the rembetists were apolitical and nonproductive.

Rembetika had a resurge of popularity a few years back and today is enjoyed by all strata of society, from blue-jeaned students to the uppercrust. A number of clubs feature rembetika music, with an emphasis on the lighter tunes of the 1950s and 1960s, rather than the earlier soulful songs favoured by purists.

boosted by the face-lifting carried out by recent mayors in the form of parks, greenery and the exclusion of traffic from certain streets. **Frestide** and **Votsalakis** beaches have been landscaped and facilities improved; if ecological campaigns to combat pollution are successful, they will become even safer places in which to swim.

Neighbourhoods behind **Zea Marina** and on Kastella hill have become "gentrified". Graceful neo-classical houses have been lovingly restored and much of the construction has been tasteful and in harmony with the landscape.

Piraeus's multinational mixture of permanent and temporary residents—shipowners, office workers, seamen, yacht brokers, shopkeepers and factory workers—adds a cosmopolitan flavour to everyday life. The nearness of the sea seems to mellow the inhabitants' natures. All these factors make Piraeus an appealing city in its own right.

Seeing the sights: The **Municipal Theatre**, located on Agiou Konstanti-

nou across from the prefecture, is a magnificent 800-seat neo-classical structure built between 1884 and 1895. Based on the plans of the Opéra Comique in Paris, its acoustics are said to be the best in the Balkans. The theatre houses the **Municipal Art Gallery** and the **Theatrical Museum** of Panos Aravantinos. The latter has attractive paintings and models of theatrical sets from the artist's career when he worked mainly in Germany.

The **Archeological Museum** at 31 Harilaou Trikoupi is highly regarded by both scholars and tourists. Its prize exhibits are two bronze statues found by workmen digging a nearby drain: a magnificent *kouros* (sixth-century BC figure) of a young man, and a fourth-century helmeted Athena, looking oddly soulful for a warrior goddess. Both are thought to have come from a shipment of loot overlooked by Greece's Roman conquerors in the first century BC.

The **Maritime Museum** at Akti

Themistokleos, Freattis, Zea Marina, has 13,000 exhibit items; scale models of galleys and *triremes*, Byzantine flags, figureheads, uniforms, shells, documents, and actual sections of famous boats. One stunning exhibit highlights part of the "Long Walls" which happens to be incorporated right into the building's foundation. Sections of the walls run along **Akti Themistokleos**. Many of the ancient ruins have recently been reconstructed.

The **flea market**, on Sunday mornings until about 2 p.m., is on **Dragatsaniou** and **Mavromichali Streets**, a five-minute walk from the electric train station. An entertaining stroll throws up an eclectic mixture of household items, second-hand clothes, electronic equipment, video cassettes, sports clothes and occasional white-elephant treasures. Be sure to bargain.

Good **antique shops** are located on the block bounded by **Alipedou**, **Plateon**, **Skylitsi** and **Ippodamias Square**, just a short distance from the electric train station. About half a dozen shops specialise in old furniture, jewellery, lamps, icons, copper and bronze and embroideries. Yiorgos Yiorgas' store "Ta Mikra Teixoi" at 2 Pilis and Skylitsi is one of the most interesting. He specialises in wooden chests, butter churns and cradles. The back wall of his crowded shop is a section of one of the fifth-century "Long Walls".

Fruit vendors, bakeries, dried-fruit and nut shops, cheese, and cold cuts are sold in the market behind Akti Posidonos on **Navarinou Street** and others around it. If you are taking a ferryboat ride it is best to stock up on these items, as the food on the ferries is both expensive and tasteless.

Restaurants by the sea: Many Athenians head for Piraeus's cluster of caves and harbours to enjoy the cool breezes and some of the tastiest food to be found in the capital. The three principal harbours are individual in their appeal, and many people, once they have found a favourite taverna by the sea, return to

Ask for the catch of the day.

the same spot over and over again. For a complete list of recommended restaurants in these areas, see *Travel Tips*.

Zea Marina is Piraeus's largest yacht harbour. In the fourth century BC, it held 196 *triremes*; now it has berths for 365 yachts. The harbour's original name was "Pasalimani", which means "Pasha's Harbour", so-called because the Turkish pasha used to harbour his flagship here. The area is lined with chic restaurants, bars, yacht supply shops and ships' offices. The side streets have nice clothing shops and hairdressers.

Piraiki is a winding coastal area before Zea Marina, along which are remnants of the "Long Walls". Some cafés and tavernas overlook the Walls.

Mikrolimano (the "Little Harbour") is a charming but much-visited crescent-shaped harbour where one can dine under awnings at the water's edge and watch the water lap against the colourful fishing boats. There are at least 22 restaurants in this little cove. All the menus are fairly similar but walk along the row and see which restaurant (or waiter) enchants you. Ask for the catch of the day. Afterwards, take a stroll on **Kastella**, the hill above Mikrolimano which has a spectacular view of the Saronic Gulf and islands.

Special events: *Posidonia* is a week-long bi-annual shipping exhibition which usually takes place in June. Set in an exhibition complex next to the customs house, more than 900 companies take part. **Nautical Week** is celebrated bi-annually in cooperation with Posidonia. The **Peace and Friendship Stadium**, nicknamed "The Shoe" because of its shape, is often used for these events. The stadium, located in neighbouring **Neo Phelaron**, is closest to Mikrolimano and even has its own electric train station. Sporting events, concerts, conventions and exhibitions are also held here.

The **Veakio Festival** is held at the hilltop **Veakio Theatre** in Kastella. Foreign dance troupes and orchestras perform for two months in the summer.

ONE-HOUR EXCURSIONS

KAISARIANI MONASTERY: This ancient monastery's strategic location causes a dilemma for modern visitors. Hidden in a ravine in the slopes of **Mount Hymettos** while allowing for unobstructed views of the surrounding area, Kaisariani is virtually invisible, even from a short distance away. Although this protection was needed by the monastery's inhabitants during the 11th century, when the enclave also served as a refuge from invasion, the fact that it cannot be seen from the road can, without warning, turn the 10-mile (16-km) journey from Syntagma Square into a three-hour trawl up and down Hymettos.

Road signs, if they exist at all, can be read from one direction only, and enquiries along the way often draw blank stares. If planning a trip to this exquisite site, ask for precise directions before setting out, or take a taxi direct from Syntagma Square and save the mysteries of the bus system for the return journey to Athens.

Once this has been accomplished, Kaisariani is unrivalled as a short excursion away from the city centre. Its grounds are extensive. Nature trails thread through groves of cypress and pine trees, and wildflowers grow in abundance. These groves teem with wildlife and, although dense, give way to clear fields with the sweeping views which were once so important to earlier Athenians.

The monks who originally inhabited Kaisariani were engaged as their principal source of revenue in apiculture, or bee-keeping. Mount Hymettos, with its slopes nourished by underground springs, was known in antiquity for its high-quality honey. So widespread was this fame that the philosophy schools which once flourished on the hill were mockingly accused by the bishop Synesios as attracting students by means of the locally-produced honey rather than

through the excellence of their scholarly teachings.

The monastery's buildings are centred around an attractive, flagstoned courtyard. On the west is the refectory and the old kitchen; on the south the bath-house, unrecognisable until fairly recently, having been converted into an olive press during the reign of the Turks. To the east of the courtyard is the church itself, built of stone and brick in the form of a Greek cross. Murals cover the cupola and much of the upper walls; paintings tend to be executed in the Cretan style—strong, bold colours and balanced compositions. The parable of the Good Samaritan, found in the south vault of the narthex, is particularly rich in detail, if a little on the gory side.

The bath-house, built around a natural spring, is contemporary with the 11th-century church. The bath-house is one of the very few examples to date from this period, its construction based on the idea of Roman baths.

Springs have always played a role in

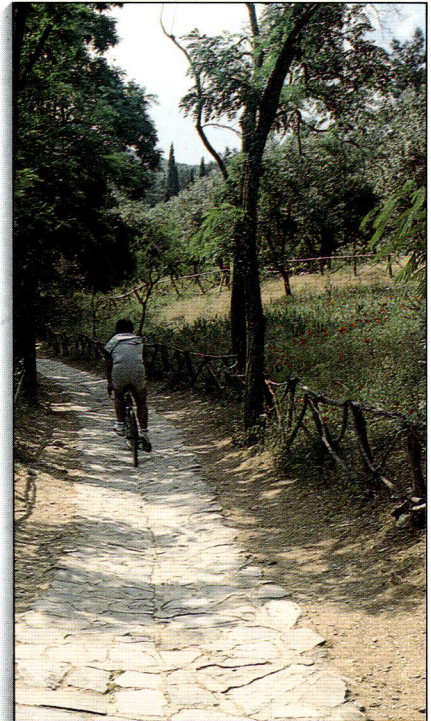

the development of Mount Hymettos, and not only for their honey-inducing properties. Since antiquity various temples and shrines on the mountain have been built and dedicated to the source of the river Ilissos. On an outside wall of the monastery is a fountain, constructed in the shape of a ram's head. The head is only a cast, the original having been moved down the hill to the Acropolis Museum. Kaisarianí's water is fed from another fountain further up the mountain, referred to by Ovid in lines of the *Ars Amatoria*. This spring, known as **Kyllou Pera**, once supplied all of Athens with drinking water. Now, it is for local use only, and water gushes from the ram's head in a pretty trickle.

One of the delights of a visit to Kaisarianí is to eat lunch in a nearby field, enjoying the sweeping panorama of Athens, the entire plain and the far-away islands of the Saronic Gulf. Donkeys or horses might become uninvited but hungry companions. Travellers who have neglected to pack a lunch can hike about one mile further up the main road to a tiny café serviced by a fast-talking Greek. While heating up Nescafé on a camp cooker, this genial chef will offer insights and speculations on a variety of subjects, then serve sandwiches on a picnic table near another cool spring.

MOUNT PARNITHA: For walking and spectacular wildflowers, the best target is Mount Parnitha, an hour north of town. Spring is best in all respects, summer crowded, but barring bad weather any day of the year spent on its forested slopes is rejuvenating; the alpine zone is a national park with numerous marked trails unaffected by the unsightly installations on every peak.

Take a number 726 bus from the corner of Stournári and Aharnón streets near Omonia, changing after 45 minutes to a number 724 bus from Aharnés village to Thrakomakedónes. From the last stop, walk five minutes uphill to a hairpin right turn marked by a retaining wall and a new house. Squeeze between

Roadside shrines are a common rural sight.

214

the two, descending into the mouth of the Hoúni gully, and pick up the clear trail on the far bank.

From Mediterranean scrub you climb gradually for 50 minutes, guided by frequent markers, to a signed junction (bear left) and the start of a fir forest. After two hours' walking you'll arrive at the alpine refuge at **Báfi**, open Friday evenings and weekends year-round and at other times by arrangement (tel: 246-1528). Except in mid-winter you can always get water from a spigot.

To continue the Parnitha loop, reach the paved ring road via the shelter parking lot, and turn right. After 300 metres, turn left onto the trail marked "Móla", which quickly negotiates the saddle between Ornio (crowned by a monstrous telecommunications tower) and Karambóla, the summit, with an air force installation on top. Change sides of the mountain at a chapel, crossing the ridge road to follow the path downslope through the thickest forest yet. Snow lies late here; from December to March

you'll appreciate the advantages of gaiters and a walking stick.

At another signed junction 45 minutes past Báfi, bear left (right goes to Móla recreation area) to follow the recommended circuit toward **Skípiza**. The next hour is spent beautifully skimming the north, then northwest, flanks of the mountain; after an initial level stretch, climb up and over the ridge just below the pathetically camouflaged radar dome, and drop steeply down to the Skípiza spring.

The fountain, in the heart of the range, is also a four-way junction; with your back to the spout, take the left-hand, southeast-bearing path (white, then red waymarks) toward **Agia Triáda**. First roller-coaster through successive ravines, then descend steadily southwards for another hour, along a creek bed, to emerge on the ring road at the Paleohóri spring.

Here turn left (east) and walk along the asphalt 15 minutes more to Agia Triáda itself, where the highway up

Mount Parnitha is a spectacular place for wildflowers.

from Aharnes meets the ring road. The **Chalet Kiklamina** is just the thing for a post-hike coffee or meal, assuming an early start—the last (no. 714) bus down to Aharnés leaves from the stop next to the chapel and spring at 4 p.m. sharp.

If you miss it, hitching down is relatively easy, or there is a path from near the **Xenia** inn (1 km south) down the ravine. At the bottom, either descend to the strip of hotels and tavernas in Ano Aharnés served by the no. 729 bus, or cut across to Thrakomakedónes for the no. 724 bus, and the hour-long journey back to Athens.

DAPHNI MONASTERY: Situated just seven miles (11 km) west of Athens, Daphní lies about half-way along the Sacred Way, the ancient route taken by revellers from the city to the pagan centre of worship at **Eléusis**. The site, at the foothills of the mountains Aigaleo, Poikilon and Korydallos, had once been occupied by a sanctuary to Daphneios, but in the fifth century this temple was torn down by Christians and the materi-als used to erect a basilica on the same spot. This was in the hope of winning over to the ways of Christ curious pagans on their way to celebrate the Eléusinian Mysteries.

Pagans of a different sort now flock to Daphní each year, from July until late August, when the grounds just by the monastery are given over to merrymakers out to enjoy the **Daphní Wine Festival**. The festival offers more than 60 wines, many straight from the barrel, and is held at a rather gaudy venue. The sounds during these hot summer nights hark back to a bawdier age which might have appealed to Daphní's original, pre-Christian landlords.

In the 12th century an octagonal **church** was built to replace Daphní's older basilica. This church, embellished with mosaics and marble, was crowned by a glorious dome covering virtually the entire building. The immense height of the dome, over 52 ft (16 metres) at the centre, flooded the church with light pouring through its 16 windows.

A rather severe Almighty in the dome of Daphní monastery.

Daphní is distinguished from other Byzantine churches in the Athens area by the collection of mosaics in the dome. Much of the interior was stripped bare by the Turks, so there is little to distract the eye upwards. Looking down is a rather severe Almighty, clutching a Bible to his chest with great, elongated fingers. Just beneath this figure, and positioned between each window, are 16 prophets, much like the statues from the Acropolis in attitude and posture. In the four corners of the dome four religious festivals are depicted: the Annunciation, the Nativity, Baptism and Transfiguration.

Glowing in soft blue and gold colours, the dome is so transfixing that it's hard to look away to the smaller paintings, or to escape the feeling of being judged by a glowering Christ. These wall paintings are scattered throughout the monastery, 76 themes in all, which illustrate the teachings of the church in the 11th and 12th centuries.

Visitors who have already been to the monastery at Kaisarianí might be disappointed by Daphní, because, mosaics aside, the latter makes for a less interesting excursion. Outside the church's walled grounds the modern world encroaches with a vengeance. The **Sacred Way** is now a busy thoroughfare, thundering with traffic only a stone's throw from the entrance. The site of the wine festival, too, is bizarre—like a miniature theme park sporting a taverna with plastic sun roofs and enormous wine barrels in the car park.

One way to take advantage of being out away from the city centre is to walk around the wooded hills which rise up behind the church. Be sure to take walking shoes as the slopes can be slippery with pine needles. Daphní can be reached in less than an hour by public bus. The ruins of ancient Eléusis, seven miles (11 km) further on, are unfortunately surrounded by very heavy industry, although the museum itself is well worth a visit.

CITY BEACHES: One aim of a good

Athens' seaside is not just for swimming.

guidebook is to give travellers the benefit of local insight. But in the case of the beaches of Athens, "inside" knowledge may deter beachgoers altogether. Many Athenians, remembering the cleaner waters and freer highways of just a few years ago, now refuse to swim within 40 miles (64 km) of the centre. Traffic is a problem in summer, but uppermost in their minds is the threat of pollution which has come with the city's population explosion and industrialisation.

The question of whether pollution can be safely ignored will be discussed later. The traveller who has the *sang froid* to go swimming at a nearby beach will find plenty of like-minded souls—enough to cover the beaches in summer. So what are the beaches like?

There are plenty, both with or without services, theoretically within an hour's ride of the city centre. Beaches, in common with cars or bathroom decor, inspire connoisseurship and many people have quite a personal image of what constitutes an ideal beach. For that

reason it would be foolish to say which are "best", but while there are many attractive spots beach-idealists should be warned they are unlikely to find the elusive locales of their fantasies in land-locked Athens.

Basically there are two choices: the west coast, to the south of the city, and the east coast, which is certainly the preferable direction for motorists seeking quieter bays and more solitude. The main beaches on both sides are served regularly by public buses, although they are often extremely crowded, especially at the height of the summer.

To the southeast, the inner beaches are dominated by highly-organised pay-beaches, though there are many walk-on beaches in between, such as that at **Kavouri**.

The five beaches under the administration of the National Tourist Organisation (EOT) are situated at Alimos, Voula (2), Vouliagmeni and Varkiza and take 25 to 45 minutes to get to in light traffic. They provide showers,

The east coast is for those seeking quieter bays.

refreshments, self-service restaurants, children's playgrounds, basketball, volleyball and tennis courts. The sunshades, of course, are monopolised by the early arrivals. These beaches also hire out canoes and pedal boats.

While it's tempting to make for the very nearest beaches, the further ones are generally preferred. The nearest of all, at **Paleo Faliro**, should be avoided unless its exquisite view of oil tankers queueing to enter Piraeus is found irresistable. The only advantage of beaches at **Alimos** and **Glyfada** is they are close to Glyfada's cosmopolitan shopping centre—and many consider this a disadvantage. They are also near a very busy and noisy airport.

By **Voula** the coastline becomes a little greener and **Vouliagmeni**, 15 miles (25 km) distant from the town centre, offers the best choice of all. Apart from **Oceanis**, the EOT beach, there is **Asteras**, a more expensive, sandier pay-beach run by the Astir Palace hotel next door. It has slightly better facilities, including three pontoons anchored offshore for energetic swimmers. Vouliagmeni also boasts a waterskiing and windsurfing school.

Crowds on all these beaches are thoroughly assorted in terms of types, shapes and ages. However, many family groups have been put off by the higher admission charge at fashionable Asteras and younger people and couples seem to predominate there, though it's by no means exclusive. Vain bathers who don't mind ogling with the locals and those with bizarre swimwear to show off will probably feel most at home at Asteras.

At the other extreme, there is **Vouli-agmeni Lake**, an outdoor spa-pool where the murky waters are said to be therapeutic and beneficial to the health. The lake, in a beautiful rocky setting which inevitably catches the shadows of aircraft on their approach to Athens airport, is usually peaceful and a plethora of sunhats and bathing caps often makes the scene extremely colourful.

Seaside sights.

Here, as might be expected, older people predominate, but again not at all exclusively.

While the Voula to Vouliagmeni range of beaches has been well-planted with trees to provide a green backdrop for swimmers, the east coast has thicker pine forests and smaller, sheltered bays. Generally speaking, the sea is also thought to be a fraction cleaner, but this probably doesn't apply to **Rafina**, which is a port, and **Nea Makri** where the water has to cope not only with a lot of tourists but with major military camps as well.

For those who prefer a well-serviced beach, EOT has one at **Porto Rafti**, about an hour's ride away, but many people head for the long sandy beach at **Skinias**, a similar distance away towards the north. However, more secluded spots can be difficult to hunt out without private transport.

Visitors who choose beaches other than those with self-service restaurants needn't fear. Virtually all main beaches on both coasts have good fish tavernas nearby, if not actually on the sand.

Finally, how about the pollution? It's not a visible threat. There are few tales of pollution actually swimming up to aghast bathers in identifiable globs and the water at many of the city beaches often looks clear.

Even along the most crowded Voula-Vouliagmeni range, bathers can be pleasantly surprised by the feathery touch of fish around their ankles. After all, fish should know... shouldn't they? Other experts, such as scientists at the Oceanographic Institute located on Voula beach, are known to regularly frolic in the waters that more scare-prone Athenians now avoid.

But, holidaymakers should be warned, there have been many cases of bathers catching diseases from the seas around Athens. At this moment not one beach in Attica meets the exacting criteria of Europe's "Blue Flag" scheme for cleaning up bathing areas in the Common Market.

Safety first: Swimming once or twice at the city beaches is probably less risky than crossing the road in the centre of town—and certainly safer than hiring any kind of motorised transport oneself. But for those who are plagued both by the heat and by misgivings about the exact microbiological make-up of the sea around Athens, there are a couple of alternatives.

One possibility is to use a hotel swimming pool. Several of the best hotels in Athens charge day admission to their pools. Another option is simply to go further away.

Anyone wanting cleaner swimming waters on a day excursion can make for somewhere like **Oropos**, up the east coast, and the bays just the other side of the **Temple of Sounion**, down the west coast. The rewards are considerable. For many people, the extra mileage is not much more of an ordeal than sampling the closer beaches as the traffic thins out a great deal further along the beach roads.

Some of the best beaches are reached by boat. Right, a visitor to nearby Glyfada.

ONE-DAY EXCURSIONS

DELPHI: Of the ancient sites of Epidavros, Corinth and Nafplion which can be visited in one-day excursions from Athens, Delphi, the spiritual centre of the classical world, is by far the most popular choice. Its stunning location overlooking valleys and fertile cypress groves makes for an extremely pleasant day out.

The journey can be tiring, however, and organised trips allow at most two hours for a visit to both the site and the museum. Overnight accommodation can be arranged in the nearby town of Delphi, also called **Kastri**. If planning to stay the night, ask ahead in Athens for a hotel which overlooks the valleys, to enjoy the same view which mesmerised the ancients.

It is claimed that, in antiquity, Delphi was the "navel" of the world, the spot where two eagles released by Zeus at opposite ends of the earth chose to meet and converge. Zeus's son Apollo is given credit for having founded the sanctuary which bears his name, although recent evidence implies that the site might have had earlier inhabitants, perhaps from Crete, around the eighth century BC. Very few early sources give a complete picture of Delphi during its heyday, for the simple reason that the oracle was so famous throughout Greece that little documentation was necessary. People travelled throughout the land for consultations.

The ritual was simple. After the sacrifice of an animal, questions were written on leaden tablets and handed in to an old woman (called a *Pythia*). This priestess would squat over a tripod—to the modern eye a rectangular rock approximately three and a half feet long (one metre) with three primary and a few secondary holes chiselled in it. Breathing in intoxicating vapours from the chasm below the tripod, the *Pythia* would utter incomprehensible phrases

to a waiting poet. The poet would, in turn, transcribe the sounds and present them to the inquirer—unfortunately in hexameter verse.

Interpretations were notoriously inaccurate (see the history section of this book), but Delphi's power and riches continued to grow. Despite a fair number of muddled predictions Strabo was moved to write: "Of all oracles in the world [Delphi] had the reputation of being the most truthful."

Setting off from Athens, the present-day route leads first to the ancient city of **Thebes**. In the fourth century BC Thebes ruled all of Greece and was to become the home of both Dionyssos and Pindar, and the scene for the downfall of King Oedipus (who murdered his father and married his mother). Thebes is now a fitful modern town surrounded by gypsy encampments.

The precise spot on **Mount Parnassos** where Oedipus's tragedy is said to have taken place is often pointed out *en route*. Beyond the workaday town of

Left, the Sanctuary of Athena (Marmaria). **Right**, the Sphinx of the Naxians.

Livadia (noted for its clocktower presented by Lord Elgin) and approaching the summit of the mountain, three crossroads converge on a red-tiled shepherd's hut. The road to the right leads to Thebes; the road to the left to Delphi; the other road leads to the north. Whether this site is the actual spot of the murderous deed or merely the fancy of imaginative tour guides remains anyone's guess, but certainly it is an isolated, even moody view of the valley, perfectly suited for a tragedy.

The largest town before reaching Delphi is **Arachova**, reminiscent of a Tuscan village with its red-roofed houses spilling down the mountain. If tour guides are to be believed, the women of Arachova engage in nothing save the weaving, looming or embroidering of fabric; the men in raising mink and tanning leather for jackets. Good savings can be made here if bargaining for sweaters or *flokati* (hand-dyed woollen rugs), although anyone with a car might try their luck in other mountain villages where prices, away from the tourist trail, will probably be cheaper. A particularly fine detour, incidentally, is to drive west from Livadia to the beautiful Byzantine monastery of **Hosios Loukas**.

And so to **Delphi**, arguably the most famous site of classical Greece. The oracle's incalculable wealth came, not only from Greek city-states, but from rulers as far away as Egypt and Sicily. Delphi's era of greatest prosperity was probably around 582 BC, when the Pythian Games, held every four years in the stadium built on the highest point of the sacred city, were rivalled only by the games at Olympia. Lavish treasuries were constructed along the city's Sacred Way to house the gifts given in tribute to Delphi's power. A coloured drawing, on the staircase in the museum, shows Delphi as it might have looked in its heyday—lavish, awash with temples and statues, and really rather gaudy.

Dominating the modern site is the

The Temple of Apollo: six are said to have been erected on this site.

great **Temple of Apollo**, restored in 1940 to its partial but imposing state. No fewer than five other earlier temples to Apollo are thought to have been erected on this site; the first of laurel leaves and branches; the second of feathers and wax. Others were fortunately of more substantial building material, including local limestone. The present temple was in the usual Doric hexastyle with 21 columns in total. Much of its fourth-century façade is in place, evidence of the temple's immense grandeur.

The **Treasury of the Athenians**, thought to have been constructed around 490 BC, stands on a terrace reached by a staircase from the Sacred Way. It is the only treasury to have been re-built at Delphi, partially from funds raised around the turn of this century by the city of Athens. Made of Parian marble, the Doric building is covered by more than 150 inscriptions.

The most photographed of Delphi's ruins stands, not in the sacred city itself, but in a ravine to the east. The **Sanctuary of Athena** (Marmaria) had as its most imposing building the **Tholos**, a magnificent circular peristyle of 20 Doric columns on a platform of three steps. Three of these columns have been re-erected. The Tholos was constructed of white marble with sumptuous black limestone for effect.

No-one is sure of the function or purpose of the dazzling Tholos. Possibilities include a treasury, a civic building, or even an ancient restaurant. Modern thought seems to go along with the latter theory, for just above the Sanctuary of Athena is a small café which serves snacks.

Delphi's museum contains finds from the ancient city, the sanctuaries and the general area of Phocis. Curiously, all exhibit signs are in Greek and French only, although guidebooks in all languages are available. Among the collection of fine sixth and fifth-century sculptures, the two most outstanding are the winged Sphinx of the Naxians, and the Charioteer, a life-size, life-like bronze (note the immaculate toe-nails) made in 475 BC.

CAPE SOUNION: Attica's southernmost promontory lies just 43 miles (70 km) from Athens. The Cape can be reached in less than two hours by car, or by organised coach trip which leaves most mornings or afternoons from the city. The journey follows the coastline immediately upon leaving Athens' suburbs, so the best views from a coach can be observed by sitting in a right-hand seat. These organised excursions, although fairly comprehensive, leave little time to explore the less-visited regions around the Cape which, littered with ancient ruins, provide wonderful walks which could easily stretch to a full day out of heat-infested Athens.

Approximately seven miles (12 km) from the Cape, the landscape leaves behind a series of tacky beach resorts to become rugged and really quite grand. Long fingers of black rock reach out the grab the sea, and bungalows give way to windswept cliffs. At the very summit of

The **Charioteer** is one of the few statues to retain its onyx eyes.

the promontory, on an isolated headland, stands the **Temple of Poseidon**, a magnificent ruin built around 444 BC, possibly as an extension of Pericles' public building programme which included the Acropolis. Almost half of the temple's original 34 Doric columns remain, nine on the much-photographed south side and six on the north. The columns differ from their Athenian counterparts in having 16 rather than the more common 20 flutes.

The view from the Temple is commanding. As well as the Peloponnesian coast and the Saronic Gulf islands, the Cycladic islands of Kithnos, Serifos and even far-flung Milos can be seen on a clear day. Unless the weather is very hot, though, the site can be windy, so take along a sweater.

Sounion has long been popular with foreign travellers and was a mandatory stop for 19th-century gentlefolk on the Grand Tour. One curious visitor was Lord Byron. Before or after carving his name on one of the temple's columns, the 6th Baron Byron composed the following lines:

Place me on Sunium's marbled steep,
Where nothing, save the waves and I,
May hear our mutual murmurs
sweep;
There, swan like, let me sing and die.

Anyone wishing to follow in Lord Byron's footsteps should visit the temple during the winter months, or early in the morning. At most other times, any hint of "mutual murmurs" are drowned by the unfortunate sound of multi-lingual tourist commentaries.

THE AEGEAN ISLANDS: One of the pleasures of Athens is its nearness to the sea. Several Greek islands are ideal for short excursions, whether by ferryboat, cruiseship or hydrofoil. Distances are deceptive in the Aegean, however, and a common misunderstanding is that islands such as Santorini, Crete, and Mykonos can be visited in a limited amount of time. This is not the case; the ferry journey to Mykonos can take up to eight hours in itself, and even a weekend

Byron's "marbled steep" at Sounion.

isn't long enough for an enjoyable stay. Airline flights to the islands, although convenient, tend to be booked up weeks ahead by canny Athenians.

With one exception the islands most suitable for short excursions are located in the **Saronic Gulf**, just southwest of Piraeus. The exception is the little-known Cycladic island of **Kea**, reached by efficient long-distance bus to the port of **Lavrion**, then by ferry. The total journey time takes just three hours. Its typical, white-cubic capital, **Ioulis**, spills down the mountainside in best Greek-island style, and its beaches are sandy. Outside of the summer months little English is spoken, however, which may be ideal for travellers wishing to enjoy island life at its simplest, but the lack of instant communication may cause problems for others.

Most people opt for the Saronic Gulf islands with good reason. Ferries leave from Piraeus several times daily, and most can be reached in under three hours. The nearest island, **Salamis**, al-though only half an hour away by boat and in 480 BC the site of a famous sea battle between the Greeks and the Persians, offers little of interest to the casual visitor. The pretty island of **Spetsai**, with its main square festooned with lights and its horse-drawn carriages a primary source of transport, is, at four hours away, more suited to a long week-end rather than a day excursion. Although hydrofoils make the trip daily from Zea Marina harbour near Piraeus to Spetsai, cutting down the time spent travelling, the seas can be choppy and hydrofoils are often cancelled.

After Delphi, the most popular excursion from Athens is an all-inclusive cruise to three islands: Aegina, Hydra and Poros, visited in a single day. With at most a 90-minute stop-over on each island, anything more than a quick tour becomes impractical, despite extravagant tourist brochure claims of "harbourside dining" and "a swim off the azure coast." To avoid disappointment, one idea is to view this one-day cruise as

The greenery of the Saronic Gulf islands.

an "island sampler": making the most of the time spent ashore (by opting for lunch on the ship, for instance) and returning for a longer stay if any of the islands appeal.

Poros, the first port of call, is actually two islands connected by a bridge. **Kalavria**, the northern section is verdant and green, at least 10 times the size of **Sferia**, the volcanic islet on which most of the population lives. The town is built around several hills, the nearest crowned by a distinctive blue and white clock-tower.

In the hour allotted during the stopover, a visit to this tower will be a rewarding, if slightly strenuous climb. The rather workaday harbour recedes, and in its place a sunny tranquillity takes over—melons, grapes and lush flowers overhang domestic verandas and from the top, it's possible to observe, smugly, the frenzied activities of other tourists far below.

Should there be time, a visit to the **Monastery of Zoodochos Pighi**, or the remains of a **Temple to Poseidon** (*circa* 500 BC) can be recommended.

Once aboard the boat, remain on deck for one of the best adventures of the day. Henry Miller, in the book *The Colossus Of Maroussi,* describes it best: "Suddenly I realized that we were sailing through the streets…the land converges on all sides and the boat is squeezed into a narrow strait from which there seems to be no egress. The men and the women of Poros are hanging out of the windows just above your head…The loungers on the quay are walking with the same speed as the boat; they can walk faster than the boat if they choose to quicken their pace."

Miller's "streets" are actually 1,300 ft (400 metres) of water which separate Poros from the mainland and from which the island takes its name. (The word *poros* means "passage" or "ford"). From Poros's straits it's a one-hour sail to **Hydra**, a cosmopolitan island where the best souvenir shopping takes place. In the 1960s, artists, att-

These ceramic decorations are unique to Aegina.

These ceramic decorations are unique to Aegina.

racted by the symmetry and clear, bright light of the port, took up residence—which in turn attracted well-heeled hippies. Hydra became a minor jet-set destination and even today, the movie stars and artists long gone, the island is a fashionable one where visitors tend to dress up, rather than "down" for the beach.

In the 17th century Hydra was the merchant marine centre of the Eastern Mediterranean. Sea-faring captains built huge mansions around the harbour, one of which is now a branch of the **Athens School of Fine Art**. The cobbled streets which twist inland from the sea are filled with chic boutiques and restaurants. White-washed walls give way to elegant doors (brass knockers much in evidence) which are no doubt the summer homes of wealthy Athenians, and small squares tucked into corners provide refuges for quiet drinks. If plans include a longer stopover, Hydra's interior contains many lovely churches, reachable only on foot as cars are banned on the island.

Aegina, the final cruise destination, was first settled around 3000 BC. These ancient inhabitants chose to settle on **Colona hill**, near the town of Aegina. Although only one column remains from a temple built to honour Apollo, archaeologists have unearthed evidence which indicates that the island was continuously inhabited for the next 2,000 years. In the seventh century, Aegina minted its own coinage.

The wealth and power of this small island grew, and in 1828 it became the capital city of free Greece. The first governor, John Capodistrias, ordered the building of many fine homes, some of which still line the island's graceful boulevards.

If there is time to visit only one attraction, opt for the coach excursion to the **Temple of Aphaía**, seven miles (12 km) northeast of Aegina town. Dedicated to the goddess of wisdom and light, Aphaía is thought to have been built between 510 and 480 BC. It is constructed on the highest point of the island, and commands a breath-taking view out to sea. Winds can be high, however, so dress appropriately.

Of the original 32 columns, 24 have been preserved, as well as the foundations of an altar and the remains of a priests' chamber. The sculptured pediments depicting scenes from the Trojan War are now housed in Munich, although lesser finds from Aphaía are on display in the **Archaeological Museum** in town.

Aegina is rich in locally-produced pistachio nuts, which come in handy on the cruise back to Athens, but a return trip to the island is recommended. Not only are its fish tavernas excellent and its horse-drawn carriages scenic, but a particularly fine excursion is to the Byzantine hill town of **Palaiochora**, riddled with churches and ruins. Another enjoyable side-trip (best in mid-week to avoid the crowds of Athenians) is to the delightful islet of **Moni**, reached by caique from the resort of **Perdika**.

Some islands offer rides in horse-drawn carriages. Following pages: *palaiodzidika* **(flea market wares).**

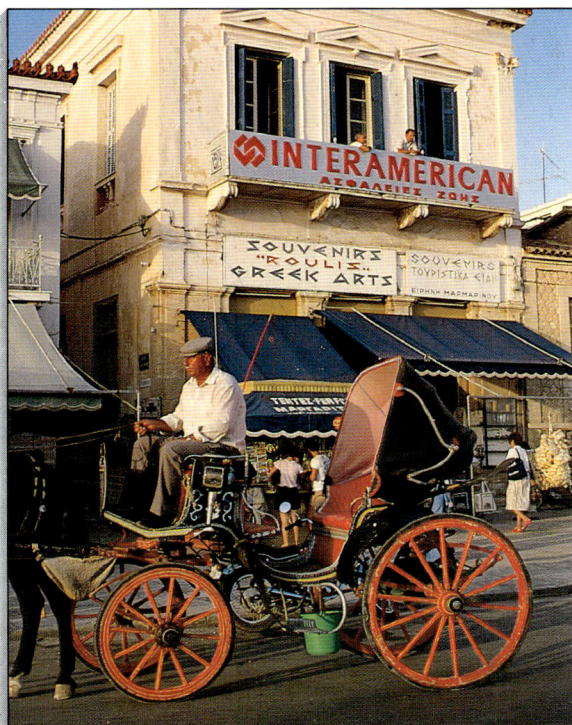

TRAVEL TIPS

GETTING THERE

BY AIR

Greece has good air connections with all five continents and is serviced by numerous international airlines. Olympic Airways, the national carrier, has frequent flights to most major capitals; flying Olympic is also the most convenient way to arrange connecting flights to the islands. The cheapest way to travel is by buying a charter flight, which can cost as little as £100 return from London. These usually arrive in the middle of the night (and depart in the middle of the night), are uncomfortable and can be chaotic.

Athens has two air terminals. The East Air Terminal is for international and charter flights; the West Terminal is for Olympic Airways flights and flights to the islands. Taxis or buses connect the two.

During the peak summer season it is impossible to walk through the East Terminal hangar which services charter flights without tripping over sleeping forms and rucksacks. All part of the fun.

BY SEA

The majority of visitors entering Greece by sea arrive from the west, that is from Italy. You can catch a boat to Greece from Venice, Ancona, Bari and Ontario, but the most regular service is from Brindisi. Daily ferry lines (somewhat less frequent in the low-season) connect Brindisi with the three main western Greek ports: Corfu, Igumenitsa and Patras. Corfu is a nine-hour trip; Igumenitsa 11 hours; and Patras 16 to 18 hours, depending on whether it is a direct boat or one making stops at Corfu and Igumenitsa. From Corfu it is possible to get a ferry, then a bus directly to Athens (about 11 hours), but Patras is best for travelling to Athens, as regular buses and trains connect the two (about four hours by bus). If you plan to take your car with you on the boat you should make a reservation well in advance. Otherwise, arriving a few hours before the departure time should suffice, except during peak seasons when booking in advance is advisable.

Italy and the west, however, are by no means the only provenance for Athens-bound sea travellers. Southward, boats connect Alexandria and Piraeus once every 10 to 15 days: eastward, boats run weekly between Haifa, Limassol and Piraeus, and once every five days between Volos, Cyprus and Syria, not to mention the numerous crossing-points between the East Aegean islands and the Turkish coast. Northward, frequent boats connect Piraeus and Istanbul, and in the summer boats run twice a month between Odesssa (USSR) and Piraeus.

BY LAND

The overland route from northwestern Europe to Greece is a long one–some 1,900 miles (3,000 km) from London to Athens. It is an arduous and impractical travel option if you're just trying to get to Athens for a brief holiday, but it can be an interesting trip if you make the journey a part of your vacation. By car there is an E route that runs through the interior of Yugoslavia, entering Greece just above Thessaloniki. There are also inexpensive bus services, along the lines of the famous Magic Bus, which connect Athens and Thessaloniki with many European cities–a three and a half day trip from London. The various trains that you can catch from northwest Europe will take about as long as the bus, will cost considerably more, but may get you to Greece feeling more intact. Hitching to Greece is also a possibility, though hitching through Yugoslavia is reported as being difficult.

If you're travelling to Greece from Asia you'll pass through Istanbul and cross into Greece at the Evros River. The recommended route is by car or bus. The road is good and the journey from Istanbul to Thessaloniki takes approximately 15 hours; various bus companies run the route. The train has the mythic appeal of running the route of the old Orient Express, but unless you're a great train fan the time may be prohibitive; some 25 hours from

Thessaloniki to Istanbul. This trip crosses the fascinating region of Thrace; a fine adventure if you have the time and the spirit for it.

Travel Essentials

VISAS & PASSPORTS

A valid passport is required for all travellers except the following:
1. Holders of a United Kingdom "British Visitor's" passport.
2. Holders of National Identity Cards from Austria, Belgium, France, West Germany, Italy, Luxembourg, the Netherlands and Switzerland.
3. Holders of either a Military Identity Card (issued by Nato) or of Laissez Passer (issued by the United Nations).
4. Seamen, travelling on duty, who hold a Seaman's book.
No visa is required for citizens of the following countries:

For a stay of three months: United Kingdom, United States, Australia, New Zealand, Canada, Andorra, Argentina, Austria, Bahamas, Barbados, Belgium, Brazil, Cyprus, Denmark, Finland, France, Gambia, West Germany, Granada, Ireland, Iceland, Israel, Italy, Japan, Luxembourg, Liechtenstein, Malta, Mexico, Monaco, Morocco, the Netherlands, Norway, South Korea, Spain, Sweden, Switzerland.

For a stay of two months: Portugal, Republic of South Africa, Venezuela, Chile, Colombia, Dominican Republic, El Salvador, Haiti, Honduras, Guatemala, Ecuador, Kenya, Mozambique, Nicaragua, Panama, Paraguay, Peru, Uruguay, Zambia.

For a stay of one month: Tunisia and Hong Kong.

RESERVATIONS

The dual perils of Greek civil aviation strikes and package tour operators' double-booking practices mean that nothing should be left to chance. Confirm travel arrangements and hotel accommodation with your tour operator or travel agent approximately three days before leaving for Greece. When returning home, call the airline or the appropriate authority from Athens to confirm again. Leave plenty of time to get back to Athens if visiting an island; distances can be deceptive. Inexpensive charter flights are often subject to several hours' delay, so be sure to slip a good novel or a pack of cards into your hand luggage and be prepared to sit it out, probably on the floor of the airport.

TRANSFERS

For information on domestic airlines, or on how to reach Athens or Piraeus from the airports, see the "Getting Around" section.

CUSTOMS

If arriving from EEC countries: You are allowed to import free of duty the following items: 300 cigarettes or 75 cigars or 150 cigarillos or 400 grams of tobacco; 1.5 litres of alcoholic drink or 5 litres of wine; 75 grams of perfume, and gift items to a total value of 55,500 drachmas.

If arriving from non-EEC countries: You are allowed to import free of duty: 200 cigarettes or 50 cigars or 100 cigarillos or 250 grams of tobacco; 1 litre of alcoholic beverage or 2 litres of wine; 50 grams of perfume and gift items to a total value of 7,000 drachmas.

You may also bring one of each of the following: a camera and film; a movie camera and film; a projector; a pair of binoculars; a portable musical instrument; a portable radio, phonograph or tape recorder, a bicycle, and sports gear (tennis racquet, etc).

It is prohibited to import narcotics, medicine (except limited quantities prescribed by a licensed physician for your own use); explosives, weapons and (yes, that's right) computers or windsurfers—

unless a Greek national residing in Greece guarantees these will be re-exported.

For other specific restrictions regarding the importation and exportation of such things as animals, plants, shotguns, pleasure craft and antiquities contact the nearest Greek embassy, consulate or tourist organisation.

BAGGAGE

Only the poshest hotels have mini-bus services to and from the airport or the harbour. Neither of Athens' two air terminals provide facilities for left luggage. Here's a handy tip if you plan to travel using Athens as a base: carrying a basket or packing a smaller suitcase inside a larger one can be useful. The smaller one can be brought out for the beach or for short trips out of town, while the larger one and its contents stay safely stored in the hotel.

WHAT TO BRING

Athens is a cosmopolitan city. People tend to dress up, and only young women wear trousers. Athenians never wear shorts, even in the hottest weather. Tourists in informal dress are tolerated, even courted, at most restaurants and tavernas, but if you want to blend in with city life, dress up a bit. A jacket or cardigan should be packed in case of chilly nights.

Footwear: Sandals are appropriate day or night. Plastic shoes are invaluable for swimming in water containing rocks, garbage or sea urchins; these can be bought locally. Rubber soled shoes are recommended for climbing the Acropolis and Athens' slick, steep streets.

HEALTH TIPS

Residents of EEC countries are eligible to receive free emergency medical care. British residents should obtain a form from the DHSS before leaving home, so check this out beforehand. Medical insurance is always a good idea for additional coverage. If touring, be sure your policy covers the cost of an air taxi as this is the quickest way, in an emergency, off the smaller islands to the nearest hospital. If you plan to hire a car, a motorcycle or a moped, ensure that your policy covers all motoring accidents. The number of accidents, especially on mopeds, rises annually.

DRINKING

Although tap water is essentially safe to drink, having a private water supply is much handier as drinking fountains are few and the sun is fierce. Bottled water can be bought almost anywhere that sells food, even in beach cafés and tavernas.

INSECTS & PESTS

The most common pest is the mosquito, which loves virgin white skin. Avoid perfumes and deodorants (it attracts them even more) and invest instead in either of two items. The first is a coil, which, when lit and placed by the window, acts as an effective means of combat by smothering the mosquito in foul-smelling smoke. The second method is more modern: a plug-in, electric coil which burns smokeless tablets called *Spira*. Practically odourless, it's worth seeking out in chemists or hardware shops .

SUNBURN

Each year hundreds of tourists are badly burned by ignoring the obvious rule: take your tan slowly. For the first few days wear a sunhat and a sunblock. Observe, like sensible Greeks, the afternoon siesta when the sun is at its hottest, and stay on the beach or visit the Acropolis for just a couple of hours in the mornings or late afternoons. Gradually work up to staying out longer, and remember to reapply suntan lotion whenever you come out of the sea. It's possible to get burned while swimming or sightseeing, too. Wearing a tee-shirt over your swimsuit the first couple of days or dressing in dark colours and long sleeves, avoids senseless burning. That said, most of Athens' buildings are constructed to keep out the worst rays. Finding a sunny café in the dull winter months can be a challenge.

DRUGS

All prescribed drugs should be packed in their original bottles, carefully labelled and marked. Failure to do so could result in arrest for the possession of dangerous drugs. Greek authorities take the unauthorised use of drugs very seriously indeed; this is not the country in which to score cannabis, no matter how small the quantity. Err on the side of caution at all times.

MONEY MATTERS

The Greek unit of money is the drachma. The Bank of Greece issues bank notes of 50, 100, 500, 1000, and 5000 drachmas, and coins of 1, 2, 5, 10, 20 and 50 drachmas. The National Bank of Greece has three branches in London. The addresses are: 50 St. Mary Axe, EC3, tel: 01 626 3222; 6 Queensway, W2, tel: 01 229 1413; 204 Tottenham Court Road, W1, tel: 01 637 0876.

EXCHANGE RATES

Rates of exchange go up or down daily. In Athens, to find out the current rate of exchange, call the National Bank of Greece, tel: 323 1802.

At the time of going to press, the rates of exchange were:

UK Pound: 263 drachmas
American Dollar: 157 drachmas
Australian Dollar: 126 drachmas
Japanese Yen: 1.2 drachmas
German Mark: 85 drachmas

CREDIT CARDS

The plusher hotels, shops and restaurants of Athens and the larger islands all recognise the major international credit cards, but many tavernas will not. Stickers in the front windows will advise on which cards are acceptable, but be sure to check *before ordering or buying* that the arrangement is still valid.

TRAVELLER'S CHEQUES

As with credit cards, only the more popular places will have facilities to cash travellers' cheques. This can be done in banks and in larger hotels by submitting proof of identity. A passport is the most accepted form of proof; be sure to retrieve this from your hotel reception desk before setting off for the bank.

ANIMAL QUARANTINE

Dogs and cats require health and rabies inoculation certificates issued by a vet in the country of origin before being allowed to enter Greece. The certificate must be issued not more than 12 months before arrival in the case of dogs and six months in the case of cats, and *not less than* six days before arrival. Parrots and other birds must have a health certificate stating they are free from psittacosis.

EXTENSION OF STAY

Aliens with no visible means of support and/or without return tickets may be refused an extension of stay. Otherwise, apply to have your visa extended from the Aliens Bureau at 9 Halkokondili Street, tel: 362 8301. If applying from one of the islands, contact the nearest police station for details of how to apply.

GETTING ACQUAINTED

GOVERNMENT & ECONOMY

Strikes are a way of life in Greece. Should there *not* be one of the following, consider yourself lucky: a postal strike; a garbage strike; a strike by telephone operators; an air traffic controllers' strike; a civil aviation strike, a bus strike or a taxi strike. Any stay in Athens of more than three days will involve witnessing at least one demonstration and probably several. These are passionate but peaceful affairs and a vital outdoor activity. Consulting one of the English-language publications might or might not tell you what they are about; most

Athenians treat demonstrations as part of the urban landscape.

Prime Minister Andreas Papandreou and his Panhellenic Socialist Movement were involved in allegations of corruption during 1988 and 1989. His party (PASOK) has yet to recover from the scandals, losing two 1989 general elections after an eight-year term to the New Democracy party led by Constantine Mitsotakis. More elections are expected to follow. With fewer than 50 percent of its nearly four million residents being true Athenians, the capital on election day is blissfully quiet. Residents leave in droves, back to their islands or mountain villages where, by law, they are required to vote.

The latter half of the 1980s saw a huge rise in inflation throughout the country; a shock for anyone who remembers Greece as a "cheap and cheerful" vacation destination. Inflation rose by 20 percent in 1986; by 16 percent in 1987; and by 12 percent in 1988. The drachma has fared well against other currencies, however, and the country remains reasonably good value for travellers.

GEOGRAPHY & POPULATION

Greece is one of the southernmost European countries, ensuring a high sunshine rate throughout much of the year. The combined population of Greater Athens and Piraeus at the last census was nearly four million.

TIME ZONE

Greek time is two hours ahead of Greenwich Mean Time. So, when it is noon in Greece it is 10 a.m. in London, 5 a.m. in New York, and 8 p.m. in Sydney. Like the rest of the Common Market, the clock is advanced one hour during summer to give extended daylight hours.

CLIMATE

If you visit Greece in the summer months you'll want to bring lightweight clothing. If you visit Greece during the winter months bring the same kind of clothes you would wear during spring in the northern part of the United States or central Europe: that is, be ready for rainy, windy days and temperatures ranging between 40° and 60° Fahren-

heit (3° and 16° degrees Centigrade).

On the whole, islands are ill-equipped for visitors during the winter months. Heating can be basic or non-existent, boats infrequent, food tinned and amenities scarce. The tourist season is officially "over" in early October, when Olympic Airways lays on extra planes from the islands to Athens to cope with the hundreds of workers returning to the city for the winter. Athens in winter becomes a calmer place, and people are friendlier to visitors generally. Rates in hotels and even in some restaurants are lower than in the summer.

SPELLINGS & PLACE NAMES

Syntagma Square is also known as Constitution Square. The island of Lesvos is known variously as Lesbos, Mytilene, or Mytilini. Corfu can be called by its Greek name Kerkira, or Kerkyra; Itaki by its English name Ithaca. Attempts have been made in this book to formalise a system which has no national standard. If you are confronted by a place name which is unfamiliar, check on more than one map or ask at a local ticket office if the destination has another name or spelling.

TIPPING

Most restaurants and tavernas add a 15 percent service charge to the bill, so a tip is not expected, although it is customary to leave the small change on the plate after a bill has been paid. If the serving boy (*micro*) has been particularly good about clearing away empty plates, etc., reward him separately by placing change on the table rather than on the plate. *Micros* rely on tips as a supplement to rather meagre wages. Just as important as any gratuity, however, is your appreciation of the food. Greek restaurant owners are often proud when you tell them you like a particular dish.

SIESTA

Siesta is strictly observed during the summer months, but has been abolished in the winter. The hours between 2 p.m. and 5 p.m. are the ideal time to take a nap or extend a leisurely lunch into the afternoon. Most shops will close, perhaps to reopen again in the evening. Although the sun is fierce during these hours, anyone with a strong constitution and protective clothing will be rewarded if choosing siesta time to visit busy archaeological sites; crowds will have diminished considerably.

CLOTHING

Be aware of the social significance of the way you dress, and of how the Greeks perceive it. Greece, like any other country, has a set of codes, both stated and implicit, which defines the socially acceptable range of attire. The Greeks will not expect you as a tourist to dress as they do (in dark colours, for instance–Greek women rarely wear white and never wear backless sun-dresses). In certain places, however, you will encounter requirements or conventions concerning dress which *do* reflect on you as a visitor. To enter a church, men must wear long trousers and women, sleeved dresses. These will occasionally be provided at the church entrance if you do not have them. Not complying with this code will be taken as insulting irreverence on your part.

NUDE BATHING

Nude bathing is another activity which merits discretion. Nude bathing is legal on very few Greek beaches, though socially acceptable on the more remote island beaches. The main rule-of-thumb is this: if the beach is secluded and/or a beach that has become a commonly accepted locale for nude bathing, you probably won't be bothered by, nor offend, anyone.

ELECTRICITY & VOLTAGE

220 AC is the standard household electric current throughout Greece. This means that appliances from the United States require converters. Greek outlets and plugs are different from both American and most European types, so you'll probably need an adapter as well.

BUSINESS HOURS

The schedule for business and shop hours is a complicated affair, varying according to the type of business and the day of the week.

The main thing to remember is this: if shopping for something important, buy it between 10 a.m. and 1 p.m. The store may or may not be open that afternoon; it may well open in the evening. Again, it may not. Athens is experimenting with "straight" hours during the winter to bring the country more in line with the EEC. Stay tuned.

Winter opening hours
Non-food shops: Monday, Wednesday. Open 9 a.m. to 5 p.m. Tuesday, Thursday and Friday: 10 a.m. to 7 p.m. Saturday: 8:30 a.m. to 3:30 p.m.
Food shops: Monday 9 a.m. to 2:30 p.m. Tuesday to Friday: 9 a.m. to 6:30 p.m. Saturday: 9 a.m. to 3:30 p.m.

Summer opening hours
Monday, Wednesday, Saturday. Most businesses are open 8 a.m. to 2:30 p.m.
Tuesday, Thursday, Friday. Most businesses are open from 9 a.m. to 1:30 p.m, reopening from 5 p.m. to 8:30 p.m.

The stores in Plaka continue trading in the summer until 10 p.m. or longer to take advantage of any late-night shoppers. Dry cleaners and specialty shops have yet another schedule of opening hours, which is not covered here. Chemists operate on a rota system so there will be at least one chemist open for emergencies; check in the window of the nearest pharmacy for the list.

BANKING HOURS

All banks are open to the public from 8 a.m. to 2 p.m. Monday to Thursday; 8 a.m. to 1 p.m. Friday. In much visited areas like central Athens and the popular islands, however, you may find at least one bank open on some summer evenings and/or weekends for currency exchange. On the small, rarely-visited islands, expect only the minimum of banking facilities and travel with emergency supplies of cash.

Around Syntagma Square, at press-time, these banks offered extended hours: General Bank of Greece, 1 Ermou St, tel: 324 6451, and the National Bank of Greece, 2 Karagiorgi Servias St, tel: 323 6481.

The East and the West Air Terminals in Athens have several banks each, all with extended opening hours:

East Air Terminal:
  Agricultural Bank of Greece, tel: 962 2791. Open 24 hours, seven days a week
  Bank of Crete, tel: 962 1010. Open 9 a.m. to 9 p.m., seven days a week
  Commercial Bank of Greece, tel: 961 3611. Open 8 a.m. to 8 p.m., seven days a week
  General Bank of Greece, tel: 961 3700. Open 7 a.m. to 9:30 p.m., seven days a week
  National Bank of Greece, tel: 961 2728. Open 7 a.m. to 11 p.m., seven days a week

West Air Terminal:
  Agricultural Bank of Greece, tel: 984 1282. Open 8 a.m. to 8:30 p.m., seven days a week
  Commercial Bank of Greece, tel: 981 1093. Open 8 a.m. to 7 p.m., seven days a week
  Ionian Bank of Greece, tel: 982 1031. Open 8 a.m. to 2 p.m. Monday – Friday
  National Bank of Greece, tel: 982 4699. Open 7 a.m. to 11 p.m., seven day a week

Athens is the centre for banks with international branches, and money can often be transferred straight from your account at home into your pocket in Greece by visiting the appropriate headquarters. The industrial disputes which plague Greece can lead to local banks locking their doors for days at a time. Knowing the Athens headquarters of your home bank can prevent finding yourself penniless.

American Express Bank:
31 Panepistimou St, tel: 323 4781–6
Arabian Express Bank:
369 Singrou Ave, tel: 942 9901
Bank of America:
39 Panepistimou St, tel: 325 1901–9
Bank of Nova Scotia:
37 Panepistimou St, tel: 324 3891–8
Banque National de Paris:
5 Koumpari St, tel: 364 1880
Bank Paribas:
39 Panepistimou St, tel: 325 5021
Barclays Bank International:
15 Voukourestiou St, tel: 364 4311
Chase Manhattan Bank:
3 Korai St, tel: 323 7711–9
Citibank:
8 Othonos St, tel: 322 7471
Kolonaki Sq, tel: 361 8619

Credit Bank:
2 Stadiou St, tel: 322 0141
9 Panepistimou St, tel: 323 4351–5
Credit Commercial de France:
20 Amalias Ave, tel: 324 1831
Ergobank:
36 Panepistimou St, tel: 360 1011
Grindlays Bank:
7 Merlin St, tel: 362 4601
Midland Bank:
1A Sekeri St, tel: 364 7410
National Westminster Bank:
24 Stadiou St, tel: 324 1562–7
Societe Générale:
23 Ipokratous St, tel: 364 2010–9
Trader's Credit Bank:
3 Santaroza St, tel: 321 2371

RUSH HOURS

One reason for experimenting with "straight" opening hours is to combat Athens' horrendous rush hours, which can take place up to four times a day: when businesses open, when they close for siesta, when they open again, and then when they close for the evening. The twin perils of traffic jams and pollution reached such heights in Athens that a law was introduced: on certain days of the week only cars with even-numbered license plates were allowed into the city centre; on other days only those cars with odd-numbered license plates. Rather than decrease the number of cars on the roads, however, the numbers have increased, as everyone who could afford the cost bought another car with the opposite type of license plate.

PUBLIC HOLIDAYS

1 January: New Year's Day
6 January: Epiphany, when the seas around Piraeus are blessed
Shrove Monday: First Day of Lent
25 March: Feast of the Annunciation/Independence Day
1 May: Labour Day and Flower Festival
Good Friday
Greek Orthodox Easter
15 August: Assumption of the Holy Virgin
28 October: *Okhi* Day (when Greece said "no" to Mussolini)
25 December: Christmas Day
26 December: Boxing Day

SEASONAL FESTIVALS

(Dates subject to change each year)

February – March (three weeks before Lent): Carnival season, with special festivities in Athens and on the islands of Skyros and Zakynthos
June – September: Athens Festival at the Herod Atticus Theatre. Information and tickets from 4 Stadiou St, tel: 322 1459
July: Rethymnon Wine Festival at the Municipal Garden on Crete. Information and tickets from 100 Kountouriotou St, Rethymnon, tel: (083) 129148
July – August: Daphni Wine Festival (on the outskirts of Athens). Information and tickets from 4 Stadiou St, tel: 322 7944
July – August: Thassos Festival (ancient drama in an ancient theatre). Information and tickets from 2 Filellinon St in the town of Kavala, tel: (051) 223958
September: Cricket season begins on Corfu

RELIGIOUS FESTIVALS

The Greek Orthodox Church exerts enormous influence on contemporary life. The most important holiday is Easter, celebrated according to the Greek Orthodox calendar and usually several weeks later than our own Easter. Traditional foods include *tsourekia*, plaited bread with red eggs inside, and *koulouria*, a special type of cookie. It is advisable to find out before booking a spring holiday exactly when Easter might be, as services, shops and even airplane flights experience disruptions in the week before and during this holiday.

Nearly every day is a cause for celebration for someone in Greece. Instead of marking birthdays, Greeks have *yiorti*, name days, which celebrate Orthodox baptismal names. When the day is to commemorate a popular name like John or Helen, practically the whole nation has a party. You'll hear locals say: *"Yiortazo Simera"* (I'm celebrating today). To which you may reply: *"Xronia polla"* (Many years).

COMMUNICATIONS

POSTAL SERVICE

Signs denoting post offices are usually bright yellow, as are post boxes. Post boxes are tiny and can be hard to find; often they are on the outside walls of tavernas or shops and are obscured. Look carefully. Most Athenian post offices are open Monday to Friday between 8 a.m. and 1 p.m. The main post office in Syntagma Square is open from 7 a.m. to 8:30 p.m. Monday to Saturday; 9 a.m. to 1 p.m. Sunday. Usually.

Stamps can be bought at post offices and most kiosks, although occasionally a service tax may be added by the kiosk. If sending the attractive, large-format postcards, additional postage may be required, so it's best to have them weighed first.

Parcels sent abroad must be inspected by the post office, so do not wrap them beforehand. Brown paper can be bought from the post office itself or from kiosks. The mail service is riddled with discrepancies: three parcels containing identical contents were sent to London at the same time. The sender was charged three different postal rates. Why? This is Greece. Give in gracefully.

TELEPHONE/TELEGRAMS

OTE offices are the cheapest way to make local or international calls. To do so, walk in and wait for a booth to be free. A desk operator will switch on the phone, the metre registering zero units. After dialling, talk for as long as you like, either locally or internationally. At the end of the call, the desk operator will present you with a bill in drachmas. Connections from the islands vary, but persevere. Telegrams can also be sent from OTE offices. Two OTE offices in Athens are located at 15 Stadiou St, just behind Syntagma Square, open 9 a.m. to 10 p.m. Monday to Saturday; 9 a.m. to 8 p.m. Sunday; and at Omonia Square, open 24 hours a day.

Local and international calls can also be made from some kiosks. Calls made from hotels or pensions are often subject to extra tariffs, so it is cheaper to use OTE offices. Hotels, however, are likely to contain the only telex machines around.

The dialling code from Greece to the UK is 0044. From Greece to the USA or Canada it is 001.

RADIO & TV

Athens, naturally, offers the best English-speaking transmissions. Most hotels now broadcast satellite TV. Channel 3 is Sky (movies and sit-coms): Channel 4 is Super (mainly music): Channel 7 is CNN (news). There may be a fee for private TV if you are staying in a posh hotel; otherwise a communal set in the lobby is available free for visitors' pleasure.

The two state-owned and operated TV stations in Greece are ERT 1 and ERT 2. These channels often transmit English-language movies and programmes with Greek sub-titles.

ERT 1 and ERT 2 are the two Greek radio channels. ERT 1 is divided into three different "programmes". The First (728 KHz) and Second (1385 KHz) both have Greek popular music and news, some foreign pop and occasional jazz and blues. The Third Program (665 KHz) plays classical music. ERT 2 (98 KHz) is much like the first two programmes. News can be heard in English, French, German and Arabic on the First Program every morning of the week; in English twice a day on ERT 2 at 2 p.m. and 9 p.m. The BBC World Service offers news on the hour (plus other interesting programmes and features). To find out the best short wave (MHz) frequencies on which to pick up the BBC, ask at your hotel reception. The U.S. Armed Forces Radio (AFRS) operates 24 hours a day on 1594 KHz and 1484 KHz with news on the hour. Pirate radio in Athens is a young, vigorous force which offers quality, English-language programming. To hear one of the contributors to this book broadcast the news, tune into Antenna 97.1 FM Stereo.

THE PRESS

Kiosks around Syntagma Square receive most British newspapers the day of or the day after publication; two days following a weekend. American papers are represented, too. Two local publications provide news and information in English for both tourists and residents alike. The daily *Athens News* contains a smattering of world news taken from wire services, Greek news coverage plus interesting small ads.

The Athenian is a monthly magazine providing coverage of various aspects of life in Greece (politics, culture, travel) and useful information on what's happening in the arts. *Greece's Weekly* concentrates on business and finance for the English-speaking community. All these publications are readily available from kiosks in areas of Athens frequented by tourists.

The tiny *Week in Athens* has been published for 41 years by the National Tourist Organisation of Greece. It contains a list of useful addresses of amenities and entertainments. Pick up one free at any NTOG desk.

LIBRARIES

The following libraries in Athens contain books in English, French, German, Spanish or, in the case of Greek institutes, perhaps all the above. Call for opening times (and/or an appointment) as hours are subject to change. A tip: in the case of the smaller libraries, be sure to take the street number as well as the street name, i.e, 17 Valaoritou St. As with much of industrialised Athens, libraries do not necessarily look like libraries from the outside and specific places can be difficult to find.

American Library, American-Hellenic Chamber of Commerce, 22 Massalias, tel: 363 8114. Two libraries, one on the fourth floor, one on the seventh floor

Benaki Museum Library, 1 Koumbari St, tel: 362 6462

Blegen Library, American School of Classical Studies, 54 Souidias St, tel: 723 6313

British Council Library, Kolonaki Sq, tel: 363 3215

French Institute Library, 31 Sina St, tel: 362 4301

Gennadius Library, American School of Classical Studies, 61 Souidias St, tel: 721 0536

German Archaeological Institute, 1 Fidiou St, tel: 362 0270

Goethe Institute Library, 16 Omirou St, tel: 360 8114

Italian Institute Library, 47 Patission Street, tel: 522 9294

Loberdios Library, Othonos & Eleptheriou Venizelou, Kifisia, tel: 801 3861

National Library of Greece, Panepistimou, tel: 361 4413

BOOKSHOPS

Athens contains numerous bookstores which sell quality books in English. Distributors often import from America, so some publications unavailable in Britain can be found on sale here. Not to be overlooked are the paperbacks sold in some outdoor kiosks. Diligent browsing can unearth surprisingly good books.

The Bookstall, 6-10 Har. Trikoupi, tel: 361 9933. Modern shop in swish complex; good on Penguin classics.

Compendium, 33 Nikis, in Plaka, tel: 322 6931. Friendly and helpful, owner is an ex-pat with good taste.

Eleftheroudakis, 4 Nikis, behind Syntagma Sq, tel: 322 9388. Most English-language books are upstairs in this comprehensive, convenient shop.

Kakoulides – The Book Nest, 25-29 Panepistimou, tel: 322 5209. Upstairs in this old-fashioned shop in the Stoa Megarou Athinon arcade are shelves and tables piled high with books. Good for publications in French and other languages, too.

Pantelides, 11 Amerikis, tel: 362 3673.

Turtle Bookshop, 24 Patriarcho Ioakim, Kolonaki. Books for children in English, French and Greek.

EMERGENCIES

SECURITY & CRIME

Crime is rare, and the petty theft which does occur might well be the result of other tourists, rather than locals. Although it is not advisable, luggage left temporarily in cafés will probably remain untouched. For the 24-hour Tourist Police dial 171 on your telephone. Someone should speak English.

Police stations in Athens/Piraeus:
4 Leoharous St, tel: 323 0263
3A Veikou St, tel: 923 9224
58 Sokratous St, tel: 522 6067
2 Ipsilandou St, tel: 722 0216
37 Iroon Politehniou St, tel: 412 0325 (Piraeus)
East Air Terminal, tel: 969 9523
West Air Terminal, tel: 981 4093

LOSS/THEFT

If something of value has been stolen, contact the Tourist Police on 171. If something has been left in an Athens taxi or bus, call 523 0111.

LEFT LUGGAGE

There are no left luggage facilities at either of the Athens Air Terminals. Most hotels in Greece, however, will be willing to store locked suitcases for up to a week if you want to take any short excursions. This is a free service, and the hotel accepts no responsibility in the unlikely event of theft. Commercial left luggage offices operate in many harbour towns on the islands. For a small charge space can be hired by the hour, by the day, by the week or longer. Although contents will probably be safe, take any valuables with you.

HOSPITALS & DENTISTS

Athens operates a roster for doctors and dentists. A list of local practitioners should be posted in the nearest chemist window. In emergencies call the Tourist Police on 171.

In Athens, the doctor's roster can be obtained by dialling 105; the 24-hour pharmacy roster can be obtained by dialling 107.

General hospitals:

General State Hospital of Athens, Messogion Ave (located across from the Pentagonon-Papagou), tel: 777 8901

Red Cross (Erythros Stavros) hospital at Ampelokipi, tel: 691 0512

Children's hospitals:

Agia Sofia, Thivon & Mikras Assias St. tel: 777 1612

Aglaia Kyriakou, Thivon & Levadias St. tel: 777 5610

GETTING AROUND

TRANSPORT FROM AIRPORT

To Athens

By taxi: From the East Terminal the taxi fare to Athens is around 550 drachmas; from the West Terminal around 450 drachmas. Many charter flights to Athens arrive at the East Terminal in the early hours of the morning. From 1 a.m. to 5 a.m. taxis are allowed to charge "double time", i.e. 51 drachmas per kilometre. From 5 a.m. to 6 a.m. there is an additional charge of 30 drachmas. For each piece of luggage there is a 15 drachma charge.

By bus: From the East Terminal, Express lines A and B travel into Syntagma or Omonia Squares every 20 minutes from 6 a.m. to midnight. The fare is 100 drachmas.

From midnight to 6 a.m. the buses run every hour and the fare is 150 drachmas. From the West Terminal the fares and the hours are the same; the buses, however, are marked A and B with a diagonal slash through each letter.

To Piraeus

By taxi: From the East Terminal to Piraeus the taxi fare is around 550 drachmas. From the West Terminal to Piraeus the taxi fare is roughly 400 drachmas. From the centre of Athens to Piraeus, expect to pay around 500 drachmas.

By bus: From the East Terminal to Piraeus the Express line No 19 runs every 30 minutes from 6 a.m. to midnight. The fare is 100 drachmas. From midnight to 6 a.m. buses run every 90 minutes and the fare is 150 drachmas. From the West Terminal, catch the same No 19 bus and pay the same fare, as the Express line makes one continuous "loop". The journey is a slow one, but the only alternative is a taxi.

By metro: It is possible to get to Piraeus in about 25 minutes by catching one of the clean, tidy and safe metro trains. The stations nearest centre of Athens are Victoria, Omonia, Monastiraki, Thissio. The fare is cheap and the metro is open until around midnight.

TAXIS

Taxis in Greece, especially in Athens, merit a guidebook all to themselves. It may well be that your taxi "experience" will figure among the most prominent memories of your holiday. Perhaps the Greek taxi experience is best divided into three stages for analytical purposes.

First: getting a taxi. It's nearly impossible at certain times of the day, and probably worst before the early afternoon meal. When you hail a taxi, try to get in before stating your destination. The drivers are very picky and often won't accept you unless you're going in their direction. If you have to say a destination, say it loudly and clearly (and with the right accents) as they may well otherwise just pass you by. If you see an empty taxi, run for it; be aggressive. Otherwise you'll find that some quick

Athenian has beaten you to it.

Second: the ride. Make sure the taxi meter is on when you start out, and not on "2"–that's the double-fare which is permitted only from 1 a.m. to 5 a.m. Once inside you may find yourself with company. Don't be alarmed. It is traditional practice for drivers to pick up two, three, even four individual riders, provided they're going roughly to the same area. In these cases, make a note of what the meter-count is. In fact, because taxis are so cheap they end up functioning as mini-bus services (although a series of recent strikes in Athens is trying to redress this situation.)

Packed in with a Greek housewife with her shopping bags overflowing with groceries, a chic businessman and a radical bohemian university student, you may find yourself in the middle (literally) of some rather interesting conversations. Or, you may find yourself chatting with an ex-seaman who tells you a few yarns from his days in the United States, or perhaps with a driver who speaks no English at all.

Third: paying up. If you've travelled with company make sure you aren't paying for that part of the trip that happened before you got in. Otherwise the meter will tell you the straight price which may be adjusted according to the following tariff regulations:

Minimum fare – 200 drachmas.
Fare starts at – 25 drachmas.
Rate per km. Inside city limits – 30 drachmas.
Rate per km. Outside city limits – 51 drachmas.
Waiting time, per hour – 300 drachmas.
Surcharge from airports, seaports, railway stations, bus terminals – 30 drachmas.
Night hours: 1 a.m. to 5 a.m. – Double day rate, 51 drachmas per km; 5 a.m. to 6 a.m. – 30 drachmas surcharge.
For each suitcase – 15 drachmas.

There is also a pick-up charge if you order a taxi from your hotel.

Some drivers will quote the fair price, others will try to rip you off. If the amount is clearly above the correct price, don't hesitate to argue your way, in whatever language, down to a normal price.

In recent years various Radio Taxi services have started up in Athens. They can pick you up within a short time of your call. These taxis, however, are often more expensive than the regular ones.

CARS

Car hire and petrol is expensive in Greece. If hiring a car, shop around for the best price. In Athens, expect to pay 72 drachmas per litre for ordinary petrol; 77 drachmas per litre for super. Outside of Athens increases in prices vary from two to four drachmas per litre.

The Automobile and Touring Club of Greece (ELPA) provides foreign motorists with assistance and information. In Athens ELPA offices are located at 2–4 Messoghion Ave, tel: 779 1615, and at 6 Amerikis & Panepistimou Streets, tel: 363 8632

Driving a car in town can be unpleasant and confusing. Greek tempers are short and road signs practically non-existent. Cars are, however, fun for day-trips out of the city. Avis, Hertz and Budget have rental desks at both the East and West Air Terminals. Otherwise, head for Singrou Avenue in town, which is chock-a-block with car hire firms.

Avis
46-48 Amaias Ave, tel: 322 4951-8
Budget
8 Singrou Ave, tel: 921 4771-3
Hertz
12 Singrou Ave, tel: 922 0102-4
Just Rent A Car
43 Singrou Ave, tel: 923 9104
Speedo Rent A Car
8 Singrou Ave, tel: 922 6102
Thrifty Rent A Car
24 Singrou Ave, tel: 922 1211-3

MOTORCYCLES & BICYCLES

For a reasonable price motorcycles and mopeds give you the freedom to travel independently, and to pretend to be a genuine Athenian. Rates are cheaper by the week than by the day. Before setting off, however, make sure your vehicle works safely. Ask to take it for a test spin down the street. Otherwise you may get stuck with a lemon or, worse, they may hold you responsible for its malfunctioning when you return. Above all, be careful: Athenian streets are mean. Wear protective clothing and check that your holiday insurance covers any problems.

Motorbikes and bicycles can be hired from two companies:

Meidanis Rent A Moto at 4 Dion, Areopagitou St, tel: 323 2346, and at Motorent, 5 Falirou St, tel: 923 4939

BUSES

Terminal A is at 100 Kifissou St. To get there take Express Line A from Syntagma or Omonia Squares. Alternatively, take bus No 051 from the corner of Zinos & Menandrou St near Omonia Square.

Terminal B is at 260 Liossion St. To get there take Express Line B from Syntagma or Omonia Squares. Alternatively, take bus No 024 from Amalias Ave, in front of the entrance to the National Garden.

Bus services:

Athens to Piraeus: Green bus No. 040 from Filellinon St (operates 24 hours a day). Alternatively, take the metro from Victoria, Omonia, Monastiraki or Thissio stations.

Athens to Daphni Monastery: Blue bus No. 873 from Deligiorgi St.

Athens to Kaisariani Monastery: Blue bus No. 224 from Vass. Sophias Avenue

Athens to Mount Parnitha: Bus No. 714 from Aharnon St. Trip takes one hour and 30 minutes.

Athens to Sounion via coast road: Orange bus from 14 Mavromateon St, Areos Park. Trip takes one hour and 45 minutes.

For a list of buses to local beaches, see the section on "Sports"

RAILWAY

To go to either Larissis or the Peloponissou railway stations, take the yellow trolley bus No. 1 from Amalias Ave (in front of the Parliament Building). Alternatively, take the blue bus No. 405 from Alexandras Ave.

INLAND AIR TRAVEL

Travelling on one of the domestic planes operated by Olympic Airways to an island is a delightful alternative to the ferryboat. The air fare, by European standards, is inexpensive, and the time saved is huge: it can take up to eight hours to sail from Piraeus to Mykonos; only 50 minutes to fly. The cost is around £25 one-way. The flights are fun, too; the planes too tiny (sometimes only 16 seats) to treat the journey as anything but a bus-ride in the sky. Carry your own luggage aboard, store it where possible, then grab a window seat for a magnificent view of low-lying hills, sparkling seas, and evocative islets crowned by chapels. Upon arrival, a modern or a dilapidated bus will transfer you to the principal harbour town. There is sometimes a fee, sometimes not.

There are drawbacks to inland air travel, however. Demand can be greater than the number of seats, as Athenians with island homes "block book" seats in the summer, often more than two months ahead.

Having said that, the experience itself is a delight. Early morning flights have the most advantages. Not only do you gain extra time to book on the next available flight, but flying into the sun as it rises over the Aegean, or arriving on Mykonos in time to watch the revellers go to bed and the old ladies sweep the streets clean, is an island adventure on its own.

Pick up a timetable and reserve seats at any Olympic Airways office. The headquarters is at 96 Singrou Avenue, tel: 929 2111. The most central office is at 6 Othonos St, Syntagma Sq, tel: 929 2489. Major credit cards accepted.

FERRIES

Advanced ferry schedules are listed in the *Greek Travel Pages* which can be purchased in the bookstore Eleftheroudakis at 4 Nikis, behind Syntagma Square or from the address in the "Hotels" section of this book. Revised ferry schedules are published weekly, and given out at Tourist Information Offices. Most offices hang a schedule in a conspicuous place, so even though the desk itself might be closed the information is still obtainable.

Unless you want a berth or first class seat,

there is no need to book in advance. Simply arrive at Piraeus a couple of hours before departure and cruise the various ticket agencies. Agencies handle different boats which are often sailing to the same destinations at the same times. Many agents will claim "their" boat is the quickest, most powerful, sometimes the only way to get to an island that day. Do some shopping around; it pays off. Seasoned travellers will add at least one hour to the time any Greek claims it takes to sail to a specific destination.

The telephone number for the Port Authority in Piraeus is 451 1311 or 452 7107 (Zea Marina).

HYDROFOILS

Hydrofoils ("Flying Dolphins") are quick and twice as expensive as ferryboats. A service between Piraeus and the Saronic Gulf islands continues throughout the year. Modern hydrofoils sometimes show videos and have bar facilities, but rough seas and bumpy rides are common. As hydrofoils need a calm sea to travel, they are prone to cancellation due to weather or technical difficulties.

WHERE TO STAY

HOTELS

The National Tourist Organisation of Greece governs the construction and classification of all hotels. The classification awarded is determined by the size of the rooms, size of public area including lobby, decor and funishings of the rooms and services provided by the hotel. All hotel accommodation is divided into classes: deluxe (luxury class), then classes A-E. The price in each category is fixed, i.e., an A-class hotel will always cost more than a B-class hotel, even with seasonal variations in price. As the classifications are so formal, anyone who rates charm above lobby-space, or yogurt and honey above an all-inclusive breakfast, will probably be just as happy in a lower-class hotel as in one of the deluxe versions; almost all accommodation from C-class upwards can be guaranteed to have a good standard of cleanliness.

NTOG offices around the world can help with hotel accommodation. See "Useful Addresses" section for names and addresses of international NTOG offices. The book *Greek Travel Pages* includes 124 pages of detailed information on accommodation in Greece supplied by the hoteliers themselves, and pictures are included of many establishments. *Greek Travel Pages* costs 1,200 drachmas an issue, and is available abroad from Timsway Holidays, Nightingales Corner, Little Chalfont, Buckinghamshire HP7 9QS. In West Germany contact Ikon-Reisen, Schwanthalerstrasse 31, 8000 Munchen 2. To receive a copy in any other country, write to BAS Overseas Publications Ltd, BAS House, 48–50 Sheen Lane, London SW14 8LP, England.

Reservations can be made in writing directly to the desired hotel; in writing to the Hellenic Chamber of Hotels, 6 Aristidou St, Athens; or in person by calling in at the Hellenic Chamber of Hotels at 2 Stadiou and Karageorgi Servias St, inside the National Bank of Greece at Syntagma Square.

There is normally a 10 percent increase for a stay less than three nights and a larger increase for an extra bed in the room. Tax and VAT are also added. As a guide, here are the *minimum* hotel rates which were charged in 1989. Add around 15 percent for each subsequent year and note that maximum rates may vary, even within the same class.

Deluxe class – single: 3800 drachmas; double: 5520 drachmas.
A class – single: 2940 drachmas; double 4090 drachmas.
B class – single: 2070 drachmas; double 2630 drachmas.
C class – single: 1440 drachmas; double 2120 drachmas.
D class – single: 1240 drachmas; double 1590 drachmas.
E class – single: 1040 drachmas; double 1570 drachmas.

PENSIONS

A pension tends to be a casual, family-run establishment. As this type of accommodation is often in older, picturesque buildings providing only basic amenities, rates are on the whole lower than in hotels. As with hotels, they are divided into classes A-E. First class pensions are listed in the NTOG hotel guide and can be pre-booked directly. Lists of pensions in lower categories can only be obtained on the spot in Athens.

HOTELS & PENSIONS IN ATHENS

Deluxe Class Hotels:

Astir Palace, Vass. Sophias & El. Venizelou corner, Syntagma Square area, tel: 364 3112. All rooms with TV and video, plus there is a newsstand, sauna, health care, beauty parlour, conference and banquet facilities, restaurant, bar and coffee shop.

Athenaeum Inter-Continental, 89-93 Singrou Ave, tel: 902 3666. Air conditioned throughout, two bars, three restaurants, swimming pool, TV in all rooms with in-house movies, health studio, bank facilities.

Athens Hilton, 50 Michalakopoulou St, tel: 724 8322. Just opposite the National Gallery, with air conditioning, central heating, American bar, restaurant, coffee shop, discotheque, bowling. The restaurant inside, Ta Nissia is recommended.

Grande Bretagne, Syntagma Square, tel: 323 0251. Lovely building with a distinguished history. 450 rooms plus 25 suites. Air conditioned, central heating, two bars, three restaurants, 24-hour room service, convention and function facilities.

Ledra Marriott Hotel, 115 Singrou Ave, tel: 952 5211. All rooms have individual climate control, radio & colour TV, in-room movies, minibar, 24-hour room service. Rooftop swimming pool, hydrotherapy pool, three restaurants and a ballroom.

Class A Hotels:

Acropolis View, 10 Galli & Webster Streets, tel: 921 7303. Small hotel with roof garden, central heating, air conditioning, bar, restaurant.

Astor Hotel, 16 Karageorgi Servias, tel: 325 5555. Just two blocks from Syntagma, the Astor has a marble and mirrored lobby as well as a marble reception desk. The 234 rooms are comfortably furnished; ask for one with a private terrace overlooking the Acropolis.

Hotel Electra, 5 Ermou St, Athens, tel: 322 3223. Situated on a busy shopping thoroughfare just off Syntagma (fortunately quieter in the evening), the Electra has a lobby with a marble lion, and boasts a "clubby" atmosphere in the evening, ie, lots of small tables dotted about.

Esperia Palace, 22 Stadiou St, Athens 10564, tel: 323 8001. As popular with visiting Greeks as with more far-flung travellers, this hotel on a busy street which connects Syntagma Square with Omonia Square is air-conditioned and has 185 bedrooms. Most have balconies or extended terraces, best used at night when the noise quietens down. The dining room and downstairs bar are panelled in pale wood and have a cozy style.

Novotel Mirayia Athenes, 4-6 Michail Voda St, tel: 862 7133. Underground car park, roof garden with swimming pool, mini-bar in rooms, satellite colour TV and radio in rooms.

Class B Hotels:

Acropolis House, 6-8 Kodrou, Plaka tel: 322 2344. A favourite with academics and writers, this pension was once a family mansion. Warm, friendly atmosphere with good conversation in the lobby. All manner of rooms (and all standards) upstairs, although the place does tend to book up quickly with repeat visitors.

Adonis Hotel, Voulis & 3 Kodrou, Plaka, tel: 324 9737. Across the pedestrian street from the Acropolis House, this attractive, functional pension serves breakfast on the roof garden which overlooks the Acropolis. The terrace reopens in time for drinks at sunset. Downstairs at reception, the staff are unfailingly helpful and friendly.

Athenian Inn, 22 Haritos, Athens, tel: 723 8097. Just two blocks from fashionable Kolonaki Square, this family-run pension advertises itself as "your home in Athens". Very nice it is, too, with an open fire, paintings on the wall by local artists, and wall-to-wall carpets in the bedrooms.

Athens Gate, 10 Singrou Ave, tel: 923 8302. This modern hotel near the Temple of Oympian Zeus has a roof garden restaurant with a stunning view, spacious rooms (some with terraces offering the same panorama), and serves American buffet breakfasts.

Omiros Hotel, 15 Apollonos St, tel: 323 5486. In a street filled with hotels just on the edge of Plaka, this handy little establishment boasts chocolate-brown walls, a cafeteria, and a roof garden with an Acropolis view.

Class C Hotels:

Aphrodite Hotel, 21 Apollonos St, tel: 323 4357. A better-than-average C-class hotel, with air conditioning (uncommon even in many B-class hotels), polite staff, room telephones, large lobby with bar and good, buffet-style breakfast for an extra fee. The rooms on the top floors in the rear offer lovely views of tiled roofs and the Acropolis. Although somewhat lacking in style, it's a good, centrally-located hotel for business people on a budget.

Hotel Hermes, 19 Apollonos St, tel: 323 5514. Next door to the Aphrodite, the Hermes is more intimate than its neighbour and offers somewhat similar facilities. The lobby has a bar with tall stools like on the American TV show *Cheers*, but the hotel is popular with tour groups and can get noisy or booked up.

Hotel Niki, 27 Nikis St, tel: 322 0913. A compact, functional little hotel on the street which connects the Syntagma area with Plaka. The adjoining snack bar is cozy and darkly furnished, a haven from the bright sunlight outside. Further along the same street is one of Athens' best English-language bookstores.

Hotel Phoebus, 12 Peta St, Athens, tel: 322 0142. A family-owned, flower-filled hotel which might provide a touch of *déja vu.*: the BBC epic drama *Fortunes of War* was partially filmed here. As the hotel is tiny (only 23 bedrooms, some of them quite pretty) and popular with returning visitors, it's best to book in advance.

Phaedre Hotel, 16 Cherefontos St, Athens, tel: 323 8461. The Phaedre Hotel looks like everyone's dream of ancient Greece, but crumbling with it. The relatively large rooms in the front overlook towering palm trees and a lovely church; the scene is so tranquil during siesta it's impossible to believe the hotel is only a couple of blocks from the noisiest part of Plaka. But the olde worlde charm continues inside the hotel,

too–none of the rooms has a private bathroom, just a sink.

A list of D and E class hotels can be obtained from offices of the National Tourist Organisation of Greece. Here are a few names and addresses:

Class D Hotels:
Hotel Arta, 12 Nikitara St, tel: 362 7753
Hotel Corfu, 21 Psaron St, tel: 523 5069
Hotel Lato, 91 Fylis St, tel: 823 5342
Hotel Parnassos, 27 Sofokleous St, tel: 321 1551
Hotel Victoria, 9 Aharon St, Vathi Square, tel: 524 6587
Hotel Zenith, 13 Xouthou St, tel: 522 3533

Class E Hotels:
Hotel Aegeon, 10 Thermidos St, tel: 321 0297
Hotel Ephessos, 30 Agiou Konstantinou St, tel: 522 3508
Hotel Kosmikon, 7 Socratous St, tel: 321 2681
Hotel Makedonia, 17 Agiou Konstantinou St, tel: 522 2275
Hotel Pentelicon, 7 Nikiforou St, tel: 522 2624
Hotel Vassilikon, 5 Iktinou St, tel: 522 8133

HOTELS IN PIRAEUS

Many hotels in Piraeus are hired out by the hour. For a list of these establishments, look to a different kind of guide book. Here are a few reputable hotels near the sea which provide useful accommodation before catching a ferry to one of the islands. Piraeus hotels are also a refreshing alternative to the hot sticky atmosphere in Athens.

The only Deluxe hotel near Piraeus is the huge (720 beds) Athens Chandris at 385 Singrou Avenue, in Paleo Phaleron, tel: 941 4824. There is a view of the sea, air conditioning, restaurants and bars.

B Class Hotels:
The Cavo D'Oro, at 19 Vassileos Pavlou, Kastella, (tel: 411 3742) is a 74-bed hotel with views of the sea.

The Diogenis Hotel, 27 Vassileos Georgiou, (tel: 412 5471) is a large hotel in Piraeus proper. For cooler breezes and the best view, ask for a room on the upper floor at the Homeridion Hotel, 32 Harilaou Trikoupi & 2 Alkiviadou, tel: 451 9811.

C Class Hotels:

The Kastella, at 75 Vassileos Pavlov, Kastella (tel: 411 4735); the Leriotis at 294 Akti Themistokleous, Piraiki (tel: 451 6640) and the smaller Scorpios Hotel down the street at 156 Akti Themistokleous (tel: 451 2172) all offer sea views at budget prices. The Scorpios even looks out over the ancient "Long Walls".

VILLAS & APARTMENTS

Self-catering is increasingly popular in Greece, especially for those with young children. Villas and apartments are clean, and comfortably, if sparsley, furnished. These, too, are graded according to fixed-price categories. Expect to pay just under the same amount of money for a first class apartment as for a deluxe hotel room. Two rental agencies specialising in the Athens area are the Accommodation Centre, 3 Filelinon St, tel: 322 0000 and the A1 Travel-All at 8 Ermou Street, tel: 322 7668. Both offer flats for hire throughout Athens.

YOUTH HOSTELS

A member's card is required in order to stay at a Greek Youth Hostel. An international membership card (approximately 1300 drachmas) can be obtained by applying to the Greek Youth Hostels Association, 4 Dragatsaniou St, 10559 Athens, tel: 323 4107. An overnight stay costs from 450 drachmas to 1000 drachmas.

Athens Youth Hostels are located at:
1 Agiou Meletinou & 57 Kipselis St, Kipseli, tel: 822 5860
Alexandras Ave & Drossi St, tel: 646 3669
52 Peoniou St, Stathmos Larissis, tel: 883 2878
75 Damareos St, Pangrati, tel: 751 9530
Y.W.C.A. Youth Hostel, 11 Amerikis St, tel: 362 6180

FOOD DIGEST

WHAT TO EAT

Dining out is a social affair. Whether it is with family or *paréa*, that special circle of friends, a meal out is an occasion to celebrate, a time for *kefi*. This may have something to do with the fact that eating out continues to be affordable and popular, not something restricted to those who have American Express cards. And the predominance of the taverna, that bastion of Greek cuisine, reflects this popularity. These casual eating establishments have more or less the same style and setting throughout Greece, and the menu is similar. Which is to say no frills, no packaging which tries to convince the "consumer" that this taverna is different from the others, or special and distinct. The place, and your being there, is somehow taken for granted: you eat the good food at Yanni's or Yorgos', you enjoy yourself, and you don't pay an arm and a leg for it.

There is, of course, some variation. The taverna is by no means the only kind of eating establishment. You'll also encounter: the *éstiatorio,* a more conventional restaurant–fancier and more polished than the taverna, with linen tablecloths and higher prices; the *psistaría*, a barbeque-style restaurant which specialises in lamb, pork or chicken on a spit; the *psarotaverna* which specialises in fish; the *ouzeri* which is mainly an establishment for drinking, but which also serves *mezédes*, snacks of various types; the *gyros* stand with *hiro* sandwiches and the ubiquitous *souvlaki*, sometimes a sit-down place with salads, sometimes a take-away on the corner.

There's also regional variety in Greek cuisine and you should keep an eye out for those specialties of the house which you haven't seen before. Another thing is how strikingly different the same dish can be when it's prepared well or prepared badly, for example, a *melat-sanasalata*, or stuffed tomatoes. It's worth shopping around in much visited areas for the best taverna, asking the locals where they eat. Even better–invite a Greek to dinner and ask him to choose the restaurant; the food is bound to improve immeasurably.

A few notes about Greek eating habits. The main meal is eaten at midday, between 1:30 p.m. and 2:30 p.m. and is usually followed by a siesta break lasting until 5 p.m. The evening meal can either be another full meal, or an assortment of *mezes*. This is eaten late, between 9 p.m. and 11 p.m. (Breakfast in Greece is rather meagre, usually consisting of bread, butter, jam and coffee. Try ordering yogurt and honey as a delicious alternative.)

Greeks never simply "go out drinking". Even if an evening involves heavy drinking of retsina or ouzo, these will be accompanied by food–a habit which minimises the effects (and after-effects) of the alcohol. When it comes to ordering wine, check to see if they serve wine from the barrel (ask for *chima*). This is the inexpensive local drink not normally served to tourists. *Aspro* is white wine, *mavro* is red, and *kokkinelli* is rosé.

GREEK WINES

Greek wines will never obtain the status of their French or Italian counterparts, but much local wine can be quite palatable. Some of the better Greek labels are: Rotonda, Cambas, Boutari, Calliga.

Retsina: the best-known Greek wine. Flavoured with the resin from pine trees and an acquired taste. Inexpensive.
Demestica: the popular alternative to retsina. White is the most common; also comes in red and rosé.
St. Helena: a reliable medium-dry white wine which can be found in many restaurants.
Cava Clauss: a full-bodied dry red wine, aged in oak barrels in the cellar of Gustav Clauss. Available in limited quantities of numbered bottles; try it if you get the opportunity.
Château Clauss: another vintage from the Achaia Clauss bottlers. Goodish dry red wine.

Nemea: a palatable red table wine; can be found on many menus.
Danielis: slightly spicy dry red wine, less common than Nemea.
Bon Viveur: a newish dry white wine with a fruity taste.
Patras: a robust white made from the grapes of the Patras region.

GREEK FOODS

Here is a partial list of the more popular dishes you'll find in Greece.

Starters–usually eaten as appetizers with bread (*psomí*)
kdokithákia–deep-fried courgettes (zucchini)
melitsánasálata–aubergine (eggplant) dip
rossikisaláta–cold potato salad with lots of mayonnaise
taramasaláta–fish roe pâté/dip
tzazíki –yogurt/cucumber dip, heavy on the garlic

Vegetables
anginária–artichokes
arakádes–peas
bámies–okra
dolmáde –stuffed grape leaves
fasoláki–snap beans
horiátiki–"greek" salad
maróuli–lettuce
patzária–beetroot (beets)
yemistés–stuffed tomatoes or peppers
yíantes–large haricot beans

Meats
Note the following terms: *psitó*–roasted; *sti soúvla*–barbecued on the spit; *tiganitó* –fried; *sto foúrno*–baked; *skáras*–grilled; *vrastó*–boiled; *kapnistó*–smoked
arní–lamb
biftélo–beefsteak
brizóla–pork or beef chop
keftédes–meatballs
kokorétsi–stuffed innards, spit-roasted
kotópoulo–chicken
loukaniká–sausages
mialó–brain
paidákia–lamb chops
sikotákia–grilled liver
souvlaki–chunks of lamb or pork, spit-roasted

Soups & Specialties

avgolémono–chicken stock with egg and lemon
fasoláda–bean soup
moussaka–aubergine (eggplant) and lamb casserole
pastítsio–macaroni casserole
patsás–tripe stew sold at special stalls
salingária–snails fried in oil and herbs
stifádo–any kind of stew, stewed meat
souzoukákia–baked meat rolls
yiorvoulákia–meat-and-rice balls

Seafood

astakos–lobster
bakaliáros–cod
galéos–shark meat
garídes–shrimp
glóssa–sole
gópes–small, fried fish
kalamária–squid
ksifías–swordfish
ktapódi–octopus
péstrofa–trout
sinagrída–red snapper

Desserts

Rarely will you find dessert served where you eat dinner. You'll find sweets instead at *zachariplastía* (sweet shops) and some *galaktopolía* (dairy stores).
baklavá–filo dough leaves, honey, nuts
kataifí–nuts and honey wrapped in shredded wheat
krema–plain custard
loukoúmi–Turkish Delight
moustalevria–grape pudding (autumn)
rizagalo–rice pudding

Snacks

kalambóki–corn on the cob, sold at stalls
kastana–roast chestnuts, sold at stalls
koulouria–sesame-sprinkled "pretzels"
kreatópita–meat pie
spanakópita–spinach pie
tirópita–cheese pie
tost–toasted sandwiches sold at stalls

Other useful words

aláti–salt & pipéri (pepper)
boukáli–bottle
potiri–glass
pirouni–fork
koutáli–spoon
mahéri–knife

katálogo/lista–menu
to logaviasmó–the bill

WHERE TO EAT

Many visitors head straight for Plaka, where there are plenty of tavernas and a guaranteed "jolly" atmosphere in open-air comfort. The food is, almost without exception, indifferent and over-priced. For the most comprehensive selection of good restaurants buy a copy of the Greek publication *Athinorama* and ask someone to translate. Failing that, consult the listings of the English-language *The Athenian* magazine. Here is a list of recommended eating places, divided into areas.

Plaka area:
O Kouklis, 14 Tripodon St, tel: 324 7605. Folkloric gallery-cum-eatery specialising in herring and sausage flambé. Red barrel wine from Tripolis.
O Kostis, 18 Kydathineon, tel: 322 9636. Just about everything possible to be found on a Greek menu. Centrally located, it's also a good place to watch all of Plaka parade by in the evening.
O Xynos, 4 Angelou Yeronda, tel: 322 1065. Good food with good music.
Socrates' Prison, 20 Mitseon St, tel: 992 3434. Fashionable and pleasant restaurant behind the Herod Atticus Theatre.
Zafiris, 4A Thespidos, tel: 322 5460. A very old establishment noted for its wild game.

Mets/Pangrati area:
Manesis, 3 Markou Moussourou, Mets, tel: 922 7684. Stews and special dishes from the Ionian islands. Evenings only with a garden in the summertime.
O Mandis, 68 Evgeniou Voulgareos, just off Moussourou, Mets. Elegant fare, can be expensive unless you stick to *mezes*. Similar to Manesis in many respects.
Ta Pergoulia, 16 Markou Moussourou, Mets. The most elaborate of the trio of reasonable Mets tavernas.
Myrtia, 35 Markou Moussourou, Mets, tel: 701 2276. Famous local landmark dishing up Greek fare and guitar music
Vellis, Platia Varnava, corner of Stilponos, Pangrati. Old-fashioned, cheap wine-with-oven-baked-food establishment

in a 1920s building. Pavement seating in summer; open for dinner only.

To Kalivi, 39 Proklou, just above Varnava, Pangrati, tel: 752 0641. Excellent, inexpensive *mezes* taverna in an old house. Also open on Sundays.

O Megaritis, 2 Ferekidou, corner of Aratou, Pangrati. More elaborate and expensive than Vellis, but similar type of fare.

O Ilias, corner of Stasinou and Telesilis, near the Truman statue, Pangrati. In an ancient building dwarfed by a ridiculously high chimney built to carry away cooking smoke. O Ilias is cheap and popular, with outdoor seating in the summer.

O Dhiasmos, 16 Grig. Theologo, far eastern edge of Pangrati. Barrel wine and home cooking.

Kolonaki area:

Gerofinikas, 10 Pindarou, tel: 983 9093. Down a long corridor which looks as if it's leading nowhere lies this well-established Athens restaurant, popular with businessmen and visitors alike. Featuring wonderful desserts Gerofinikas specialises in Constantinople/Greek dishes which cannot be found elsewhere in Athens. Bring your credit card.

Vladimiros, 12 Aristodimou St, tel: 721 7407. Continental specialties on the way up to the téléferique on Mt. Likavitós. Garden in summer.

Thekaokto (18), 51 Souidias, tel: 723 5561. Intimate continental atmosphere and bar.

Baltazar, 27 Tsoha and Vournazou Sts, tel: 644 1215. A modern, very trendy place for Greek cultural yuppies. Features a long, see-everyone-who-is-anyone bar in the garden.

I Rouga, 7 Kapsali (side alley). Small, moderately priced taverna. Open only in the evenings in winter.

Kostas, 64 Athineon Efivon, tel: 722 1489. Red mullet and other fresh fish plus luncheon specialties.

O Vrahos, 8 Likavitou. Dirt cheap, weekday lunchtimes only. Taverna run by a friendly old couple.

Dimokritos, 23 Dimokritos, corner of Tsakalof. Moderately priced *mezes* taverna open for both lunch and dinner. Closed in late summer, however.

Exarhia area:

Bagasakos, 67 Killidromiou. Moderately-priced taverna, neighbourhood clientele, very rich entrées. Closed Sundays.

Hlorofili, 12 Soultani, near corner of Solomou. As a change from Greek food, try this elegant vegetarian restaurant (dinner only) which also has a health food shop attached.

Seven Steps, 49 Arahovis. A newish bistro run by Greek-Americans catering to the homesick and/or the trendies by serving dishes like chilli con carne.

Kostoyannis, 37 Zaimi, tel: 821 2496. Famous (and quite pricey) taverna featuring game dishes and yummy desserts. Closed lunchtimes and Sundays.

Galatea, 50-52 Valtetsiou, tel: 360 1930. Serves the dishes you expect to find in a taverna but never do, like hummus and fried cheese. That's because it's Cypriot, not Greek.

Piraeus:

Eating in Piraeus is a popular activity with Athenians, who enjoy the change of scene and the cooling sea breezes. Perhaps the best of all restaurants in this area is Vasilenas at 72 Etolikou, tel: 461 2457. This family-run business hasn't changed since the 1920s, and has been the haunt of kings, movie stars, and Aristotle Onassis. Diners reserve space, arrive, and are served some 16 to 24 courses, all under the direction of George Vaslinas. Other good restaurants/tavernas are scattered throughout Piraeus' many harbours and hills. Here's a selection by area:

Piraiki:

This coastal area just before Zea Marina provides a good after-dinner stroll along the ancient "Long Walls". O Diasimos at 306 Akti Themistokleos, tel: 451 4887, features hanging plants and views of the sea. Excellent salads and seafood. The Piraiki, at 324 Akti Themistokleos, tel: 451 1231, is the place for fish, especially fresh squid or crayfish.

Zea Marina/Pasalimani:

The largest of Piraeus' yacht harbours is lined with restaurants and yacht supply shops. Go to Garth's, at 36 Akti Tr. Moutsopoulou, tel: 452 6420, or to the Landfall Club, 3 Makriyianni, tel: 452 5074 for seafood and Greek dishes.

Mikrolimano:

A charming crescent-shaped harbour where one can dine right at the water's edge and admire the colourful fishing boats. There are at least 22 restaurants in this little cove. All menus are fairly similar so walk along the row and see which restaurant (or which waiter) appeals. Some restaurants of interest include Zorba's at 14 Akti Koumoundourou; Mykonos at No. 20 on the same street; and the Psaropoulou next door at No. 22. Nearby at 23 Nafarhou Votsi (also spelled Navarxou Botsi) is the Kuyu-Kaplanis, tel: 411 1623 which offers fresh fish and can be topped off by heavenly chocolate soufflé.

Kastella:

The hill above Mikrolimano has a spectacular view of the Saronic Gulf and islands. Good restaurants include the Panorama, at 18 Irakliou, tel: 417 3475 across from the Veakio Theatre, and Patiniotis at 7 Pythagora, tel: 412 6713 for fresh fish and seafood. Ziller's at 1 Akti Koundouriotou, tel: 411 2013 is nicely decorated and offers a full menu. The view is superb: it overlooks the sea at Votsalakia beach.

THE GREEK EXPERIENCE

Some culinary activities are truly Greek. Sipping *patsas* (a soup made from beef hooves and intestines) is one of them. Although it sounds unpalatable, *patsas* is, in fact, the perfect cure for hangovers. As a result Monastiri, inside the central meat market off Athinas Street near Monastiraki, is open at any hour, and is packed with the high, the mighty, and the lowly. Ask the way.

Ouzeries are another local tradition. Apotsos, inside the arcade at 10 Panepistimou is a legend. Founded in 1900, Apotsos serves both hot and cold *mezes*, plus beer and wine. The atmosphere is hard to beat.

Coffee houses in Athens are justifiably well-known. The most popular is probably the Brazilian Coffee Stores at 1 Voukourestiou. A stand-up affair, the coffee is good and the pastries fresh. The Café de Brazil, inside the arcade cutting through to Stadiou from Kar. Servias, is a favourite place for illicit lovers. For a view of the Acropolis along with your coffee, try Orea Ellada (Beautiful Greece), a gem of a café. It resides upstairs off the stoa/arcade which houses the Center of Hellenic Tradition.

THINGS TO DO

CRUISES

Apparently one in six of all visitors to Greece embarks on an Aegean cruise. Cruises can range from one-day trips to the Saronic Gulf islands, to 21-day packages on a "floating hotel" departing from Piraeus and taking in Gibraltar, Morocco, and Barbados. Many people elect for a seven-day excursion, which offers an opportunity to see a couple of islands in the Cyclades, a few Dodecanese islands, and a stop-over in Turkey or Morocco for good measure. Accommodation, prices and standards vary widely and it might be an idea to shop around. Ticket agencies in Athens are the places to visit, with cruise opportunities prominently displayed in windows. (However, if you have ever been at Mykonos harbour when the ships arrive, and watched the frantic preparations of shop managers adjusting their prices upwards, it may change your mind about a cruise entirely.) Sun Line are one of the most comprehensive companies and are accustomed to dealing with foreigners. Their rates are advertised in dollars, beginning at $460 for a three-day trip, or $1165 for a seven-day cruise, excluding taxes. Details can be found from any travel agent or by contacting Sun Line's headquarters at 3 Iasonos St, Piraeus, tel: 452 3417.

A more casual atmosphere can be found aboard the boats used by Viking Tours, a long-established company with a fine reputation. Only 36 passengers can be carried in Viking's 118-foot ships, so the feeling is more like travelling on a private yacht than being aboard a mammoth ship.

For more information contact Viking at 3 Filellinon St, in Athens. Rates begin at around $850.

EXCURSIONS

Day-trips to Delphi, Epidavros, Nafplio and the Saronic Gulf islands are popular excursions from Athens. The day can be a long one, however, beginning at 7:30 a.m. and concluding around 6 p.m. Agencies near Syntagma can offer guidance and tickets, but here's a tip: don't book for lunch, which is always offered as an optional extra. The lunch is expensive and unspectacular; usually the coach stops in a town where there is a choice of restaurants anyway. This does not apply to the islands excursion, however; passengers on cruise ships are virtual prisoners, and lunch offers a welcome respite from the long voyage.

SOUND & LIGHT SPECTACLES

Throughout the summer, Athens offers "sound and light" shows projected onto the Acropolis. These performances are perfect for children, and the lights are exciting to watch from a nearby terrace-top. The words, however, are dire. Try attending a performance in a language other than your own.
Acropolis Sound and Light: 9 p.m. (English); 10:15 p.m. (French–except for Tuesdays and Fridays); 10 p.m. (German–Tuesday and Fridays only). Tickets 500 drachmas, students 200 drachmas, available at the Pnyka before the show. For information, tel: 332 1459.

TOUR GUIDES

A tour guide is a good idea for anyone who wants to study Athens in detail, who has no transport, or who enjoys the idea of spending several hours in close proximity with a local. Whether all the "facts" are actually true remains anyone's guess, but an entertaining companion can be worth the price. Guides generally hire themselves out by the half day, full day or even week; enquire with the Tourist Police or ask around at various ticket agencies. Many people tout for business; some are official guides and some are not. Be sure to negotiate everything in advance, including petrol and lunch.

CULTURE PLUS

MUSEUMS

Museums and archaeological sites permit the taking of photos if a portable camera is used. Foreign students are allowed into most sites for half price on production of their student cards. If an archaeological site is particularly crowded, try walking around it backwards, against the crowds. All opening hours are subject to change without notice, and most island attractions are closed on Mondays and most afternoons. Always check before setting out.

Opening hours–Athens:
The Acropolis, tel: 321 0219. Open daily 8 a.m. to 5 p.m. Saturdays, Sundays & holidays 8:30 a.m. to 3 p.m. Entrance fee: 600 drachmas (including fee to the museum).
Acropolis Museum, on the Acropolis, tel: 323 6665. Open daily (except Mondays) 8 a.m. to 5 p.m. Saturdays, Sundays & holidays 8:30 a.m. to 3 p.m. Mondays 11 a.m. to 5 p.m. Entrance fee: 600 drachmas (including fee to archaeological site).
Ancient Agora Museum in the Stoa of Attalos, entrance from Thission Sq. & 24 Andrianou Sts, tel: 321 0185. Open daily 8:30 a.m. to 3 p.m. Closed Mondays. Entrance fee: 400 drachmas (including fee to archaeological site).
Athens City Museum, 7 Paparigopoulou St, tel: 323 0168. Open Mondays, Wednesdays & Fridays 9 a.m. to 1:30 p.m. Entrance fee: 100 drachmas. Admission free on Wednesdays.
Benaki Museum, Vass. Sophias Ave, tel: 361 1617. Open daily 8:30 a.m. to 2 p.m. Closed Tuesdays. Entrance fee: 200 drachmas.
Byzantine Museum, 22 Vass. Sophias Ave, tel: 721 1027. Open daily 8:30 a.m. to 3 p.m. Closed Mondays. Entrance fee: 300

drachmas.

Cycladic Arts Museum, 4 Neof. Douka St, tel: 723 4931. Open daily 10 a.m. to 4 p.m., Saturdays 10 a.m. to 3 p.m. Closed Tuesdays & Sundays. Entrance fee: 150 drachmas.

Paul and Alexandra Canellopoulos Museum, Theorias and Panos Streets, Plaka area, tel: 321 2313. Open 8:45 a.m. to 3 p.m. Saturdays, Sundays & holidays 9:30 a.m. to 2:30 p.m. Closed Tuesdays.

Epigraphical Museum, 1 Tossitsa St, tel: 821 7637. Open daily 8:30 a.m. to 3 p.m. Closed Mondays. Admission free.

Centre of Folk Art and Tradition, 6 Angeliki Hatzimihali St, Plaka area, tel: 324 3987. Open Tuesdays & Thursdays 9 a.m. to 9 p.m., Wednesdays, Fridays, Saturdays 9 a.m. to 1 p.m. & 5 p.m. to 9 p.m., Sundays 9 a.m. to 1 p.m. Admission free.

Museum of Greek Popular Art, Plaka, tel: 321 3018. Open daily 10 a.m. to 2 p.m. Closed Mondays. Entrance fee: 200 drachmas.

Hellenic Theatre Museum & Studies Centre, 50 Akademias St, tel: 362 9430. Open daily exc. Saturdays, Sundays 9 a.m. to 3 p.m. Monday 5 p.m. to 8 p.m. Sundays 10 a.m. to 1 p.m. Entrance fee 150 drachmas.

Hist. and Ethnological Museum, Stadiou St, tel: 323 7617. Open Tuesdays to Fridays 9 a.m. to 2 p.m., Saturdays & Sundays 9 a.m. to 1 p.m. Closed Mondays. Entrance fee: 100 drachmas. Admission free on Thursdays.

Keramikos Museum, 148 Ermou St, tel: 346 3552. Open daily 8:30 a.m. to 3 p.m. Closed Mondays. Entrance fee: 200 drachmas (including fee to archaeological site).

Keramikos Cemetary, Ermou & Pireos corner, tel: 346 3552. Open daily 8:30 a.m. to 3 p.m. Closed Mondays. Entrance fee: 200 drachmas (including fee to museum).

Jewish Museum of Greece, 36 Leof. Amalias. Open daily 9 a.m. to 1 p.m. Closed Saturdays.

National Archaeological Museum, 1 Tossitsa St, tel: 821 7717. Open daily 8 a.m. to 5 p.m., Saturdays, Sundays & holidays 8:30 a.m. to 3 p.m., Mondays 11 a.m. to 5 p.m. Entrance fee: 500 drachmas (including fee to the exhibits from Santorini & the Numismatic Museum).

National Gallery and Alexandros Soutsos Museum, 46 Vass. Sophias Ave, tel: 721 1010. Open daily 9 a.m. to 3 p.m., Sundays

& holidays 10 a.m. to 2 p.m. Closed Mondays. Entrance fee: 30 drachmas.

Goulandris National History Museum, 13 Levidou St, Kifissia, tel: 808 0254. Open daily 9 a.m. to 1 p.m. & 5 p.m. to 8 p.m. Closed on Fridays. Sundays & holidays an entrance fee is charged. Entrance fee: 100 drachmas.

Numismatic Museum, 1 Tossitsa St, tel: 821 7769. Open daily 8:30 a.m. to 1:30 p.m., Sundays & holidays 9 a.m. to 2 p.m. Closed Mondays. Admission free.

Roman Agora, end of Eolou St, tel: 321 0185. Open daily 8:30 a.m. to 3 p.m. Closed Mondays. Entrance fee: 200 drachmas.

Temple of Hephaistos and Ancient Agora, tel: 321 0185. Open daily 8:30 a.m. to 3 p.m. Closed Mondays. Entrance fee: 400 drachmas.

Temple of Olympian Zeus, Olgas and Amalias Ave, tel: 922 6330. Open daily 8:30 a.m. to 3 p.m. Closed Mondays. Entrance fee: 200 drachmas.

Temple of Dionyssos, D. Areopagitou Ave, tel: 323 6665. Open daily 8:30 a.m. to 3 p.m. Closed Mondays. Entrance fee: 200 drachmas.

War Museum of Greece, Vass. Sophias Ave, tel: 729 0543. Open daily 9 a.m. to 2 p.m. Closed Mondays.

Piraeus:

Maritime Museum of Piraeus, Akti Themistokieous, tel: 451 6822. Open daily 9 a.m. to 12:30 p.m., Sundays & holidays 10 a.m. to 1 p.m. & 5 p.m. to 8 p.m. Closed Mondays, Tuesdays & Fridays. Admission free.

Piraeus Archaeological Museum, 31 Char. Trikoupi St, tel: 452 1598. Open daily 8:30 a.m. to 3 p.m. Closed Mondays. Entrance fee: 200 drachmas.

SITES NEAR ATHENS

Corinth Archaeological Site and Museum, tel: 0741 31207. Open daily 8:00 a.m. to 5 p.m. Saturdays, Sundays & holidays 8:30 a.m. to 3 p.m. Museum open Mondays 11 a.m. to 5 p.m. Entrance fee: 400 drachmas inclusive.

Daphni Monastery, tel: 581 1558. Open daily 8:30 a.m. to 3 p.m. Closed Mondays. Entrance fee: 200 drachmas.

Delphi Archeological Site and Museum,

tel: 0265 82313. Open daily 8 a.m. to 5 p.m., Saturdays, Sundays and holidays 8:30 a.m. to 3 p.m. Entrance fee: 400 drachmas. Museum also open Mondays 11 a.m. to 5 p.m. Entrance fee: 400 drachmas.

Epidavros Archaeological Site and Museum, tel: 0753 22009. Open daily 8 a.m. to 5 p.m. Saturdays, Sundays & holidays 8:30 a.m. to 3 p.m. Museum open Mondays 11 a.m. to 5 p.m. Archaeological site closed Mondays. Entrance fee: 500 drachmas.

Eléusis Museum, tel: 554 6019. Open daily 8:30 a.m. to 3 p.m. Closed Mondays. Entrance fee: 200 drachmas (including fee to archaeological site).

Kaisariani Monastery, tel: 723 6619. Open daily 8:30 a.m. to 3 p.m. Closed Mondays. Admission free.

Nafplion Museum, tel: 0752 27502. Open daily 8:30 a.m. to 3 p.m. Closed Mondays. Entrance fee: 200 drachmas.

Nafplion Palamidi Fortress, tel: 0752 28036. Open daily 8 a.m. to 5 p.m. Saturdays, Sundays & holidays 8:30 a.m. to 3 p.m. Entrance fee: 200 drachmas.

Nafplion Popular Art Museum, tel: 0752 28379. Open daily 9:00 a.m. to 7 p.m. Closed on Mondays. Entrance free.

THE ISLANDS

The Ionian Islands:
Corfu
Archaeological Museum, tel: (0661) 30680. Open daily 8:30 a.m. to 3 p.m. Closed Mondays. Entrance fee: 200 drachmas.

Museum of Asiatic Art, tel: (0661) 23124. Open daily 8:30 a.m. to 3 p.m. Closed Mondays. Entrance fee: 400 drachmas.

Saronic Gulf Islands:
Aegina
Temple of Aphaía, tel: (0297) 32398. Open daily 8 a.m. to 5 p.m., Saturdays, Sundays and holidays 8:30 a.m. to 3 p.m. Entrance fee: 300 drachmas.

Island Museum, tel: (0297)22637. Open daily 8:30 a.m. to 3 p.m. Closed Mondays. Entrance fee: 200 drachmas (including fee to the Temple of Apollo).

Cyclades Islands:
Andros
Archaeological Museum, tel: (0282) 23664. Open daily 8:30 a.m. to 3 p.m. Closed Mondays. Entrance fee: 200 drachmas.

Museum Basil & Elisa Goulandris (Modern Art) tel: (0282) 22650. Open daily 10 a.m. to 1 p.m and 5 p.m. to 8 p.m. Closed Mondays. Admission free.

Delos
Archaeological Site, tel: (0289) 22259. Open daily 8:30 a.m. to 3 p.m. Closed Mondays. Entrance fee: 500 drachmas (including fee to museum).

Island Museum, tel: (0289) 22259. Open daily 8:30 a.m. to 3 p.m. Closed Mondays. Entrance fee: 500 drachmas (including fee to archaeological site).

Milos
Archaeological Site & Museum, tel: (0287) 21620. Open daily 8:30 a.m. to 3 p.m. Closed Mondays. Entrance fee: 200 drachmas.

The Catacombs, tel: (0287) 21620. Open daily exc. Wednesdays & Sundays 9 a.m. to 2:30 p.m. Entrance fee: 200 drachmas.

Santorini (Thira)
Akrotirion Thiras Archaeological Site, tel: (0286) 81366. Open daily 8:30 a.m. to 3 p.m. Closed Mondays. Entrance fee: 500 drachmas.

Archeological Site, tel: (0286) 22217. Open daily 8:30 a.m. to 3 p.m. Closed Mondays. Admission free.

Island Museum, tel: (0286) 22217. Open daily 8:30 a.m. to 3 p.m. Closed Mondays. Entrance fee: 200 drachmas.

Northeast Aegean Islands:
Samothraki
Archaeolgical Site, tel: (0551) 41474. Open daily 8:30 a.m. to 3 p.m. Closed Mondays. Entrance fee: 200 drachmas.

Island Museum, tel: (0551) 41474 Open daily 8:30 a.m. to 3 p.m. Closed Mondays. Entrance fee: 200 drachmas.

Dodecanese Islands:
Kos
Asclepieion and other Archeological Sites, tel: (0242) 28763. Open daily 8:30 a.m. to 3 p.m. Closed Mondays. Entrance fee: 300 drachmas.

Island Museum, tel: (0242) 28326. Open

daily 8:30 a.m. to 3 p.m. Closed Mondays. Entrance fee: 200 drachmas.

Kos Castle, tel: (0242) 28326. Open daily 8:30 a.m. to 3 p.m. Closed Mondays. Entrance fee: 200 drachmas.

Restored Ancient Dwelling, tel: (0242) 28326. Open daily 8:30 a.m. to 3 p.m. Closed Mondays. Entrance fee: 200 drachmas.

Lesvos

Eressos Archaeological Museum, tel: (0251) 22087. Open daily 8:30 a.m. to 3 p.m. Closed Mondays. Admission free.

Mytilini Archaeological Museum, tel: (0251) 22087. Open Wednesday & Thursday 3 p.m. to 5 p.m. Saturdays & Sundays 9 a.m. to 6 p.m. Entrance fee: 200 drachmas.

Theofilos Art Museum, tel: (0251) 28179. Open daily 9 a.m. to 1 p.m. & 4:30 p.m. to 8 p.m. Closed Mondays. Entrance fee: 30 drachmas.

Patmos

Island churches and other monuments, admission free.

Monastery of St. John and Library, Vestry, tel: (0241) 21954. Open daily 8:30 a.m. to 3 p.m. Closed Mondays. Admission free.

Rhodes

Acropolis, Theatre and Stadium, tel: (0241) 21954. Open daily 8:30 a.m. to 3 p.m. Closed Mondays. Admission free.

Acropolis of Ialyssos, tel: (0241) 21954. Open daily 8:30 a.m. to 3 p.m. Closed Mondays. Entrance fee: 200 drachmas.

Acropolis of Lindos, tel: (0241) 21954. Open daily 8:30 a.m. to 3 p.m. Closed Mondays. Entrance fee: 400 drachmas.

Decorative Collections, tel: (0241) 21954. Open daily 8:30 a.m. to 3 p.m. Closed Mondays. Admission free.

Island Museum, tel: (0241) 21954. Open daily 8:30 a.m. to 3 p.m. Closed Mondays. Entrance fee: 300 drachmas.

Kamiros Archaeological Site, tel: (0241) 21954. Open daily 8:30 a.m. to 3 p.m. Closed Mondays. Entrance fee: 200 drachmas.

Palace of the Knights, tel: (0241) 21954. Open daily 8:30 a.m. to 3 p.m. Closed Mondays. Entrance fee: 300 drachmas.

Perimeter of the Medieval Walls, tel:

(0241) 21954. Open to visitors accompanied by a guide on Tuesdays & Saturdays from 3 p.m. to 5 p.m. Visitors should gather in the courtyard of the Palace of the Knights. Entrance fee: 200 drachmas.

Crete

Ag. Nikolaos Museum, tel: (0841) 22462. Open daily 8:30 a.m. to 3 p.m. Closed Mondays. Entrance fee: 200 drachmas.

Aghia Trias Archaeological Site: tel: (081) 226092. Open daily 8:30 a.m. to 3 p.m. Closed Mondays. Entrance fee: 200 drachmas.

Gortys Archaeological Site, tel: (081) 226092. Open daily 8 a.m. to 5 p.m. Saturdays, Sundays & holidays 8:30 a.m. to 3 p.m. Entrance fee: 200 drachmas.

Hania Museum, tel: (0821) 20334. Open daily 8:30 a.m. to 5 p.m., Sundays & holidays 8:30 a.m. to 3 p.m., Mondays 11 a.m. to 5 p.m. Entrance fee: 300 drachmas.

Iraklion Archaeological Museum, tel: (081) 226092. Open daily 8 a.m. to 5 p.m., Saturday, Sundays & holidays 8:30 a.m. to 3 p.m., Mondays 11 a.m. to 5 p.m. Entrance fee: 500 drachmas.

Iraklion Harbour Fortress (Koules), tel: (081) 286228. Open daily 8:30 a.m. to 3 p.m. Closed Mondays. Entrance fee: 200 drachmas.

Knossos Archaeological Site, tel: (081) 231940. Open daily 8 a.m. to 5 p.m., Saturdays, Sundays & holidays 8:30 a.m. to 3 p.m. Entrance fee: 500 drachmas.

Mallia Archaeological Site, tel: (0841) 22462. Open daily 8:30 a.m. to 3 p.m. Closed Mondays. Entrance fee: 200 drachmas.

Phaestos (Festos) Archaeological Site, tel: (0892) 22615. Open daily 8 a.m. to 5 p.m., Saturdays, Sundays & holidays 8:30 a.m. to 3 p.m. Entrance fee: 300 drachmas.

Rethymnon Museum, tel: (0831) 29975. Open daily 8:30 a.m. to 3 p.m. Closed Mondays. Entrance fee: 200 drachmas.

Tylissos Archaeological Site, tel: (081) 226092. Open daily 8:30 a.m. to 3 p.m. Closed Mondays. Entrance fee: 200 drachmas.

Zakros Archaeological Site, tel: (0841) 22462. Open daily 8:30 a.m. to 3 p.m. Closed Mondays. Entrance fee: 300 drachmas.

Other Archaeological Sites (St. Titus,

Gournia), tel: (081) 226092. Open daily 8:30 a.m. to 3 p.m. Closed Mondays. Admission free.

NIGHTLIFE

REMBETIKA CLUBS

After the fall of the junta, live as well as recorded *rembetika* (Greek blues) music enjoyed a revival in Athens. The first, and still extant club, was Marabout, which was closed by the police and reopened in its present position at 113 Panormou, Ambelokipi in 1980. (Rumour has it that the club is to close again.) The fashion peaked in 1981–82, when over a dozen clubs enlivened the music scene, many around the Exarhia area. *Rembetika* can still be heard in a relatively intimate setting in Athens, but venues do open and close with regularity.

Always call first to check and to make reservations (essential on weekends; tables usually seat four people). Most performances start late–don't bother arriving before 10:30 p.m–and things really liven up after midnight. There's generally a 1 a.m. interval which is the polite time to change clubs if you wish. Such an outing although fun, can be quite expensive, with your wallet at least 3,000 drachmas lighter after two sets.

These are the best-known rembetika clubs:

Frangosyriani, 57 Arahovis, Exarhia, tel: 360 0693. Closed Thursdays. The band's emphasis (good female vocalist, 1950s instrumentation of *bouzouki, baglama,* accordian) is on Bellow/Tsitsanis material, with a dash of Vamvakaris and earlier composers, but the delivery is uneven. No food, and drinks cost around 800-1,000 drachmas per head.

Taksimi, 29 Isavron off Harilaou Trikoupi, Exarhia, tel: 363 9919. Closed Wednesday. Crowded place on third floor of old house; no food, and the bar bill will run

700-1,200 drachmas a person minimum. Young bands relying on 1950s material, but with too much *laika* (light, trivial *rembetika*) thrown in to please purists. Still, an unpretentious crowd and people tend to have fun.

Rembetiki Istoria, 181 Ippokratous, Exarhia, tel: 642 4937. Closed Monday through Wednesday.

Minore, 34 Notara, near the Archaeological Museum, Exarhia, tel: 823 8630. Closed Monday and Tuesday.

Rembetiki Nichta, 102 Formionos, Pangrati, tel: 766 9903. Closed Wednesday.

Anifori, 47 Vass. Yeorgiou, Piraeus, tel: 411 5819. Listen to *rembetika* in the town where it first began.

OTHER MUSIC CLUBS

Here is a selection of Greek folk, jazz, and international music clubs. Though some, like the Half Note, are city fixtures, other come and go like mushrooms on a lawn, and the music programme is equally unpredictable. Music clubs tend to be more expensive than the *rembetika* places–count on 4,000 drachmas to get in and out of the door. If you can read Greek, buy a copy of the weekly listings magazine *Athinorama* to make sure venues are still in business.

Half Note, corner of Nikiforou Duranou and Patriarhou Fotiou, Kolonaki, tel: 364 1841. Closed on Tuesdays. Name jazz acts at a club which recently moved here after many years in Ilissia.

Latin, 69 Kallidromiou, Exarhia, tel: 364 5978. New, innovative (for Greece) venue, with Peruvian folk, *salsa*, etc on different nights. Open all week.

Ravanastron, 60 Dimitsanas, Ambelokipi, tel: 644 9534. Recently opened venue for Greek and Turkish folk music on traditional instruments.

Esmeralda, 50 Kefallinias, Kipseli, just north of Areos Park, tel: 867 1290. Featuring *bouzouki* artist Babis Gkoles. Closed Tuesdays.

Paniyiri ton Trellon, 97 Evelpidon, Kipseli, next to Areos Park, tel: 884 3595. One of the longest-established food-and-music tavernas. Greek and island music. Closed Tuesdays and all summer.

Ambelofyllo, 3 Samothrakis at Karayanni, Kipseli, tel: 867 8862. Another durable music taverna. Closed Wednesday and from midsummer onward.

GREEK FOLK DANCES

The renowned Dora Stratou Group perform at the Filopappou Theatre every summer night at 10:25 p.m. On Wednesdays and Sundays there is an extra performance at 8:15 p.m. Tickets are 950, 850 or 750 drachmas each. Information may be obtained by calling 324 4395.

OUTDOOR MOVIES

One of the delights of an Athenian evening is to sit under a starry sky and enjoy an outdoor movie. Like an American drive-in without the cars, Greece's outdoor cinemas do not attempt to compete with mainstream movie houses, screening instead old favourites, Westerns, Hollywood war movies and films you've never heard of. Usually in English with Greek sub-titles, the noise in the theatre (Greeks talk through screenings) often makes the movie dialogue incomprehensible but doesn't spoil the evening a bit. Take snacks, a jacket and wear lots of anti-mosquito spray. Addresses can be found in the English-language newspaper *Athens News*.

SHOPPING

WHAT TO BUY

Most tourist tat is instantly forgettable. Much better to concentrate on small local items like sponges from Kalymnos, leather bags from Rhodes, hand-made pottery from Sifnos, and extremely attractive silver jewellery from a number of islands. Much of this jewellery is made by local craftsmen, and styles range from the traditional to the fashionable. All of these island crafts can be bought in the shops and stalls around Monastiraki in Athens.

Other good buys include baskets, copper pots and other copperware, honey, olive oil, and the ubiquitous *loukoúmia,* (Turkish Delight). Wool sweaters from the mountains are remarkably good value, as are fur coats. Prices can be fully two-thirds less than the cost of the same item if bought in Europe or the USA.

Bargaining is expected in marketplaces and stalls. In these places, even if an item has a price tag, try offering a lower price. Even better, show interest and then walk away. (You can always return if the ploy doesn't work.) Bargaining is unacceptable in deparment stores, chain stores and most boutiques.

Department stores implement a complicated service system not recommended for anyone in a hurry. If you happen to go to a large stationers to purchase a notebook, a pencil, a couple of envelopes and perhaps a birthday card, you could find yourself standing in six different queues: one for each department (where an assistant writes a receipt for each item), one to pay the cashier the total amount, and one for delivery of the goods. If you're lucky, all four items will have arrived from their various departments (only a few steps from each other) at the delivery desk, wrapped or placed into four separate bags with four separate receipts taped on top.

PERIPTERA (KIOSKS)

Open days, nights, holidays and Sundays, life in Greece would be unmanageable without a neighbourhood *periptera*. Although they may appear limited by their diminutive structures, kiosks are really multi-purpose powerhouses. Besides filling the function of newsagent/tobacconist, these businesses, many family-run, also double as mini amusement parks with kiddie rides, or sporting goods stores, iron-mongers or locksmiths. For many customers with problems, the proprietor may dispense psychiatric or medical advice. Here, too, is a quick place to buy tourist requisites: shampoo, nail clippers, postcards.

There are over 3,000 kiosks in Athens alone. It is not unusual for a *periptera* to work shifts of 12 hours in conditions which vary from furnace-like in summer to chill and damp in winter. The kiosks started as gifts from the government to wounded veterans of the Balkan and First World Wars. Many people remark on the similarity between the architecture of kiosks and that of military guardposts such as those used by the honour guard in front of Parliament on Syntagma Square. In a symbolic way the *periptera* also serve as guard houses where old soldiers prolong their duty, emerging from the military into the commercial sector, watching over and serving the community.

SPORTS

Greece's sports tend to revolve around water. There are only four golf courses in the entire country. In Athens, the course at Glyfada (tel: 894 6875) charges 3,000 drachmas or 2,000 before 11 a.m. during the week. Weekends and holidays the charge is 5,000 drachmas or 18,000 for the week.

Many beaches offer a range of water sport facilities, from surf boards to water bikes. The Greek Windsurfing Federation can be contacted by calling 413 7351. The Greek Water Skiing Federation is on 523 1875. Telephone numbers for NTOG beaches within striking distance of Athens include:

Alimos – tel: 982 7064
1st Voula – tel: 895 3248
2nd Voula – tel: 895 9569
Vouliagmeni – tel: 896 0906
Varkiza – tel: 897 2102
Porto Rafti – tel: 0299 72572

City buses to Athens' beaches:
West Coast
Glyfada – Nos. 121, 128, 129 from Vass. Olgas Ave, Zappeion.
Voula – No. 122 from Vass. Olgas Ave, Zappeion.
Vouliagmeni – Nos. 118, 153 from Vass. Olgas, Zappeion.
Varkiza – Nos. 115, 116, 117 from Vass.

Olgas, Zappeion.
Sounion – (orange bus) No. 14 from Mavromateon St, Areos Park.

East Coast
Nea Makri-Skinias-Marathonas-Oropos – (orange bus) No. 29 from Mavromateon St, Areos Park.

YACHTS

The NTOG publishes an excellent booklet called *Sailing the Greek Seas*. Included is information on weather, coastal radio telephone stations, entry and exit regulations. The pamphlet is particularly detailed on marinas, bunkering ports and supply stations. There are four marinas within striking distance of Athens. Information on services or facilities may be obtained by calling:
Vouliagmeni marina – tel: 896 0012
Zea marina – tel: 451 3944
Alimos – tel: 982 8642
Flisvos – tel: 982 8537
If you prefer to charter a yacht, the NTOG can provide lists of yacht brokers and consultants. All charter agreements have to be made in this manner and on the official form prescribed by the Greek government. The following organisations can also offer help and advice:
Greek Yacht Brokers & Consultants Association, 36 Alkyonis St, tel: 175 61.
P. Faliro, tel: 981 6582.
Greek Bareboat Yacht Owners Association, 56 Vass. Pavlou St, Kastela, Piraeus, tel: 452 5465.
Hellenic Professional Yacht Owners Association, 43 Freatidos St, Zea Marina, Piraeus, tel: 452 6335.

Here is a list of island ports where fuelling facilities and other provisions may be available:
Adamas (Milos); Aegina; Agios Nikolaos (Kea); Agios Nikolaos (Crete); Argostoli (Kefalonia); Corfu port; Ermoupoli (Syros); Hania (Crete); Hios; Hydra; Kalymnos; Kamares (Sifnos); Kapsali (Kythera); Kastelorizo; Kastro (Andros); Katapola (Amorgos); Kos; Lakki (Leros); Lefkas; Linaria (Skyros); Mirina (Limnos); Mytilini (Lesvos); Mykonos; Naxos; Parikia (Paros); Pigadia (Karpathos); Poros; Mandraki (Rhodes); Skala (Patmos); Skiathos;

Skopeos; Spetses; Tinos; Vathi (Ithaki); Zakynthos.

LANGUAGE

USEFUL WORDS & PHRASES

yes – *né*
no – *ókhi*
okay – *en dáksi*
thank you – *efharistó*
(very much) – *para polí*
excuse me – *signómi*
it doesn't matter – *dhen pirázi*
it's nothing – *típota*
certainly – *málista*
good day – *káli méra*
good evening – *káli spéra*
good night – *káli níhta*
goodbye – *addio*
Greetings! – *yá sou, yá sas* (plural or formal)
"health to you!" (a toast) – *yá sou, yá sas* (plural)
bon voyage – *kaló taksídhi*
welcome – *kalós ilthathe*
good luck – *kalí tihi*
How are you? – *ti kánis, ti kánete* (plural or formal)
fine (in response) – *kalá*
so so (in response) – *étsi kétsi*
pleased to meet you – *hárika*
Have you...? – *éhete...?*
Is there...? – *éhi...?*
How much does it cost? – *póso káni?*
It's (too) expensive – *íne (polí) akrivó*
How much? – *póso?*
How many? – *pósa?*
Do you have a room? – *éhete éna domátio?*
Can I...? – *boro na...?*
When? – *póte?*
Where is...? – *póu ine...?*
Do you speak English? – *milás/miláte angliká?* (singular/plural or formal)
Do you understand? – *katálaves?*
What time is it? – *ti ora íne?*
What time will it leave? – *ti ora tha figi?*

I don't – *dhen* (plus verb)
I want – *thélo*
I have – *ého*
today – *simera*
tomorrow – *avrio*
now – *tóra*
here/there – *edho/eki*
near/far – *konda/makria*
small/large – *mikro/megalo*
quickly – *grigora*
slowly – *argá*
good/bad – *kaló/kakó*
warm/cold – *zestó/krio*
shower with hot water – *douz me zestó nero*
hotel – *ksenodhohio*
bed – *kreváti*
key – *klidhi*
entrance – *isodhos*
exit – *eksodhos*
toilet – *touleta*
women's – *ginekón*
men's – *adrón*
store – *magazi*
kiosk – *periptero*
open/shut – *aniktos/klistós*
post office – *tahidromio*
stamp – *grammatósima*
letter – *gramma*
envelope – *falelos*
telephone – *tilefono*
bank – *trapeza*
marketplace – *agora*
pharmacy – *farmakío*
doctor – *yatros*
hospital – *nosokomío*
police – *astinomía*
station – *stathmós*
boat – *karávi, vapóri*
bike/moped – *podílato/motopodílato*
on foot – *me ta pódhia*
ticket – *isitirio*
road/street – *dhromos/odhos*
beach – *paralía*
church – *eklisia*
ancient ruins – *arhéa*
centre – *kentro*
square – *platia*
sea – *thálassa*

NUMBERS

one – *énna*
two – *dio*
three – *tria/tris*
four – *téssera*

five – *pendhe*
six – *éksi*
seven – *eptá*
eight – *oehtó*
nine – *ennea*
10 – *deka*
11 – *éndeka*
12 – *dódeka*
13 – *dekatria*
14 – *dekatessera*
etc, until 20 –
20 – *ikosi*
21 – *ikosi énna*
30 – *triánda*
40 – *saránda*
50 – *peninda*
60 – *eksinda*
70 – *evdhominda*
80 – *ogdhonda*
90 – *enneninda*
100 – *ekató*
150 – *ekatopeninda*
200 – *diakóssia*
300 – *triakóssia*
400 – *tetrakóssia*
1,000 – *hília*

DAYS OF THE WEEK

Monday – *deftéra*
Tuesday – *tríti*
Wednesday – *tetárti*
Thursday – *pémpti*
Friday – *paraskeví*
Saturday – *sávato*
Sunday – *kiriakí*

UNTRANSLATED WORDS

kéfi – to be in good spirits, having a good time with your *paréa*
paréa – one's group of close friends, your "gang"
kaimós – the opposite of *kéfi*, one's long-suffering or sadness
palikári – a good fellow (honourable, brave, intelligent, etc)
filótimo – adjective meaning literally "love of honour"
mángas – a "toughie," a "cool dude", macho
re – short for *moré*, meaning baby, kid, dummy; a word thrown in when addressing a buddy in the typically male Greek rough-affectionate manner

malákas – literally "masturbator"; often combined with *re (re malákas);* can be directed to one's friends affectionately or to others more antagonistically
paidhia – "the boys", fellows, guys
alítis – a bum, roughly the opposite of *palikári*
lipón – well, so, now then
ella! – Come! Come on!
oríste(?) – Can I help you?
po po po! – Well well! What have we here!
ópa – Look out! Also, at a music taverna for instance, "way to go!" "all right!" etc.

LANGUAGE OF GESTURES

Greek is a gestural language; you don't speak it with your hands in your pockets or with your head still. The body and its movements are signs which form an integral part of the communications process. You can learn this aspect of Greek only through close observation. Two of the most common of these gestures are those indicating "yes" and "no". "No" is often communicated by jerking the head and chin up and back sharply. This is a very slight movement, but emphatic. Sometimes, in fact, only the eyebrows or eyes make this upward gesture. The gesture indicating "yes" is a rather gentler one, a slow downward angling of the head.

FURTHER READING

HISTORY

The Living Past of Greece, by A.R. and Mary Burn, Penguin, 1982.
Byzantine Athens, by Manolis Hatzidakis, M. Pechlivanides & Co., Athens.
Greek Vases, by Dyfri Williams, British Museum Publications, London, 1986.
Medieval Greece, by Nicholas Cheetham, New Haven, 1981.
Italy's Aegean Possessions, by C.D. and I.B. Booth, London, 1928.

The Ancient Greeks, by M.I. Finley, Harmondsworth/Penguin, 1963.

Mythology, by Edith Hamilton, New American Library, New York, 1969.

Greek and Roman Life, Ian Jenkins, British Museum Publications, London, 1987.

The Elgin Marbles, B.F. Cook, British Museum Publications, London, 1986.

Athens-Auschwitz, by Errikos Sevillias, Lycabettus Press, Athens.

The Greek Dances: Our Living Link with Antiquity, by Dora Stratou, translated by Amy Mims-Argyrakis, Athens, 1966.

The Meridian Handbook of Classical Mythology by Edward Tripp, New American Library, Times Mirror, Ontario.

A History of Greece by J. B. Bury & Russell Meighs, Macmillan Press, London.

Greek Inscriptions, by B.F. Cook, British Museum Publications, London 1987.

The Olympic Games in Ancient Greece, general supervision by N. Yalouris, General Inspector of Antiquities, Ekdotike Athenon S.A., Athens.

TRAVEL BOOKS & GUIDES

Early Greek Travellers and the Hellenic Idea, by David Constantine, CUP, Cambridge, 1984.

Monastiraki: Athens' Old Market, translated by Kevin Andrews, Oceanida, Athens, 1985.

Plaka, by Liza Micheli, Panorama, Athens, 1988. (Not translated).

Nauplion, by Timothy E. Gregory, Lycabettus Press, Athens.

Greece on Foot, by Marc Dubin, Cordee, Leicester/London,1986.

Old and New Athens, by Demetrios Sicilianos, translated by Robert Liddell, Putnam, London, 1960.

Delphi, by Alan Walker, Lycabettus Press, Athens.

FOREIGN WRITERS

Prospero's Cell; Reflections on a Marine Venus; Bitter Lemons, all by Lawrence Durrell, Faber & Faber, London.

The Magus, by John Fowles, Cape, London, 1977.

Eleni, by Nicholas Gage, Collins, London, 1983.

The Flight of Ikaros, by Kevin Andrews, Harmondsworth/Penguin, 1984.

Athens (Cities of the World number 7) by Kevin Andrews, Phoenix House (J.M. Dent), London, 1967.

Athens Alive, by Kevin Andrews, Hermes, Athens, 1979.

The Other Side of the Road, by Elizabeth Herring, Lycabettus Press, Athens, 1988.

The Bananaless Republic, by Alec Kitroeff, The Athenian Press, Athens, 1988.

Hill of Kronos, by Peter Levi, Penguin, New York, 1984

The Last of the Wine, by Mary Renault, Sceptre, London, 1986.

The Colossus of Maroussi, by Henry Miller, New Directions, New York, 1958.

USEFUL ADDRESSES

TOURIST INFORMATION

National Tourist Organisation of Greece: International offices:

United Kingdom & Ireland – 195-197 Regent St, London W1R 8DL, tel: 734 5997

USA – 645 Fifth Avenue, Olympic Tower, New York, N.Y. 10022, tel: 421 5777; 611 West Sixth St, Los Angeles, California 90017, tel: 626 6696; 168 North Michigan Ave, Chicago, Illinois 60601, tel: 782 1084; Building 31, State St, Boston, Mass, tel: 227 7366

Canada – 1233 rue de la Montagne, Montreal QC, Quebec H3G 1Z2, tel: 871 1535; 80 Bloor St West, Suite 1403, Toronto ONT M5S 2V1, tel: 968 2220

Australia & New Zealand – 51-57 Pitt St, Sydney, N.S.W. 2000, tel: 241 1663

Germany – Neue Mainzerstr, 22,6 Frankfurt/Main 1, tel: 236 562; Pacellistr, 2,8000 Munchen 2, tel: 222 035; Neuer Wall, 35,2000 Hamburg 36, tel: 366 910

Austria – Karntner Ring 5,1015, Wien, tel: 525 317

Belgium – 62-66 Blv. de I'Imperatrice,

1000, Bruxelles, tel: 513 0206

Denmark – Vester Farimagsgade 3, DK 1606, Kopenhagen, tel: 1-123 063

Finland – Stora Robertsgatan 3-5 C38, 00120 Helsingfors 12, tel: 0-655 223

France – 3 Avenue de L'Opera, Paris 75001, tel: 260 6575

Italy – Via L. Bissolati 78-80, 00187, Roma, tel: 4744 301; Piazza Diaz 1, Ang. Via Rastrelli, Milano, tel: 860 470

Japan – 3-16-30 Nishi Azabu, Minato–Ku, Tokyo 106, tel: 4031 812

Netherlands – Leidsestraat 13, NS Amsterdam, tel: 2542 12

Norway – Ovre Slottsgatan 15B, Oslo 1, tel: 426 501

Saudia Arabia – Embassy of Greece, Madina Road, City Centre, P.O.B. 13262, Jeddah 21493, tel: 667 6240

Spain – Alberto Aguilera No 17, Madrid 28015, tel: 248 4889

Sweden – Grev Turegatan 2, Box 5298, 10246 Stockholm 5, tel: 203 802

Switzerland – Gottfried Kellerstr 7, CH 8001 Zurich, tel: 251 8487

IN GREECE

The 24-hour Tourist Police number in Athens is 171.

The Athens headquarters of the National Tourist Organisation of Greece is located at 2 Amerikis St, tel: 322 3111-19. Visiting hours are from 12 noon to 2:30 p.m. Monday to Friday. There is also an information desk at the East Air Terminal which is open during the day and displays ferryboat sailings even when closed. Most general literature (maps, hotel information, and so on) can be obtained from the two information bureaus located in Syntagma Square, which also post daily sailings of ferries from Piraeus.

During the peak tourist months these Syntagma bureaus are sometimes open longer hours:

Inside the General Bank of Greece, 1 Ermou St, tel: 325 2267-8. Open Monday to Friday 8 a.m. to 6 p.m., Saturday 9 a.m. to 1 p.m

Inside the National Bank of Greece, 2 Karageorgi Servias St, tel: 322 2545. Open Monday to Friday 8 a.m. to 2 p.m., then 3:30 p.m. to 8 p.m., Saturday 9 a.m. to 2 p.m

Piraeus - Marina Zeas, NTOG building, tel: 413 5716/4134709

EMBASSIES & CONSULATES

United Kingdom – 1 Ploutarhou St, Athens, tel: 723 6211

United States of America – 91 Vass. Sophias Ave, Athens, tel: 721 2951

Australia – 37 D. Soutsou St, Athens, tel: 644 7303

Canada – 4 I. Genadiou St, Athens, tel: 723 9511

New Zealand – 15-17 Tsoha St, Athens, tel: 641 0311

France – 7 Vass. Sophias Ave, Athens, tel: 729 0151-6

Germany – 10 Vass. Sophias, Maroussi, tel: 36941

Austria – 26 Alexandras Ave, Athens, tel: 821 1036

Belgium – 3 Sekeri St, Athens, tel: 361 7886

Cyprus – 16 Irodotou St, Athens, tel: 723 7883

Denmark – 15 Filikis Eterias Sq, Kolonaki, tel: 724 9315

Finland – 1 Eratosthonous St & Vass. Konstantinou Ave, Athens, tel: 751 5064

Hong Kong – 2 Vass. Alexandrou Ave, Athens, tel: 724 2666

India – 4 Meleagrou St, Athens, tel: 721 6227

Ireland – 7 Vass. Konstantinou Ave, Athens, tel: 723 2771

Israel – 1 Marathonodromon St, Paleo Psihiko, tel: 671 9530

Italy – 2 Sekeri St, Athens, tel: 361 1722

Japan – 2-4 Messogion Ave, Athens, tel: 775 8101

Luxembourg – 11 Stissihorou St, Athens, tel: 721 7948

Malta – 2 Efplias St, Piraeus, tel: 418 1501

Netherlands – 5-7 Vass. Konstantinou Ave, Athens, tel: 723 9701

Norway – 7 Vass. Konstantinou Ave, Athens, tel: 724 6173

Portugal – 44 Karneadou St, Athens, tel: 729 0096

Spain – 29 Vass. Sophias Ave, Athens, tel: 721 4885

Sweden – 7 Vass. Konstantinou Ave, Athens, tel: 729 0421

Switzerland – 2 Iassiou St, Athens, tel: 723 0364-6

Turkey – 8 Vass. Georgiou II St, Athens, tel: 724 5915

ART/PHOTO CREDITS

Ashmolean Museum	51
Athens National Museum	66
Benaki Museum	56, 57, 58, 72, 74, 75, 180
Benaki Museum, Photographic Archive	60, 61, 80, 81
British Museum	135
Brooke, Marcus	37R
Byzantine Museum	54, 55, 197
Couteau, Pierre	14/15, 16/17, 25, 26, 27, 36, 70, 78, 85, 90, 95, 100, 102, 107, 110, 112, 118/119, 120/121, 126, 127, 134, 137, 138/139, 140, 144, 145, 148, 156/157, 163, 168, 178/179, 187, 189, 200/201, 214, 215, 218, 219, 222, 224, 230/231
Decopoulos, John	34, 37L, 38, 39, 42, 44, 48, 49, 68, 136, 223, 225
Gennadios Library	59, 76
Hionos, Markos G.	18/19, 82/83, 96, 108, 111, 114, 116, 117, 147, 155, 171, 207, 208, 217, 228, 229
Macrakis, Michele	3, 28, 29, 47, 84, 91, 92, 101, 103, 106, 109, 115, 169, 196, 198, 205, 206, 213, 232
National Portrait Gallery	77
Princeton University Library	32/33
Stekovics, Janos	20/21, 23, 24, 30/31, 35, 40/41, 43, 45, 50, 52, 53L, 53R, 64/65, 69, 71, 86, 87, 88, 89, 99, 104L, 104R, 105, 109, 113, 122/123, 131, 132, 133, 138/139, 141, 143, 152L, 152R, 153, 158, 159, 162, 165, 167, 173, 174, 177, 184, 185, 186, 190, 191, 194, 202, 216, 220, 221
Tony Stone Worldwide	cover
Topham Picture Library	62, 63
Wassman, Bill	129, 151, 161, 175, 195, 227
Wilson-Smith, Marcus	9, 22, 93, 94, 97, 98, 146, 149, 154, 164, 166, 170, 181, 183, 192, 193, 199, 209, 210/211, 212, 226, 230/231

INDEX

A
C
D
E
F
G
H
I
J
a
b
d
e
f
g
h
i
j
k
l